GERMAN POETRY

AN ANTHOLOGY FROM
KLOPSTOCK TO ENZENSBERGER

This anthology of German poetry prints a representative selection from the work of seventeen poets writing from the mid eighteenth century to the present. There are poems by Klopstock, Goethe, Schiller, Hölderlin, Novalis, Brentano, Eichendorff, Heine, Droste-Hülshoff, Mörike, Hofmannsthal, Rilke, Trakl, Benn, Brecht, Celan, and Enzensberger.

The aim of the volume is to dispel whatever fears students may have about reading German poetry by suggesting that lyric poetry offers the most economical and enjoyable way of comprehending the range and variety of German literature over the past two hundred years. In his introduction Professor Swales discusses the nature of lyric poetry in general and then presents a brief historical survey of the themes and modes of German lyric poetry in this period. Notes are provided on individual poems, not with the aim of offering definitive interpretations, but in order to highlight points of theme and style and to facilitate class discussion.

Blessed be all metrical rules that forbid automatic responses,
force us to have second thoughts, free from the fetters of Self.
— W. H. Auden

Seid unbequem, seid Sand, nicht das Öl im Getriebe
der Welt!   — Günter Eich

GERMAN POETRY

AN ANTHOLOGY FROM KLOPSTOCK TO ENZENSBERGER

EDITED BY

MARTIN SWALES

Professor of German, University College, London

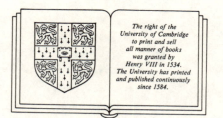

The right of the
University of Cambridge
to print and sell
all manner of books
was granted by
Henry VIII in 1534.
The University has printed
and published continuously
since 1584.

CAMBRIDGE UNIVERSITY PRESS

CAMBRIDGE

LONDON NEW YORK NEW ROCHELLE
MELBOURNE SYDNEY

Published by the Press Syndicate of the University of Cambridge
The Pitt Building, Trumpington Street, Cambridge CB2 1RP
32 East 57th Street, New York, NY 10022, USA
10 Stamford Road, Oakleigh, Melbourne 3166, Australia

First published 1987

Printed in Great Britain at
the University Press, Cambridge

British Library cataloguing in publication data

German poetry: an anthology from Klopstock
to Enzensberger.
1. German poetry   2. Lyric poetry
I. Swales, Martin
831'.04'08   PT1187

Library of Congress cataloguing in publication data

Swales, Martin.
German poetry: an anthology
from Klopstock to Enzensberger.
Bibliography.
1. German poetry.   I. Title.
PT1153.S93   1987   831'.008   86–17578

ISBN 0 521 32116 6 hard covers
ISBN 0 521 31264 7 paperback

CONTENTS

v

PREFACE

This anthology offers a selection of German lyric poetry which spans just over two centuries, from Klopstock to Enzensberger. In the choice of individual poems, and in the interpretative notes, which I have deliberately kept as brief as possible, my aim has been to take account of and to combine a number of different approaches and responses to lyric poetry. Three criteria have dictated the shape of this volume.

First, I have chosen poems that I hold to be major achievements in the lyric mode. By this I mean that each of the poems has, considered simply as words on the page, an energy and distinction that speak to us with the persuasive immediacy of all great literature. Whether the individual text comes from the recent or from the more distant past, it can be read with pleasure and profit without our having to 'make allowances' for historical distance. Of course some of the 'older' poetry may speak a language that is unfamiliar to us. But, as we know from the fact that Shakespeare's plays are widely and successfully performed, an unfamiliarity with the kind of language used need not constitute an obstacle to our appreciation of the text. Moreover, with lyric poetry the difficulty is in a sense even less troublesome than with other genres, because we do not as a rule expect poetry to be close to the patterns of everyday speech. The very appearance on the page of a set of linguistic statements printed as verse tells us that this text is of a different order from most of the linguistic material (newspapers, letters, income tax forms, etc.) that confronts us daily. That is to say we can (or at any rate we imagine that we can) speak the language of a novel or a play. But we rarely imagine that we can speak in verse. We bring certain expectations to bear on poetry and these expectations involve the sense that poetry speaks a special, stylized, heightened language, one that challenges our familiar modes of speaking, feeling, and thinking. This holds true even when a poem is manifestly close to vernacular speech: the unfamiliar context obliges us to notice our vernacular (as opposed to taking it for granted). I hope that the poems I have chosen, whether they are 'ancient' or 'modern', will speak to present-day readers. And speak they must. For, while the language of poetry is different from everyday discourse, it must also be related (and relatable) to it. Otherwise we should not be able to understand it at all. If one of the functions of poetry is, in T. S. Eliot's gloss on a phrase of Mallarmé's, 'to purify the dialect of the tribe', then it follows that poetry must necessarily encompass that very dialect in the act of challenging it.

This anthology contains selections from the work of seventeen individual poets. It would, of course, have been easy to include more poems and poets, and there are many individual omissions that I regret. But – and this was my second criterion – I have deliberately chosen poems by writers who have produced a lyric corpus that is significant in both quantity and quality. The poems are not occasional pieces, but are part of a rich harvest. This anthology will, I hope, serve as an introduction to the work of seventeen important lyric voices. And for many readers this meets, I believe, an important consideration: that the poems should be not discrete entities, but should speak with a voice, a sensibility and linguistic cadence, that bears the signature (both thematic and stylistic) of their maker. I hope that my selection will serve to whet the appetite; and that specialist readers will feel that I have produced a representative sample of the work of the poets in question.

Third (and perhaps most important): I have endeavoured to compile a selection that gives an indication of the historical variety of German lyric poetry from the middle of the eighteenth century to the second half of the twentieth century. I believe that the question of historical placing is crucially important, because I do not accept that there is a contradiction between on the one hand 'practical criticism' in I. A. Richards's sense – the close reading of an individual poem which can produce an enlargement of our linguistic and experiential horizons – and on the other hand, the perception that these particular texts were and are part of history. We do read both 'immanently' and 'historically'; just as we live our lives in a present which we can only fully comprehend in relationship to the past. Literature from the past is not simply inert matter that we carry around with us: it is something that can live with us in the present as a voice that makes imaginatively accessible to us alternative ways of seeing and feeling. We can all use our imagination in order to picture a world different from the one which we inhabit in our daily lives. And part of that imagining encompasses past alternatives, just as in science fiction we can imagine future alternatives. But any alternative is only as alive and absorbing as it relates to the present of our here and now. If I lay stress, then, on the historicity of the poems in this anthology, this is not in order to make them into museum pieces. We do not approach these poems as we do exhibits under glass. We do what all their previous users have done: we take possession of them − by reading them. Moreover, it is no disparagement of a poet's individual creativity to stress the historicity of his or her utterance. With T. S. Eliot I would argue that part of the material with which individual creativity works is the sense of historical (i.e. inherited) substance − both in respect of theme (that is, the kind of experience poets traditionally explore) and mode (that is, the kind of linguistic and formal conventions that poets traditionally employ). The poet is both inheritor and maker, both receiver and producer. And very often poetic creativity consists in both acknowledging and changing the traditional parameters of poetic statement. To say that a poet is a craftsman who learns his trade from his predecessors is not to imply that he has nothing to say. Rather, his craft enables him to say what he has to say.

To lay stress on the historicity of the lyric poem in this way may at first sight seem strange in view of the fact that, by tradition, poetry is regarded as the most private of literary utterances. Novels or plays can obviously embody much more 'social content' than is the case with lyric poems. Yet we should never forget that even the subjectivity of the lyric voice, the 'Ich' of the poem, is never raw, unmediated subjectivity: it is subjectivity that is institutionalized by the very medium of its existence, poetic language. The public conventions of language itself (its syntactical rules) and of literary form (conventions of verse form, metre, rhyme) mean that the privacy of the 'Ich' becomes public property, becomes part of history. I am not, of course, saying that a particular historical age 'had to' produce a particular poet. There is no way that one can legislate a Donne, a Baudelaire, or a Rilke into existence. But equally it would be misleading to see poetry as some kind of visitation by the Muses without purchase on or connexion with historical circumstances. Moreover, as I hope to suggest both in the introduction and in the notes, self-understanding in and through history was rarely far from the creative enterprise of many of the poets we shall be considering here. This anthology is historical not simply in the sense that it moves chronologically from Klopstock to Enzensberger but also in the sense that, for particular reasons that I wish to discuss later, German lyric poetry is especially and insistently aware of its own historicity. With the result that historicity is not just the condition of the poetry but also part and parcel of its very import.

It is my hope, then, that this anthology will have something to offer to a wide variety of readers: to those who are committed to the attentive, detailed analysis of the poetic artefact; to those who look for a unifying creative sensibility in the oeuvre of each individual poet; to those who are engaged by the history of lyric styles and themes. But in addition I would also hope that readers will find themselves responding in all three ways: that the 'words on the page' will be inseparable from the creative voice of the individual poet, and that the voice will be part of the historical continuity of lyric voices which speak eloquently to our age. The selection will, I trust, necessarily suggest points of cross-reference and comparison. To consider poetry that addresses man's relationship to transcendental experience is to concern oneself with Goethe, Schiller, Hölderlin, Novalis, Rilke (among others). To examine nature poetry (or perhaps, more accurately, we should say poetry that explores the situation of man within the orders of natural things) is to inquire into Goethe, Eichendorff, Mörike, Trakl, Brecht (among others). A concern with poetry that debates its own existence as poetry should attend to Heine, Rilke, Benn, and Brecht. Questions concerning the employment of highly wrought, classical forms (such as the elegiac couplet) will be raised by the work of Schiller, Hölderlin, and Rilke. The ballad form will entail consideration of Brentano, Heine, Hofmannsthal, Brecht. I have no wish to prescribe the uses of this anthology − or, indeed, the uses of poetry. But I hope that my selection will prevent readers from mounting the barricades in defence of any one cherished approach or interpretative method because ultimately the task of understanding a major poet presupposes a precise knowledge of his or her particular oeuvre, of other poems by contemporaries or forebears, of other poems *tout court*. Those who interpret Rilke's *Duineser Elegien* will be enriched if they also know Hölderlin's *Brot und Wein*. And to take a striking (but by no means uncharacteristic) example, to interpret Brecht's *Liturgie vom Hauch* − even as 'words on the page' − necessitates reference to Goethe's *Über allen Gipfeln*.

Much of the material in this anthology derives in one form or another from an introductory course on literary analysis which I have for some years now offered to first-year students of the German Department at University College London. Only they will recognize how extensively the discussions in that class have contributed to the making of this book. To them I offer my deepest gratitude: in very many ways they are the co-authors of this anthology.

MARTIN SWALES

University College London

ACKNOWLEDGEMENTS

The author and publisher wish to thank the following for permission:

Suhrkamp Verlag, for all the poems by Brecht taken from Bertolt Brecht, *Gesammelte Werke* © Suhrkamp Verlag, Frankfurt am Main, 1967; for all the poems by Hans Magnus Enzensberger: 'Geburtsanzeige' and 'Ins Lesebuch für die Oberstufe' from *Verteidigung der Wölfe* © Suhrkamp Verlag, Frankfurt am Main, 1967, 'Küchenzettel' and 'Weiterung' from *Blindenschrift* © Suhrkamp Verlag, Frankfurt am Main, 1964, 'Zwei Fehler' from *Gedichte 1955–1970* © Suhrkamp Verlag, Frankfurt am Main, 1971, 'Nicht Zutreffendes streichen' from *Die Furie des Verschwindens* © Suhrkamp Verlag, Frankfurt am Main, 1980; and for Paul Celan's 'Weggebeizt' from *Atemwende* © Suhrkamp Verlag Frankfurt am Main, 1967, 'Ich kann dich noch sehn' from *Lichtzwang* © Suhrkamp Verlag, Frankfurt am Main, 1970, and 'Ein Blatt' from *Schneepart* © Suhrkamp Verlag, Frankfurt am Main, 1971.

S. Fischer Verlag, for Paul Celan's 'Tenebrae' from *Sprachgitter* © S. Fischer Verlag, Frankfurt am Main, 1959.

Arche Verlag AG, for all the poems by Gottfried Benn from *Statische Gedichte* © Verlags AG Die Arche, Zürich, 1948, 1983.

Deutsche Verlags-Anstalt, for Paul Celan's 'Espenbaum' and 'Todesfuge' from *Mohn und Gedächtnis* © Deutsche Verlags-Anstalt, Stuttgart, 1952, and 'Sprich auch du' from *Von Schwelle zu Schwelle* © Deutsche Verlags-Anstalt, Stuttgart, 1955.

INTRODUCTION

In a variety of ways German lyric poetry is particularly accessible to English readers. One obvious reason for this is the fact that the English speaker will often find that he knows a good deal of German poetry without ever having studied it. The unsurpassed tradition of the German *Lied* means that anybody who enjoys classical music will have absorbed much of the feel of German poetry. The contribution of Beethoven, Schubert, Brahms, Wolf, Mahler, and Richard Strauss to the dissemination of German lyric poetry beyond national frontiers can scarcely be overestimated. Moreover, the 'feel' of German poetry is congenial in many ways to English ears. The German lyric is constituted by stress, not by syllable: in this sense it is much more akin to the English tradition than is, say, French verse. The heart beat of poetry is the interplay of repeated pattern and its modification; and the shifts in stress pattern which dictate the movement of the poem are very similar in German and English poetry. We do not need to be told where the heart beat is; we can feel it.

POETRY AND PROSE

Before embarking on specific considerations to do with the particular tradition of the German lyric, I want to begin with a discussion of first principles. What is poetry? If one turns to standard works of reference for help, it becomes immediately apparent that poetry is most often defined by contrasting it with prose. And the distinctions that emerge in this process concern both mode and theme. In terms of the mode, the distinction is often put as follows: prose is the language of everyday speech, it tends, in consequence, to be literal, often factual and utilitarian. And even when the prose is more exalted than its everyday condition would allow, it tends to be argumentative, discursive, wedded to notions of linearity, consistency, and clarity. In short, prose is felt to be less tightly organized, less overtly patterned than is poetry. Poetry, by contrast, is claimed as

1

carefully wrought, compact, stylized. The very term 'lyric' implies
in its etymology (deriving from the word 'lyre') that poetry is linked
with music and with song. It tends towards brevity, and its concentration of statement leads to the creation of rhythmic, patterned
sequences of which the repeated refrain is the most obvious. In this
sense, poetry is close not to literal statement, but to magic incantation − as in the little verse that a mother will say to comfort her
child:

> Heile, heile, Segen
> Drei Tag' Regen
> Drei Tag' Schnee
> Mach dem Kindlein nimmer weh.

In terms of their content, these lines defy any rational summary.
But their power is to be found in the incantatory rhythm (often ac-
companied by the mother's stroking the sore place on the child's
body). Poetry, it is often said, works by suggestion rather than by
statement. It exploits sound pattern to the full: it is less concerned
to be testable by the yardstick of common experience than is prose.
Its aim is to create an intact, self-defining linguistic construct. To
quote Archibald MacLeish's famous dictum 'a poem must not
mean but be.'

One of the crucial ways in which poetry exploits sound pattern
is, of course, rhyme. We are all familiar with the rhyme pattern
that occurs at the end of lines, as in the mother's incantation
quoted above where 'Segen' rhymes with 'Regen', and 'Schnee'
with 'weh'. (Where the rhyme word ends with a stressed syllable −
'Schnee'/'weh' − the rhyme is called masculine, where it ends with
an unstressed syllable − 'Segen'/'Regen' − the rhyme is called
feminine.) Whereas the unit of prose is the sentence, the unit of
poetry is both the sentence and the individual line. Rhyme can be
a powerful indicator of the end of the line. But additionally a poem
can display internal rhymes, that is, rhymes that are not confined
to the ends of lines but occur throughout the poem, thereby
generating a dominant sound pattern. Moreover, we must also be
alert to the possibility of assonance: that is, to recurrent sound
values even where the words in which they appear do not achieve
perfect rhymes. In the mother's poem of comfort we should, for
example, note the insistent assonance of the 'ei' sounds − 'he*i*le',
'he*i*le', 'dr*ei*', 'dr*ei*', 'Kindl*ei*n'. One can imagine that the 'ei'
sound originates in the child's cry of pain when it hurts itself: and
the mother takes up that cry and, by embracing it in the gentle but

insistent rhythms of her comfort, converts pain ('ei') into healing ('heile').

But rhyme or assonance are not the only means by which poetry endows language with powerful rhythmic patterns. For poetry also works with metre. I have already made the point that German verse, like English verse, is scanned according to stress pattern and not by length of vowel sounds (as is classical Latin or Greek verse) or by the number of syllables (as is French verse). As soon as we discern, in a line of German or English verse, a recurrent pattern of stressed and unstressed syllables, we are registering the metrical form of the poem. On the whole, critics (of both German and English verse) tend to borrow the technical names for scansion patterns from classical prosody. That is to say:

a stressed syllable preceded by a single unstressed syllable (∪ —) is iambic;

a stressed syllable followed by a single unstressed syllable (— ∪) is trochaic;

a stressed syllable preceded by two unstressed syllables (∪∪ —) is anapaestic;

a stressed syllable followed by two unstressed syllables (— ∪∪) is dactylic.

As soon as one sets out a scheme in this way, there is always the danger that one reduces poetry to a jingle. It is crucially important that we should not seek to make lines of verse obey invariable patterns of the 'ti-ti-tum, ti-ti-tum' kind, because we will constantly find that poetry derives its most powerful effects from the interplay of, on the one hand, our expectations of rhythmic regularity and, on the other, the flexible counter-movements of the stress pattern in natural speech. Where the natural rhythm accords with the regular metrical pulse, the line of verse will immediately strike us as powerfully stressed. But often, as the mood of a poem changes, so too the regular pulse changes its throb to signal a different kind of statement. We must notice the ways in which expectations are established, and then modified, re-instated and then modified again, because in that process is to be found the power and memorableness of verse. When, for example, a sequence of end-stopped lines, where the sense demands a pause at the end of the line, is suddenly disturbed by an enjambement – that is, by the sense flowing over the end of the line – we will register a powerful change in the rhythm of the poem. Rhythm in itself does not *mean*;

but it can enable meaning to be expressed. MacLeish's dictum expresses only a partial truth: poems cannot *be* without *meaning* unless language is used purely as a repertoire of noises. All great poets have attended to the physical force of language, to its sound values, colours, and textures. But the radical experimenters who have reduced language to mere recurrent noises have produced intriguing — but only ephemeral — effects.

Most of the technical terms associated with the analysis of poetry are used to identify various kinds of regularity that inform the poem's operation as a linguistic artefact. A couplet is a pair of (usually rhyming) lines, a triplet is a sequence of three lines. (One noteworthy form is that known as *terza rima*, which refers to a group of three lines in which the unrhymed word provides the rhyme for the next triplet — a b a, b c b, c d c, and so on.) A quatrain is a unit of four — often rhyming — lines. The sonnet is one of the most highly wrought verse forms. It is a poem of fourteen lines which often separates into a first unit of eight lines (the octave) and a second unit of six lines (the sestet), although English readers will also be very familiar with the Shakespearean sonnet which works with three quatrains and a final couplet.

Technical terms such as these are useful because they function as a short-hand which enables us to draw attention economically to recurring features of the poem before us. They may also help us to notice the organization of any given poem. Poetry, compared with prose, is language used in a highly organized way: its technical devices, its rhyme and metre, its division into regular units and sub-units (stanzas, refrains), all serve to establish patterns. Poetry, in a way that is rarely true of prose to anything like the same degree, seeks to achieve a maximum of internal coherence and rhythmic organization. If we transfer this distinction in mode between poetry and prose to the question of differences in theme, the following points of contrast emerge. Poetry, it is often said, is the vehicle for moods, for exalted and privileged conditions of the sensibility whereas prose is, to recall the everyday usage of the term, concerned with the 'prosaic'. In its relative brevity, the poem is devoted not to the extent and variety of experience but to its intensity at a particular point in time. Poetry, it is often held, stands apart from the workaday world, and thereby it captures moments of privileged sensation or vision. And just as the moment itself is separated from the temporal run-of-the-mill, so the poet asserts the autonomous, timeless splendour of his perceptions. The linguistic intensity is the correlative of the experiential intensity. The special aura which surrounds poetic themes and utterance creates the divorce from history, time, from mundane concerns. Poetry is the utterance of the lyrical self, the 'lyrisches Ich'. And this 'Ich' speaks in an unbroken monologue. The external world figures only in so far as it is registered by that 'Ich': hence the rapt subjectivity of the lyric mode to which many commentators have drawn attention. The resistances and frictions that characterize the everyday commerce of self and world are the stuff of drama and fiction: but in poetry, so we are told, the self reigns in unchallenged, privileged sovereignty.

One could sum up these arguments by saying that poetry works by and through implications. Its linguistic mode is that of implicit utterance, of indirection rather than paraphrasable clarity. Moreover, poetry invokes only that experiential terrain in which the self — 'das lyrische Ich' — is implicated. All of which engenders a plenitude that is intensive rather than extensive, a unity between speaking self and world. With the lyric, one sensibility (as it were) runs the show — in the simple sense that there is no show other than that articulated by the lyric voice.

In many ways, these traditionally espoused distinctions between poetry and prose can still be helpful in that they indicate certain contrasting impulses within literary expression. But one must beware of converting such differences of emphasis into absolute distinctions, because the implied 'either/or' simply proves an unacceptable — and ultimately unworkable — attempt at demarcation. The putative link between mode and theme, between the dominance of the incantatory 'Ich' and a thematic condition of enraptured subjectivity, simply does not hold good for countless examples of lyric poetry that will concern us in the pages that follow. Perhaps the German word 'Dichtung' can help us here. It is often translated into English as 'poetry': but this is far too restrictive. In fact, the term denotes all imaginative literature. The word itself has often been held to derive from the German word 'dicht' which means dense or compressed. The etymology is dubious, but it hardly matters because the notion of concentrated utterance is one that can serve to define a particular property of all great literature: that it makes language work at maximum pressure. Literature is concerned to articulate experience, and the word 'articulate' means both to express and to organize or shape. In this process of shaping, the language not only utters an experience: it concentrates it and embodies it. And this embodying function is, once again, true of all major literature. In so far as lyric poems display (relatively speaking) an unmistakable brevity, and with that brevity goes (by tradition) a set of expectations to do with maximal formal control, it follows that poetry can be seen as compounding that linguistic density which is characteristic of imaginative literature generally. But to conclude from this that poetry must be concerned with the thematic correlative of its linguistic mode − that, in other words, it must be about the seamless unity of self and world − is profoundly misleading. We have all met lyric poetry that is suggestive, intensely metaphorical, structurally controlled, linguistically rich and which concerns itself centrally with the experiences of disunity, deprivation, inadequacy, disenchantment. It would be foolish to put such poetry beyond the pale. Indeed, the history of the German lyric charted by the poems in this volume shows us how increasingly, in the course of the nineteenth century, the subjectivity of the lyric poem gradually changes from rapt, absorbed unreflectivity into an increasingly problematic, self-questioning condition. And to say that that movement is a process of cultural decline is sheer nonsense.

Bertolt Brecht − and he is by no means alone in this respect − had a marked dislike for the cultural notions that went with the hallowed term 'Dichtung'. What he distrusted was precisely its aura of privileged inwardness, its worship of a literary language whose value was directly proportional to its timelessness and subjectivity. Brecht regarded all this aesthetic sacramentalism as nothing but bourgeois idealogy. With Brecht (as with so many major writers) the theoretical battle lines are much clearer than the actual artistic creativity which they claim to explicate. Brecht's notion of 'Verfremdung' ('estrangement') in the theatre entails not a break with art, but its reinstatement as a fictional model that de-familiarizes and 'makes strange' certain features of our worldly experience that otherwise we might take for granted. Brecht wanted, not to make art like life, but to make art cast a questioning light on life. And his linguistic power, as a great poet, was part and parcel of that enterprise. In his choice of thematic and linguistic raw material he was polemically at variance with what he saw as a pernicious bourgeois tradition. But while his concern to de-familiarize language and experience was unashamedly in the service of political aims, it was, in itself, an aesthetic principle; and one that comes close to asserting the revelatory value of art. Which is, when one comes to think about it, one of the properties of the special (i.e. de-familiarized) discourse of 'Dichtung'.

Even if, then, any discussion of Brecht's creative practice as poet and dramatist demands that we question some of the implications of his theoretical and polemical writings, yet the sheer asperity with which he viewed bourgeois aesthetics can help to alert us to a number of problems inherent in the traditional view of poetry–versus–prose which I have summarized above. The thrust of Brecht's polemic is that the view of lyric poetry as the repository of hallowed subjectivity is by no means a definition of poetry as such, but is, rather, the product of particular historical circumstances, and refers therefore to a particular kind of poetry which was available to a particular age but which then became increasingly unworkable for the finest creative talents of subsequent ages. To this issue of the increasingly problematic subjectivity of lyric poetry I want to return shortly. What should be noted at this stage is simply that poetic creativity may indeed be the gift of the Muses: but that the specific forms that creativity takes in any particular individual have to do not simply with the particular cast of mind or temperament of the individual writer but also with the historical availability (or non-availability) of certain lyric themes and forms. This does not, of course, alter the fact that subsequent ages can and do respond to earlier modes of poetry as something immediate and valid – despite the fact that these modes no longer commend themselves to contemporary practitioners. Readers are never as conditioned in their responses to earlier literature as some critics would have us believe. Even a secular age can appreciate religious poetry.

POETRY AND HISTORY

Even though it is possible for past poets to have an imaginative contemporaneity for us (i.e. we can appreciate Goethe *and* Benn, Eichendorff *and* Trakl), we also know that these various imaginative possibilities that we can enter at will have an essential historical signature: they came into being at a particular time, under certain historical circumstances. How can we locate the historicity of the lyric poem, given that it tends to express little or no publicly historical content? We have already said that the poem has at its core the lyric voice, the 'lyrisches Ich'. How can we chart the history of the lyrical persona in poetry? On the face of it, we would not seem to have much historical evidence to go on. Certainly we are unlikely to find a great deal of help from the kind of documentary material that professional historians concern themselves with. And one further point should be borne in mind: we should never assume that the lyrical 'Ich' is identical with the historical personage who is the author of the poem. The self of the poem is part of the fiction of the poem, and does not establish biographical identity. But, paradoxical though it may sound, it is here, in the fictional identity of the lyric persona, that we shall discern the contours of the poem's historicity. For the 'Ich' is a cipher for the kind of knowable and sayable subjectivity that was available to a particular poet. We shall find ourselves asking what kind of 'Ich' speaks. How public, implicitly or explicitly, is the speaking subject? In what ways does that subject define its essential identity in the course of the poem. Is it an active self, a doer, a maker? Or passive? How intrusive is the self? How far does that self claim to speak for a generality? For mankind, for man and woman in love? These and other questions also extend to the recipient of the poem. And, in invoking the recipient, I mean not the historical audience of contemporary readers: but rather the implied reader. What kind of reader does the poem invite us to become? Is the poem addressed to a patron, a king or a prince? Is it perhaps addressed to a friend? How 'public' is the implied public? Is the poet speaking to mankind in general? Does the 'Ich' modulate into 'wir'? If so, what kind of 'wir'? A small circle of initiates or the broad spectrum of humankind? Perhaps the poem is not addressed to any reader: perhaps the 'Ich' is engaged in an act of communing with himself, and we are merely eavesdroppers on essentially private utterances? The interplay of private and public is crucial to the history of lyric forms. Karl Pestalozzi has reminded us that the notion of a separate, intact 'I' in the poem, of 'das lyrische Ich' is first established by Margarete Susman in a book entitled *Das Wesen der modernen deutschen Lyrik*. This study appeared in 1910, and Susman's insistence on the non-biographical, autonomous 'Ich' of the lyric voice derived in part from her response to contemporary poetry: the encapsulated self is the voice of the encapsulated poem. Not, of course, that this particular perception which equates the lyrical self with the hermetic self holds good for all poetry – it would certainly not apply to Goethe, for example. But the argument is important in that it alerts us to the kind of speaking self that informs the poem.

To trace the changing forms of 'das lyrische Ich' and of the kind of public which it addresses is but one way of charting the history, and historicity of poetry. One can, of course, also survey the changes in lyrical conventions and forms, the uses to which the ballad, the elegy, the ode, the sonnet have been put. Moreover, one can also register the movements of certain key themes. Nature is a case in point. Within the German tradition it recurs with great frequency from Goethe onwards. In part, the importance of nature as a theme derives from the extent to which it generates so many sub-themes. This is because nature, as mediated in poetry, is never simply an objectively recorded landscape: nature outside the human self always expresses profound human concerns and dilemmas. Amongst other things, nature can stand for community, for physicality and sensuousness, for patterns of eternal recurrence, for the strength and beauty of integral, unreflective existence, for the resistance of material reality to human wishing and willing. The poet may see man as part of nature's being; or he may see him as radically divorced from the nature around him. Under this aspect, the poet's view of nature may highlight the extent to which man is isolated and vulnerable, is endowed with (and perhaps blighted by) self-consciousness, is a spiritual being, is a historically circum-scribed, and therefore limited, self, is a free and ethically respons-ible being. Nature, we might say, is often made in the poet's image or counter-image. The theme of nature can even have political reverberations. If a poet turns away from human society to a wor-ship of nature, this may entail utopian aspirations for a more 'natural' (i.e. equal) society, or it may imply a disparagement of the social and political world. And this latter stance can imply quietistic (i.e. politically conservative) attitudes. Certainly Brecht distrusts nature poetry as being too readily associated with German inwardness, with an evasion of human problems in the name of some mendacious, because timeless, concern. Gottfried Benn distrusts the cosy domestication of nature that he perceives in so much lyric poetry: for him nature is indifferent to human thinking and striving, and he pits art, the human mind, against the chaos of nature. All of which reminds us that nature can also be implicated in the artist's sense of his own creativity. Does the poet assert the naturalness of his poetry? Is artistic creation viewed as, and made to appear, a natural process − or is it the product of uniquely human processes of self-consciousness? Once again the theme of nature serves to monitor a human concern and measures the stature of man and his works.

The question as to the character of poetic creativity is another point at which history impinges on the poet's craft. This anthology has no shortage of poets who make their poems out of a debate with the presuppositions of lyric art. For obvious reasons, German poets after 1945 were acutely conscious of this dilemma: what price poetry given that German culture, which had produced such a flood of great poetry, was not proof against the seductions of barbarism? Hence Adorno's much-quoted remark to the effect that poetry was no longer possible after Auschwitz. Brecht's and Enzenberger's answer to this dilemma is to write poetry that sternly asserts its anti-poetic character, thereby anchoring their creativity in a critical relationship to previous kinds of lyric production. In their overtly sceptical stance they take issue with a particular German problem: but the problem is by no means confined to Germany. In their distrust of euphony, beauty of diction, of the subtle and refined lyric self, in their determination to let argument prevail over fine writing, they are at one with the American poets William Carlos Williams and Marianne Moore. Perhaps such voices are the historically appropriate correctives to the poetry of the first three decades of the twentieth century, much of which is conceived in the grand manner (Eliot, Yeats, Rilke, Pound). To borrow the terms of MacLeish's dictum again, Brecht and Enzensberger are concerned to write poems that will 'mean' rather than 'be'. That is to say: for them, the 'meaning' of a poem entails its having abundant purchase on the non-poetic world around it, with the lyric 'Ich' functioning as some kind of knowable human self. Whereas, to register the 'being' of poetry would be to see the poem as some kind of icon, a sacred piece of lovingly fashioned language which houses an impersonal poetic speaker, one who explicitly or implicitly repudiates the world of prose. In the shifting emphases that have been given, over the years, to the interplay of 'being' and 'meaning' in poetry we can perceive many of the historical currents that flow through the traditions of European lyric poetry.

Poets are, as the derivation of the word 'poetry' from the ancient Greek for 'making' tells us, workers with words. Their need to pattern and shape the vernacular which they share with their fellows makes them peculiarly attentive observers of the common language of the age which must necessarily be the starting point. We must never forget that, however private the import of a poem may seem, its vehicle is necessarily language, and language is a public commodity. (The notion of a wholly private language is, quite simply, a contradiction in terms.) And very often it is the poets who bring about change and development in language. They challenge out-worn phrases, clichés, and in the process, of course, they also challenge outworn attitudes and perceptions. Moreover, poets are acutely aware of the expectations that their readers bring to bear. Literary convention often dictates that certain kinds of experience are not the appropriate subject of poetry. This makes available to the poet the chance of challenging — even shocking — his readers: by proclaiming certain kinds of theme over and done with and by replacing them by new themes, he can effect a revolution in public sensibility. The early poems of Goethe (from the 1770s) were part of that spectacular process whereby conventionality of both theme and mode were challenged in the name of a new truth to (individual) experience. What Goethe's contemporaries perceived was sheer, untrammelled feeling, feeling that was valid not in spite of — but precisely because of — the unmistakable claim to individual authority of utterance and experience. Similarly, two of the Heine poems which figure in this anthology — *Der Doppelgänger* and *Mein Kind, wir waren Kinder* — reflect on the poet's past and contrast it with the present. At one level, of course, one can read these poems psychologically: that is, we discover in them an exploration of the writer's relationship to his childhood and adolescent past. But, beyond that concern, we sense that the 'I' of the poem is registering a change in literary sensibility: a certain kind of behaviour — the childhood idyll, the simple integrity of grief — are now over and done with. The psychological argument interlocks with a broader cultural, historical, and linguistic argument. The modes of poetry that were once available to poetry (with the Romantic generation) are now no longer workable for the self who speaks in these two poems.

In these considerations of poetic self and hearer, of literary and linguistic convention, then, we shall discover the historical identity and variety of lyric poetry.

In an influential study, Hugo Friedrich has suggested one possible model for the comprehension of historical change within poetry over the last 150 years. He argues that lyric poetry in the course of the nineteenth century moves further and further away from common experience and common discourse, and into an increasingly inaccessible, 'hermetic' territory. Gradually poetry comes to constitute a world that is radically resistant to knowable human experience. The more eccentric poetry becomes, the more it repudiates any contact with the debased currency of modern living, the more it asserts that valid experience, valid language stands at the very periphery of our modern discourse. Difficulty, inaccessibility becomes the guarantee of authenticity. Hugo Friedrich's argument is a helpful one — but it only accommodates one strand within the period that concerns us, and he has little to say on German poetry. He tends to forget that there are dissenting poets who resist the tendency towards a dehumanization of poetry, who express a bad conscience about the banishment of the human self from the poem. Perhaps, for all the difficulty of his diction, Rilke is an important witness in this context. In many of the *Neue Gedichte* he attempts to write the self out of the poem, to celebrate the unity and integrity of objects, plants, animals, thereby affirming that strength of being and purpose that is denied to man. Yet in his later work, he reinstates the human voice, and poetic self as the only sayer and redeemer of the world. And Brecht defiantly insists on the public mission of the poet: he explores feelings and experiences that are (or can be made) publicly accountable. It follows from all this that we should beware of expecting a tidy linear sequence into which we can slot a particular poet's oeuvre. After all, Celan and Enzensberger were published at the same time. But, whether tidy or not, the sequence of creative selves which we shall meet in this anthology is one that enshrines the historical self-understanding of a range of major lyric talents.

METAPHORICAL LANGUAGE

In discussing Hugo Friedrich's view of modern poetry, I raised the question of difficulty: by which we must understand a willed inaccessibility of language and theme. And this brings me to the place of metaphor in poetry. Metaphorical speech entails a transference of meaning from one sphere to another. If I say that my beloved is like a violet, I am employing a simile which makes explicit the two spheres (human and botanical) which I am linking. But if I suppress the word 'like' and say that my beloved *is* a violet, I have created a metaphorical statement: that is to say, I equate the two spheres, I write of one in terms of the other. Often a poet begins with a simile but then continues in metaphor: having established the point of kinship, the poet works with the conjoined spheres as though they were interchangeable. This kind of metaphorical writing can frequently serve to unite concrete and abstract, physical and mental worlds. Of the categories of metaphorical discourse, we are probably most familiar with personification, which endows non-human situations or objects with human properties ('the river smiled'). Synecdoche entails making a part stand for the whole ('keel' for 'ship'), and metonymy uses physical proximity to make one entity stand for another (as when we refer to the White House and mean the President of the United States). It is important to realize that metaphor is by no means confined to poetic language: we understand a poet's metaphors because we ourselves are used to thinking in associations which link separate phenomena. But poetry displays a sustained inventiveness in the use of figurative language which constantly moves from one sphere of experience to another.

However much metaphorical discourse may be a perennial feature of lyric poetry, it too is responsive to the promptings of changing historical and cultural circumstances. It is a fascinating exercise to chart the shift in the relations that poets have established through metaphor between the physical world and other orders of experience, value, and meaning. When a physical object, when a palpable situation or event becomes transparent upon a realm of being and intimation beyond the common significance we speak of the literary symbol. A rose is a physical entity: but if, in a particular text, a rose is invested with more than horticultural value and connotes love, or beauty, or Christ's crucifixion, then it has become a symbol. Christianity provided Western European poetry with a whole range of publicly known symbols − bread, wine, the cross, the cock crowing and so on. But with the decline of religious belief that begins in the eighteenth century, poets increasingly had to forgo these public symbols and corporate myths, and had to create their own version of the higher or transcendental realm. In a justly famous essay, Erich Heller has defined this condition as 'the hazard of modern poetry'. For private myths, by definition, are difficult of access. Indeed, it may be that, for a modern poet, the higher realm is not only private but also opaque, resistant even to his exploratory quest. Where this happens we will find ourselves wrestling with poetry that suggests rather than spells out the realm of higher signification. And, in consequence, the symbol becomes tantalizing rather than revelatory. Moreover, in an important essay, Walter Benjamin argued that the symbol is simply no longer appropriate to the modern literary sensibility, and that allegory may be truer to our world. Whereas the symbol compresses two different orders of statement together so that matter and spirit coexist, the allegory recognizes the separation of the two orders of meaning. The symbol is itself and is also what it represents; the allegory is one thing that stands for something else. The figure of a blind-folded woman with a pair of scales and a sword stands for justice; but it does not incarnate the principle in physical terms. Benjamin's argument is that our world no longer exists with assured access to (and belief in) a spiritual world as immanent in the physical world. Hence allegory is as much as we can aspire to, because it acknowledges the gulf we must cross in moving from physical to transcendental statement. The gulf and our aspiration to cross it may be as much as we can truthfully say and know.

These arguments, when applied to lyric poetry, bring us back to 'das lyrische Ich'. Where there is a disjunction between experiencing and reflecting self, allegory will be appropriate to the inherent mismatch. And the signs that point to the higher meaning will be unsettling invitations rather than redeemed (to say nothing of redemptive) promises. Gottfried Benn enshrines his private mythology not in symbols but in what he calls 'ciphers' ('Chiffren'). At the simplest level, these are stylistic figures which recur with repetitive insistence in his oeuvre. They are highly evocative, but what do they mean? Here we find ourselves in difficult territory. For 'cipher' is another word for 'code' or 'secret language'. And the whole point of a code, when employed by spies or secret agents, is to keep the uninitiated from understanding the message. Confronted by Gottfried Benn's (and by a good deal of modern) poetry, we are aware that there is no community of believers, of initiated readers who have reliable access to the import. We are all excluded. We notice those linguistic signposts which point beyond the realm of everyday discourse: but we cannot say where they lead us. The metaphorical promise is there, but it gives us little insight. We are vouchsafed brief glimpses, unredeemed promises — but little more than that. Once again the interplay of public and private in both the lyric self and the reader, in both language and theme of the poem is central to the historical condition of the poem.

These are complex and difficult issues, and we shall need constantly to bear them in mind, for they constitute the theoretical territory within which individual poets and poems move. I want to pass now to a discussion of specific poets within the German tradition, because their works will help us to see how the various theoretical possibilities which I have outlined above took shape as specific lyric practice. The tradition of the German lyric articulates these issues with especial clarity because of the particular lyric achievement of one poet: Goethe.

THE TRADITION OF THE GERMAN LYRIC

Goethe is the first major German writer to achieve European status. In the middle of the eighteenth century German culture suffered from what one can only call a profound inferiority complex in respect of French literature. A century earlier there had been the amazing flowering of French classicism. The consolidation of power and patronage at the court of Louis XIV had produced a culture of great sophistication and distinction. In the second half of the seventeenth century Germany was still recovering from the hideous devastation of the Thirty Years War. A century later some measure of stability and prosperity returned: but there was still no national unity. German intellectual and cultural life was played out in a number of small principalities and dukedoms. The model of France was held up for dutiful acceptance and emulation. Gradually countervailing voices made themselves heard: there was a change in literary models. English literature was perceived as freer from formal constraints, as closer to the emotions and natural energies than French literature. The poet Klopstock managed to recreate the metres and linguistic patterns of classical Greek poetry in German, and to combine formal artistry with an assertion of the self, of intense individual emotion. With other poets too, the German language began to find expressive flexibility. And the process was completed swiftly and breathtakingly by Goethe. In his hands, as Eric Blackall has shown, German suddenly, explosively, came of age as a literary language. By Goethe's death in 1832 the literary, linguistic, and philosophical culture of Germany was the equal of anything in Europe. Not, of course, that Goethe can be credited with being the only begetter of this remarkable cultural flowering. But his linguistic achievement is, quite simply, unsurpassed: and it finds expression principally in his lyric gift. When the German language came of age, it did so in the hands of a man who, by temperament and cast of mind, was a superb lyric poet − a poet who has arguably not been surpassed by any poet in any language.

Goethe contributed to and absorbed a whole complex of energies that transformed the face of German culture. He came of solid bourgeois stock − he was brought up in a patrician house in Frankfurt am Main, his father held a position of esteem in the Free

City, and his mother was the daughter of a former *Bürgermeister*. When, later in life, Goethe made his home in Weimar, he once again sought out the atmosphere of bourgeois solidity, and indeed played an active role in the civic administration. In one sense, then, this was a man for whom the outer world, society, with its laws, customs, and regulations was never something inimical or alien. And he never, although his life spanned the years of European Romanticism, disparaged practical activity in the outer world. He was never the *poète maudit* of the Romantic and post-Romantic generation. And yet, as Barker Fairley's magnificent *Study of Goethe* shows, he was a person of volatile – even explosive – emotional energy. He was influenced by Pietism, with its cult of abundant inner feeling as the repository of the religious sensibility; he came into contact as a young man with Herder from whom he learnt to believe in the genius of the creative, poetic self. He was part of the 'sentimentalism' (or 'Empfindsamkeit') of his age, with its powerful advocacy of the release of the emotions from constraints and restrictions. Yet all this inwardness was tempered by an esteem for rational argument, for clarity of form and discourse. The upshot was a sensibility that was grounded in a reverence for both inward and outward things, indeed that insisted on the reciprocal interaction of self and world as the necessary and right (or, to use one of his favourite terms, natural) chemistry of living. Moreover, we should not forget that he was also intensely interested in natural science. And for him the scientific exploration of the world was not in any fundamental sense divorced from the poetic exploration of the world. Hence his fierce resistance to Newtonian science. However idiosyncratic some of his own scientific arguments may have been, he was surely right to sense the profound upheavals that modern science would bring in its train. Goethean science was the last-ditch attempt not to bridge but to close that gap between material and spiritual truth that was to become the governing feature of nineteenth- and twentieth-century European culture. It was this triumphantly undissociated sensibility that made Goethe the fine lyric poet that he was. And the correlative of that sensibility was a linguistic gift that moved easily from the colloquial and casual to the high-flown and carefully wrought. The early poems – from the 'Sturm und Drang' period – exude emotional energy and turmoil, the exultant sense of self-discovery in and through feeling. Yet even here the formal control of the poetry, the subtle ordering of sense impressions and exclamations, conveys a coherent perception of both self and world as equal partners in the experience of living. Later, with the *Römische Elegien*, Goethe produced joyously erotic verse: yet the eros was housed within the classical form of the elegiac couplet with its alternating hexameter and pentameter lines. Time and time again Goethe's poetry is characterized by an ease of diction, a naturalness that can border on the colloquial, even when it addresses philosophical topics. And the linguistic gift means not only that Goethe seems to be the presiding deity of the emergence of German as a fully fledged literary language, but also that his poetry proved eminently transferable to other sensibilities and other ages. His poetry retained its eloquence even for writers who could not share most of his convictions and beliefs.

It is this combination of linguistic mastery and experiential integrity that accounts for the undoubted, yet problematic stature of Goethe for subsequent generations. I have already said that Goethe's poetry breathes a kind of naturalness even at its most sophisticated. Within Goethe's sensibility, emotional immediacy went hand in hand with intelligence: the mind was supple, thoughtful, inquiring, and mental activity was felt and shown to be part of man's natural energies. For Goethe, the knowing mind is not a debunking agency: it sifts, combines, and connects experiences, it intensifies (rather than weakens) the truthful feel of experience on the pulses. And here the problem begins. In a quite special way, the nature and scale of Goethe's lyric achievement is felt by later poets to be unobtainable and intimidating. One could say that subsequent poets were more often than not in quest of that unity of feeling and intelligence, of sensuous and visionary poetry which Goethe took for granted. A poem such as *Dauer im Wechsel* is a good illustration of what is involved. In that poem Goethe addresses the fact of human transience. Man, the poem suggests, is more transient than other phenomena in organic nature because he is self-aware: that is, he *knows* himself to be transient, and this knowingness compounds his insubstantiality. Here we touch a cardinal theme of nineteenth- and twentieth-century European poetry: the perception that man is a disunited creature because he knows too much for him to be able to retain experiential wholeness. The knowingness amounts, then, to a betrayal of life: experience is blighted by the treachery of foreknowledge. And that condition troubles the Romantic poets, it troubles Byron, Heine, Baudelaire, it troubles the moderns (Valéry, Eliot, Yeats, Rilke). Yet, if we now return to Goethe's *Dauer im Wechsel*, we note a crucial difference. In Goethe's poem, knowledge in advance of experience is not an act of treachery; it is not a blight on the living process. Rather, consciousness compounds *and* redeems human transience, it reinforces the immediacy and the abundance of living. This is not facile optimism on Goethe's part. His poetry does not display willed naivety, an evasion of uncomfortable questions. The affirmations are earned, but they are made with a confidence in the rightness of natural, organic processes, in that wholeness of which the poetic sensibility (the 'Gunst der Musen') is part and to which it contributes. No other European poet could make that kind of affirmation. No other poet could be at once so simple, sensuous, and profound, could offer the kind of triumphant yet hard-won assertion of the final line of *Der Bräutigam*: 'Wie es auch sei, das Leben, es ist gut.' Or, to put the matter more simply, we could say that no other major European poet could write that line without it sounding either facile or ironic.

It is important to clarify what I am claiming here. I am not saying that everything that comes after Goethe is simply an anticlimax. I am not saying that he was the last whole man and complete poet in the Western European tradition (although that certainly has been claimed for him). But I do wish to suggest that the particular social, cultural and psychological circumstances that shaped Goethe's creativity produced a poet who, both linguistically and thematically, expressed a particular belief in the rightness of man's anchorage in the world of immediate experience. And the resultant oeuvre does seem to fulfil many of the definitions of — and prescriptions for — lyric poetry that I have rehearsed in the opening pages of this introduction, particularly in so far as they entail notions of poetic unity. And this poses a particular problem for German-language poets, because they find themselves confronted with the achievement of a poet which seems somehow exempt from history: in the precise sense that Goethe's oeuvre constitutes not just one important voice within the historical variety and sequence of poetic voices — but quite simply the supreme voice of lyric poetry as such. The upshot is that Goethe is seen either as an unattainable genius — or as an irrelevance to the hazardous and difficult concern of modern (i.e post-Goethean) poetry. Something of this oscillation between polar extremes can be felt in the history of the reception of Goethe in the years since his death. What the two extreme positions have in common is a sense of Goethe as an unrepeatable phenomenon. Either he is the integral humanity to which the moderns can only aspire (without ever achieving it); or he belongs, in his unity and wholeness, to a different planet from the one on which later men and women have to live, move, write and read poetry. I know of no other European literary tradition that has quite that same sense of a dominant, ahistorically dominant, literary creator whose work is felt to be (whether for good or for ill) quite simply of a different order from what came after. Of course other national literatures have their great figures: Shakespeare, Molière, Pushkin. But they are not elevated to the status of timeless arbiters of what constitutes a supreme value, both in literature and in life. It is worth noting that German culture is represented abroad by institutions known not as the 'German Institute' but as the 'Goethe Institute'. Generations of Germans have acquired little anthologies of Goethe's wisdom entitled 'mit Goethe durch das Jahr', whereby again this man's sensibility, this man's language acquires a quasi-sacramental status.

How should we respond to this phenomenon? It is, I think, important that we should not deify Goethe. Rather, we should see him in history and as a source of historical self-understanding for others. Goethe's life, anchored as it was successively in Frankfurt and then in Weimar, made possible an affirmation of many of the central tenets of bourgeois culture in a model of interacting and mutually supportive energies. In his reverence for individual selfhood, for nature, for society, for art, for commerce and handicraft, for body and mind, for physical and spiritual things, Goethe was responding to a whole complex of energies – social, economic, cultural, political and religious – towards the end of the eighteenth century in Germany. The prehistory and subsequent history of bourgois culture was marked by conflicts between these diferent aspirations, values, and allegiances. But Goethe was and is part of bourgeois culture: and lyric poetry was one of its key organs of self-understanding and self-expression. For subsequent German poets Goethe's lyric oeuvre had the function of making them reflect on the historicity of their condition – psychological, linguistic, and cultural. And, as we shall see, that historicity was not disabling but was part of their creativity.

No discussion of the historicity of creative responses to Goethe can afford to ignore what is one of the greatest critical essays of modern times. It was written by Goethe's closest friend, Friedrich Schiller, and it is called *Über naive und sentimentalische Dichtung*

(*On naive and reflective Poetry*). In this essay Schiller takes stock of Goethe's and his own creative temperament and suggests that the two contrasting modes of being and writing which they represent make possible the definition of contemporary culture. Schiller sees the condition of modern poetry as being 'sentimentalisch': that is, it is knowing, self-reflective creativity. And he contrasts this condition with that of the naive poet for whom thoughtfulness, consciousness is subsumed into a unity of feeling and being. It is of the utmost significance that Schiller, confronted by the scale of Goethe's achievement, responded not just by defining but by *historicizing* the difference in creative temperament and sensibility between himself and Goethe. Above all, his essay supplies an unsurpassed analysis of the complex and frequently uneasy kinds of relationship that are possible between the reflective temperament and human (and other forms of) nature. Above all, Schiller charts the disunity of the modern spirit, the extent to which modern man knows of a unified condition from which he is excluded. And his knowledge is both the mode and measure of his deprivation − but it also makes possible a gain in reflectivity, a new realm of cognition, ultimately of creativity. Schiller's essay alerts us to both the theme and the mode of reflective poetry: he helps us to see that, in following the theme of childhood from Hölderlin to Heine and Rilke we are tracing variations on the theme of the forfeited idyll; that, in analyzing the language of poetry from Hölderlin to Brecht we are obliged to notice the different values and colours that attend the reflective naming, and situating, of the self, the 'Ich' in the poem. Moreover, Schiller's is only one of several attempts in the period of Goethe's lifetime to chart the course of modern culture. Hegel, registering the increasing self-consciousness of modern art, predicts the end of art itself: as man becomes more self-aware, he argues, so philosophy will take the place of art as the vehicle for a culture's self-understanding. Heine some time later will view the death of Goethe as marking the 'Ende der Kunstperiode'. What comes after, he suggests, is a different age, one in which creative people will bend their talents to politics and public life, rather than to art. How far Hegel and Heine were right in their predictions matters less than the fact that they were engaged in mapping the terrain in which, for good or for ill, modern culture would find itself dwelling. Both of them see reflectivity as the crucial signature of the modern age, a reflectivity that will manifest itself in discursive writing, in philosophy, journalism, or political tracts: and (we might add) in so far as that reflectivity will seek to express itself in poetry, it will do so through modes of detachment from the experiential substance invoked — that is, through irony, cultural commentary, and allegory. For allegory, it will be remembered, makes explicit the divide that opens between the physical scene or image and its spiritual signification.

These are complex and difficult arguments. But what they all point to is the identification of a particular condition of poetry, which, in all its perils and hazards, is the truthful precipitate of the modern world. And one cannot but feel that modernity is defined as an acutely and historically self-conscious exercise; one that is made the more urgent by the need to see the stresses and strains of modern writing as not inferior to Goethe's oeuvre, but as legitimately (i.e. historically) different from it. It was Heine of all people who once wrote: 'Die Natur wollte wissen, wie sie aussah, und erschuf sich Goethe'. It is a profound, and profoundly affectionate, tribute: and it is one that stems from the knowledge that the changing interrelation between reflectivity and nature marks the end of one period of art and the beginning of another kind of culture. The change can also be felt in the different modes of selfhood. Goethe's lyric art is a tribute to the plenitude and multifariousness of the interplay of self and world. However complex the mediations are, Goethe never doubts the rightness and wholeness of this process. In a sense the 'Ich' of Goethe's poetry is a given. What Schiller's definition of the 'sentimentalisch' poet does is to make the 'Ich' a problem and a theme: because of this reflectivity that is part of its condition, the 'Ich' necessarily worries at the problem of its own definition and location (not only psychological, but historical and cultural).

Schiller offers us not only the discursive analysis of the 'sentimentalisch' sensibility: he also offers its creative exploration in the poems he writes. He is one of a number of poets in this anthology who invoke the authority of transcendental experience, of ideals, of a divinity. Constantly we find that Schiller's poetry inquires into the place of man with regard to the transcendental realm that is invoked. Do the transcendental intimations serve to indicate the place of unregenerate humanity? Or do they perhaps vindicate it? The poetic work is exalted, highly wrought, often indebted to the complex forms of classical Greek poetry. As an inflected language, German can cope with the fearsome demands of stretching the syntax of everyday speech in order to encompass the architecture of the chosen form while yet keeping the sentence statement alive. The employment of classical form and metre is often a tribute to a bygone age in which divine and earthly experience were united. And often such prosody is attended by explicit passages of reflection on the cultural history of mankind since the Greeks. Thereby the mode becomes part of the theme. Linguistically such poetry can often be difficult: and that difficulty may be the measure of the gulf that has opened between the everyday vernacular and the forms of linguistic and transcendental aspiration. The visionary poet may find himself driven to the limits of what is sayable in the common discourse. The 'Ich' may find itself in the double guise of both spokesman for quotidian humanity and quester after transcendence. The scale and pathos of this undertaking has never been more finely expressed than in the lines from Hölderlin's *Brot und Wein*:

> Aber Freund! wir kommen zu spät. Zwar leben die Götter,
> Aber über dem Haupt droben in anderer Welt.
> Endlos wirken sie da und scheinen's wenig zu achten,
> Ob wir leben, so sehr schonen die Himmlischen uns.
> Denn nicht immer vermag ein schwaches Gefäß sie zu fassen,
> Nur zu Zeiten erträgt göttliche Fülle der Mensch.
>   [. . .] Indessen dünket mir öfters
> Besser zu schlafen, wie so ohne Genossen zu sein,
> So zu harren, und was zu tun ides und zu sagen,
> Weiß ich nicht, und wozu Dichter in dürftiger Zeit?

These lines chart the heartland of what Schiller perceives as the condition of modern 'sentimentalisch' poetry, and in this sense they are the very signature of so much modern lyric creativity — of the hazardous enterprise that seeks to create, through poetry, a mythology for which there are no common terms or symbols. Hölderlin's lines establish the vision of a fuller humanity while at the same time recognizing how far man falls short of attaining that goal: in that process the lines move in their form of address between the 'du' of a close friend, the 'wir' of common humanity, and the 'Ich' of the quester-poet. The impulses from both the thematic and the poetic substance of Hölderlin's lines can be felt in such poets as Blake, Wordsworth, Coleridge, Victor Hugo, Mallarmé, Rilke, T. S. Eliot, Yeats, Valéry, Pound. From each poet the specific perception of the perilous condition of the 'Dichter in dürftiger Zeit' will be different, because the 'dürftige Zeit' will change its particular historical aspect. But the spiritual landscape of the poetry will remain recognizable through the various changes.

Where this kind of concern provides the mainspring of the poetry we find one of the cardinal experiences of the post-Goethean age. In Goethe's poetry we find no irremediable divide between inner and outer worlds, or between simplicity and sophistication. But the great majority of poetry in this volume tells a different story. I have included three (very different) poets of the Romantic generation. Novalis offers us a vision of unity — but at the price of dissolving the common world into insubstantiality. The *Hymnen an die Nacht* begin with a praise of light, but then, in the second hymn all familiar categories of value and significance are challenged. Night becomes the realm of knowable truth, death and the womb allow access to a higher realm in which sexuality and religion proclaim one and the same transcendent realm. This unity entails the dissolution of all manner of human allegiances and understanding. The poetry is impressive for its sense of expanding rapture as line succeeds line in what seems an almost never-ending sentence structure. But for other poets of the Romantic generation the rapture will not be enough to banish the resistant outer world. Brentano's religious poetry is characterized by a despair that implies (but cannot achieve) transcendence. Moreover, time and time again we sense antithetical patterns at the heart of his work. He was drawn to the folk song, but his sensibility could not dwell easily within the simple patterns (both experiential and linguistic) of the folk song. Hence the ballad form, with its simple narrative structure and refrain patterns, is married to the expression of experiences that go with complex states of psychological and sexual disorientation. The upshot is a strange concoction of sturdiness and anchorless sophistication. The abysses that Brentano perceives are present in Eichendorff's work: but often the threat is triumphantly exercised by a firmly commonsensical Christian sensibility. Enchantment can be the wellspring of poetry, but magic has its dangers, and the enchantress is to be feared. As Novalis put it, 'wo keine Götter sind, walten Gespenster'.

With much of Heine's work we enter the realm of poetry that is made, both linguistically and thematically, not of enchantment but of disenchantment. Heine wrote poetry with an extraordinary — perhaps excessive — facility. But with that facility went the sense that poetry was but an escapist exercise in an age of prose. In the finest of his poems, the knowingness, the self-consciousness expresses itself as the problematic sensibility of a lyrical persona that is divided against itself. Often he has the urbanity and scandalous zest of a Byron. But the accent of pain gives his art a psychological cutting edge and an intensity of social and cultural criticism that Byron rarely attains. In bittersweet, often outrageously tawdry lines Heine captures the sense of coming late, of standing at the end of a cultural and historical period and inheriting only the bric-à-brac of a poetry that is now out of season. To modify Hölderlin's cry: 'whither poetry in a prosaic age?' might have been Heine's motto.

With Droste-Hülshoff and Mörike we have two poets who are often held to be characteristic of the 'Biedermeier' age, of that conservative, restoration ethos that follows upon the upheavals of revolutionary aspiration. The values asserted are those of modesty, domesticity, containment within a small, familiar — indeed often familial — world. Yet the unease is never far away, the containment may be alarmingly close to constriction. With Droste this theme acquires particular poignancy by virtue of her being a woman; one thinks of *Im Turm*, of the self that has to behave like a well-behaved child and can only secretly let her hair flow in the wind. If there is a nature *within* the self that threatens the enforced self-possession of the poet, there is also an unruly nature *outside* the charmed circle of hearth and home. The moorland is a realm that can only just be — literally and metaphorically — contained. Similarly in Droste's religious poetry, the public sequences of the Christian calendar offer a housing that proves less than adequate to the spiritually threatened self. In Mörike's art we find an ethos of balance and containment that is nowhere more moving than where it proves brittle. The patterned verse, the scrupulously moulded form is an act of exorcism that (like all exorcism) acknowledges the thing that is to be banished. Even in *Auf eine Lampe*, that seemingly motionless poem that is an example of — and that speaks of — the lovely, self-sufficient containment of the work of art, we note the awareness of a world outside the charmed realm of lovely stasis. The lamp hangs from the 'Decke des nun fast vergessnen Lustgemachs'. And the final two lines of the poem read:

> Ein Kunstgebild der echten Art. Wer achtet sein?
> Was aber schön ist, selig scheint es in ihm selbst.

The closing line is one of the most famous in the whole of German literature: a validation of the self-sufficient artefact as something that partakes of the intactness and integrity of beauty. Yet directly preceding this validation of beauty we have a half line that reads

'Wer achtet sein?' The poem, itself a 'Kunstgebild der echten Art', both recognizes its own fragility within a world that pays no attention and asserts its own inviolability. Once again, much less spectacularly of course, Hölderlin's sense of making poetry in – and against – unpropitious times is heard. Similarly, in *Um Mitternacht* the magic equipoise of the midnight moment is a moment and no more. What the poem celebrates is eroded by time.

With Hofmannsthal and Rilke we come to two poets who express that spiritual impoverishment of modern life of which Nietzsche was the incomparable psychologist and diagnostician. Both are acutely aware of being late-comers, of being in receipt of an inheritance that is no longer viable. Both find themselves obliged to address the radical shifts that affect man's place in the world. Above all, the notion of selfhood is challenged, and with it the traditional, hallowed place of 'das lyrische Ich'. In 1905 Hofmannsthal wrote: 'Das Wesen unserer Epoche ist Vieldeutigkeit und Unbestimmtheit. Sie kann nur auf Gleitendem ausruhen und ist sich bewußt, daß es Gleitendes ist, wo andere Generationen an das Feste glaubten.' His sense of 'unsere Epoche' told him that modern man had lost both his centrality in respect of the phenomenal world – and his centredness within himself. There was, in other words, no reliable vantage point from which experience could be endowed with shape and coherence. Hofmannsthal grounds his whole creative career in the attempt to coax the unstable self into an acceptance of – and involvement with – the demands of social existence. And he moves away from lyric poetry into the more 'social' and public form of the drama. Rilke attempts to exorcise the problematic self by writing, in the *Neue Gedichte*, poems that are not dependent on, but indeed are resistant to, the voice of human subjectivity. The *Neue Gedichte* convey and celebrate experiences that enshrine an integrity of being and value that is denied to man: hence the poems that concern plants, animals, objects (most usually artistic artefacts). Yet ultimately human consciousness cannot be so banished. And in the *Duineser Elegien* Rilke finds a place again for man as sayer of the world, as a unique voice that transforms the visible world into poetic utterance. In many ways Rilke's answer to the devaluations and deformations of the modern world entails the establishment of a new mythology, one in which the world and man can again be justified. It is an important and moving achievement, but it may in fact justify less than it claims to do. Perhaps, to borrow terms from the early Nietzsche of the *Geburt der Tragödie*, it is not the world as such, but the world in so far as it can become an aesthetic phenomenon, that is justified in Rilke's poetry.

In the last analysis, we may remember and cherish Rilke more for the lament at the condition of the modern world than for the aesthetic redemptions of its ugliness and emptiness. Certainly, that powerful undercurrent of lament links Rilke with both Trakl and Benn. The physical decay of which both these poets speak with well nigh obsessive urgency is not merely an outward condition: it touches the very subjectivity that claims to know this collapse of being and value. And both Trakl and Benn seek solace in the utterance, part mythological, part aesthetic, of which art alone is capable. To that quest for an aesthetic or spiritual transcendence Bertolt Brecht offers an answer that is as simple as it is radical. He challenges the notion of privileged subjectivity in the lyric utterance, and makes his poetic voice overtly − even aggressively − public (and, on occasion, polemical). He brings everyday speech and everyday concerns into poetry in a way that only Goethe before him had managed. He derives poetry from the inhospitable terrain of the modern world, from the uncomfortable (and uncomforting) indifference of the natural world (implying thereby a criticism of so much 'Naturlyrik' that had preceded him); and from the political betrayals of the twentieth century. His *Schlechte Zeit für Lyrik* is a poem made out of the sense of his own historicity as poet. Similarly, Hans Magnus Enzensberger derives his lyrical oeuvre from the resistant banality of modern life. He displays a masterly ability to incorporate colloquial speech patterns into his verse and to make them yield a range of implications far in excess of their normal (i.e. non-poetic) meaning. It is a very different enterprise from Paul Celan's. For Celan poetic language is poetic precisely to the extent that is has been wrested from everyday discourse, and from silence. Celan's work is austere and forbidding. Yet, for all the vast differences of temperament and diction that separate him from Brecht and Enzensberger, what unites all three is their will, and ability, against the odds, to find a place for the 'Dichter in dürftiger Zeit'.

It has often been remarked that in communist countries lyric poets tend to adopt the voice of personal experience, whereas in more individualistic societies poets feel the need to speak through a depersonalized voice. Of course, there can be no hard and fast rules for the modes of poetic creativity, because the connexions between the lyrical self and the public world are many and variable.

But much of the work in this anthology shows that poetry can spring from an adversary relationship between the lyric voice and the common discourse of the age. Such a relationship means that poets perceive and record the hostility of their times more passionately and more precisely than anyone less.

FRIEDRICH GOTTLIEB KLOPSTOCK

1724–1803

Der Zürchersee

Schön ist, Mutter Natur, deiner Erfindung Pracht
Auf die Fluren verstreut, schöner ein froh Gesicht,
Das den großen Gedanken
Deiner Schöpfung noch einmal denkt.

Von des schimmernden Sees Traubengestaden her
Oder, flohest du schon wieder zum Himmel auf,
Komm in rötendem Strahle
Auf dem Flügel der Abendluft,

Komm und lehre mein Lied jugendlich heiter sein,
Süße Freude, wie du, gleich dem beseelteren
Schnellen Jauchzen des Jünglings,
Sanft, der fühlenden Fanny gleich.

Schon lag hinter uns weit Uto, an dessen Fuß
Zürich in ruhigem Tal freie Bewohner nährt;
Schon war manches Gebirge
Voll von Reben vorbeigeflohn.

Jetzt entwölkte sich fern silberner Alpen Höh,
Und der Jünglinge Herz schlug schon empfindender,
Schon verriet es beredter
Sich der schönen Begleiterin.

Hallers Doris, die sang, selber des Liedes wert,
Hirzels Daphne, den Kleist innig wie Gleimen liebt;
Und wir Jünglinge sangen
Und empfanden wie Hagedorn.

Jetzo nahm uns die Au in die beschattenden
Kühlen Arme des Walds, welcher die Insel krönt;
Da, da kamest du, Freude,
Volles Maß auf uns herab!

Göttin Freude, du selbst! Dich, wir empfanden dich!
Ja, du warest es selbst, Schwester der Menschlichkeit,
Deiner Unschuld Gespielin,
Die sich über uns ganz ergoß!

Süß ist, fröhlicher Lenz, deiner Begeistrung Hauch,
Wenn die Flur dich gebiert, wenn sich dein Odem sanft
In der Jünglinge Herzen
Und die Herzen der Mädchen gießt.

Ach, du machst das Gefühl siegend, es steigt durch dich
Jede blühende Brust schöner und bebender,
Lauter redet der Liebe
Nun entzauberter Mund durch dich!

Lieblich winket der Wein, wenn er Empfindungen,
Bessre, sanftere Lust, wenn er Gedanken winkt,
Im sokratischen Becher
Von der tauenden Ros umkränzt,

Wenn er dringt bis ins Herz und zu Entschließungen,
Die der Säufer verkennt, jeden Gedanken weckt,
Wenn er lehret verachten,
Was nicht würdig des Weisen ist.

Reizvoll klinget des Ruhms lockender Silberton
In das schlagende Herz, und die Unsterblichkeit
Ist ein großer Gedanke,
Ist des Schweißes der Edlen wert!

Durch der Lieder Gewalt bei der Urenkelin
Sohn und Tochter noch sein, mit der Entzückung Ton
Oft beim Namen genennet,
Oft gerufen vom Grabe her,

Dann ihr sanfteres Herz bilden und, Liebe, dich,
Fromme Tugend, dich auch gießen ins sanfte Herz,
Ist, beim Himmel, nicht wenig,
Ist des Schweißes der Edlen wert!

Aber süßes ist noch, schöner und reizender,
In dem Arme des Freunds wissen, ein Freund zu sein,
So das Leben genießen,
Nicht unwürdig der Ewigkeit.

Treuer Zärtlichkeit voll, in den Umschattungen,
In den Lüften des Waldes und mit gesenktem Blick
Auf die silberne Welle,
Tat ich schweigend den frommen Wunsch:

Wäret ihr auch bei uns, die ihr mich ferne liebt,
In des Vaterlands Schoß einsam von mir verstreut,
Die in seligen Stunden
Meine suchende Seele fand:

Oh, so bauten wir hier Hütten der Freundschaft uns!
Ewig wohnten wir hier, ewig! Der Schattenwald
Wandelt' uns sich in Tempe,
Jenes Tal in Elysium!

Die Frühlingsfeier

Nicht in den Ozean der Welten alle
Will ich mich stürzen! schweben nicht,
Wo die ersten Erschaffnen, die Jubelchöre der Söhne des Lichts,
Anbeten, tief anbeten und in Entzückung vergehn!

Nur um den Tropfen am Eimer,
Um die Erde nur will ich schweben und anbeten!
Halleluja! Halleluja! Der Tropfen am Eimer
Rann aus der Hand des Allmächtigen auch!

Da der Hand des Allmächtigen
Die größeren Erden entquollen,
Die Ströme des Lichts rauschten und Siebengestirne wurden,
Da entrannest du, Tropfen, der Hand des Allmächtigen!

Da ein Strom des Lichts rauscht' und unsre Sonne wurde,
Ein Wogensturz sich stürzte wie vom Felsen
Der Wolk' herab und den Orion gürtete,
Da entrannest du, Tropfen, der Hand des Allmächtigen!

Wer sind die tausendmal Tausend, wer die Myriaden alle,
Welche den Tropfen bewohnen und bewohnten? Und wer bin ich?

Halleluja dem Schaffenden! mehr wie die Erden, die quollen,
Mehr wie die Siebengestirne, die aus Strahlen zusammenströmten!

Aber du, Frühlingswürmchen,
Das grünlichgolden neben mir spielt,
Du lebst — und bist vielleicht,
Ach, nicht unsterblich!

Ich bin herausgegangen, anzubeten,
Und ich weine? Vergib, vergib
Auch diese Träne dem Endlichen,
O du, der sein wird!

Du wirst die Zweifel alle mir enthüllen,
O du, der mich durch das dunkle Tal
Des Todes führen wird! Ich lerne dann,
Ob eine Seele das goldene Würmchen hatte.

Bist du nur gebildeter Staub,
Sohn des Mais, so werde denn
Wieder verfliegender Staub,
Oder was sonst der Ewige will!

Ergeuß von neuem du, mein Auge,
Freudentränen!
Du, meine Harfe,
Preise den Herrn!

Umwunden wieder, mit Palmen
Ist meine Harf umwunden! Ich singe dem Herrn!
Hier steh ich. Rund um mich
Ist alles Allmacht and Wunder alles!

Mit tiefer Ehrfurcht schau ich die Schöpfung an,
Denn du,
Namenloser, du
Schufest sie!

Lüfte, die um mich wehn und sanfte Kühlung
Auf mein glühendes Angesicht hauchen,
Euch, wunderbare Lüfte,
Sandte der Herr, der Unendliche!

Aber jetzt werden sie still, kaum atmen sie,
Die Morgensonne wird schwül!
Wolken strömen herauf!
Sichtbar ist, der kommt, der Ewige!

Nun schweben sie, rauschen sie, wirbeln die Winde!
Wie beugt sich der Wald! Wie hebt sich der Strom!
Sichtbar, wie du es Sterblichen sein kannst,
Ja, das bist du sichtbar, Unendlicher!

Der Wald neigt sich, der Strom fliehet, und ich
Falle nicht auf mein Angesicht!
Herr! Herr! Gott! barmherzig und gnädig!
Du Naher, erbarme dich meiner!

Zürnest du, Herr,
Weil Nacht dein Gewand ist?
Diese Nacht ist Segen der Erde.
Vater, du zürnest nicht!

Sie kommt, Erfrischung auszuschütten
Über den stärkenden Halm,
Über die herzerfreuende Traube.
Vater, du zürnest nicht!

Alles ist still vor dir, du Naher!
Ringsumher ist alles still!
Auch das Würmchen, mit Golde bedeckt, merkt auf!
Ist es vielleicht nicht seelenlos? Ist es unsterblich?

Ach, vermöcht ich dich, Herr, wie ich dürste, zu preisen!
Immer herrlicher offenbarest du dich!
Immer dunkler wird die Nacht um dich
Und voller von Segen!

Seht ihr den Zeugen des Nahen, den zückenden Strahl?
Hört ihr Jehovas Donner?
Hört ihr ihn? Hört ihr ihn,
Den erschütternden Donner des Herrn?

Herr! Herr! Gnädig!
Barmherzig und gnädig!
Angebetet, gepriesen
Sei dein herrlicher Name!

Und die Gewitterwinde? Sie tragen den Donner!
Wie sie rauschen! Wie sie mit lauter Woge den Wald
    durchströmen!
Und nun schweigen sie. Langsam wandelt
Die schwarze Wolke.

Seht ihr den neuen Zeugen des Nahen, den fliegenden Strahl?
Höret ihr hoch in der Wolke den Donner des Herrn?
Er ruft: Jehova! Jehova!
Und der geschmetterte Wald dampft!

Aber nicht unsere Hütte!
Unser Vater gebot
Seinem Verderber,
Vor unsrer Hütte vorüberzugehn.

Ach, schon rauscht, schon rauscht
Himmel und Erde vom gnädigen Regen!
Nun ist, wie dürstete sie! die Erd' erquickt
Und der Himmel der Segensfüll' enlastet!

Siehe, nun kommt Jehova nicht mehr im Wetter,
In stillem, sanftem Säuseln
Kommt Jehova,
Und unter ihm neigt sich der Bogen des Friedens!

Dem Unendlichen

Wie erhebt sich das Herz, wenn es dich,
Unendlicher, denkt! Wie sinkt es,
Wenns auf sich herunterschaut!
Elend schauts wehklagend dann und Nacht und Tod!

Allein du rufst mich aus meiner Nacht, der im Elend, der im Tod
    hilft!
Dann denk ich es ganz, daß du ewig mich schufst,
Herrlicher! den kein Preis, unten am Grab, oben am Thron,
Herr, Herr, Gott! den dankend entflammt kein Jubel genug
    besingt.

Weht, Bäume des Lebens, ins Harfengetön!
Rausche mit ihnen ins Harfengetön, kristallner Strom!

Ihr lispelt und rauscht und, Harfen, ihr tönt
Nie es ganz! Gott ist es, den ihr preist!

Donnert, Welten, in feierlichem Gang, in der Posaunen Chor!
Du Orion, Wage, du auch!
Tönt all' ihr Sonnen auf der Straße voll Glanz,
In der Posaunen Chor!

Ihr Welten, donnert,
Und du, der Posaunen Chor, hallest
Nie es ganz, Gott, nie es ganz, Gott,
Gott, Gott ist es, den ihr preist!

Die Sommernacht

Wenn der Schimmer von dem Monde nun herab
In die Wälder sich ergießt, und Gerüche
Mit den Düften von der Linde
In den Kühlungen wehn;

So umschatten mich Gedanken an das Grab
Der Geliebten, und ich seh in dem Walde
Nur es dämmern, und es weht mir
Von der Blüte nicht her.

Ich genoß einst, o ihr Toten, es mit euch!
Wie umwehten uns der Duft und die Kühlung,
Wie verschön warst von dem Monde
Du, o schöne Natur!

JOHANN WOLFGANG VON GOETHE

1749–1832

Willkommen und Abschied

Es schlug mein Herz, geschwind zu Pferde!
Es war getan fast eh gedacht.
Der Abend wiegte schon die Erde,
Und an den Bergen hing die Nacht;
Schon stand im Nebelkleid die Eiche,
Ein aufgetürmter Riese, da,
Wo Finsternis aus dem Gesträuche
Mit hundert schwarzen Augen sah.

Der Mond von einem Wolkenhügel
Sah kläglich aus dem Duft hervor,
Die Winde schwangen leise Flügel,
Umsausten schauerlich mein Ohr;
Die Nacht schuf tausend Ungeheuer,
Doch frisch und fröhlich war mein Mut:
In meinen Adern welches Feuer!
In meinem Herzen welche Glut!

Dich sah ich, und die milde Freude
Floß von dem süßen Blick auf mich;
Ganz war mein Herz an deiner Seite
Und jeder Atemzug für dich.
Ein rosenfarbnes Frühlingswetter
Umgab das liebliche Gesicht,
Und Zärtlichkeit für mich – ihr Götter!
Ich hofft es, ich verdient es nicht!

Doch ach, schon mit der Morgensonne
Verengt der Abschied mir das Herz:
In deinen Küssen welche Wonne!

In deinem Auge welcher Schmerz!
Ich ging, du standst und sahst zur Erden
Und sahst mir nach mit nassem Blick:
Und doch, welch Glück, geliebt zu werden!
Und lieben, Götter, welch ein Glück!

Mailied

Wie herrlich leuchtet
Mir die Natur!
Wie glänzt die Sonne!
Wie lacht die Flur!

Es dringen Blüten
Aus jedem Zweig
Und tausend Stimmen
Aus dem Gesträuch

Und Freud und Wonne
Aus jeder Brust.
O Erd, o Sonne!
O Glück, o Lust!

O Lieb, o Liebe!
So golden schön,
Wie Morgenwolken
Auf jenen Höhn!

Du segnest herrlich
Das frische Feld,
Im Blütendampfe
Die volle Welt.

O Mädchen, Mädchen,
Wie lieb ich dich!
Wie blickt dein Auge!
Wie liebst du mich!

So liebt die Lerche
Gesang und Luft,
Und Morgenblumen
Den Himmelsduft,

Wie ich dich liebe
Mit warmem Blut,
Die du mir Jugend
Und Freud und Mut

Zu neuen Liedern
Und Tänzen gibst.
Sei ewig glücklich,
Wie du mich liebst!

Ganymed

Wie im Morgenglanze
Du rings mich anglühst,
Frühling, Geliebter!
Mit tausendfacher Liebeswonne
Sich an mein Herz drängt
Deiner ewigen Wärme
Heilig Gefühl,
Unendliche Schöne!

Daß ich dich fassen möcht
In diesen Arm!

Ach, an deinem Busen
Lieg ich, schmachte,
Und deine Blumen, dein Gras
Drängen sich an mein Herz.
Du kühlst den brennenden
Durst meines Busens,
Lieblicher Morgenwind!
Ruft drein die Nachtigall
Liebend nach mir aus dem Nebeltal.

Ich komm, ich komme!
Wohin? Ach, wohin?

Hinauf! Hinauf strebt's.
Es schweben die Wolken
Abwärts, die Wolken
Neigen sich der sehnenden Liebe.

Mir! Mir!
In euerm Schoße
Aufwärts!
Umfangend umfangen!
Aufwärts an deinen Busen,
Alliebender Vater!

Prometheus

Bedecke deinen Himmel, Zeus,
Mit Wolkendunst
Und übe, dem Knaben gleich,
Der Disteln köpft,
An Eichen dich und Bergeshöhn;
Mußt mir meine Erde
Doch lassen stehn
Und meine Hütte, die du nicht gebaut,
Und meinen Herd,
Um dessen Glut
Du mich beneidest.

Ich kenne nichts Ärmeres
Unter der Sonn als euch, Götter!
Ihr nähret kümmerlich
Von Opfersteuern
Und Gebetshauch
Eure Majestät
Und darbtet, wären
Nicht Kinder und Bettler
Hoffnungsvolle Toren.

Da ich ein Kind war,
Nicht wußte, wo aus noch ein,
Kehrt ich mein verirrtes Auge
Zur Sonne, als wenn drüber wär
Ein Ohr, zu hören meine Klage,
Ein Herz wie meins,
Sich des Bedrängten zu erbarmen.

Wer half mir
Wider der Titanen Übermut?

Wer rettete vom Tode mich,
Von Sklaverei?
Hast du nicht alles selbst vollendet,
Heilig glühend Herz?
Und glühtest jung und gut,
Betrogen, Rettungsdank
Dem Schlafenden da droben?

Ich dich ehren? Wofür?
Hast du die Schmerzen gelindert
Je des Beladenen?
Hast du die Tränen gestillet
Je des Geängsteten?
Hat nicht mich zum Manne geschmiedet
Die allmächtige Zeit
Und das ewige Schicksal,
Meine Herrn und deine?

Wähntest du etwa,
Ich sollte das Leben hassen,
In Wüsten fliehen,
Weil nicht alle
Blütenträume reiften?

Hier sitz ich, forme Menschen
Nach meinem Bilde
Ein Geschlecht, das mir gleich sei,
Zu leiden, zu weinen,
Zu genießen und zu freuen sich,
Und dein nicht zu achten,
Wie ich!

An Belinden

Warum ziehst du mich unwiderstehlich,
Ach, in jene Pracht?
War ich guter Junge nicht so selig
In der öden Nacht?

Heimlich in mein Zimmerchen verschlossen,
Lag im Mondenschein,

Ganz von seinem Schauerlicht umflossen,
Und ich dämmert ein;

Träumte da von vollen goldnen Stunden
Ungemischter Lust,
Hatte schon das liebe Bild empfunden
Tief in meiner Brust.

Bin ichs noch, den du bei so viel Lichtern
An dem Spieltisch hältst?
Oft so unerträglichen Gesichtern
Gegenüber stellst?

Reizender ist mir des Frühlings Blüte
Nun nicht auf der Flur;
Wo du, Engel, bist, ist Lieb und Güte,
Wo du bist, Natur.

Auf dem See

Und frische Nahrung, neues Blut
Saug ich aus freier Welt;
Wie ist Natur so hold und gut,
Die mich am Busen hält!
Die Welle wieget unsern Kahn
Im Rudertakt hinauf,
Und Berge, wolkig himmelan,
Begegnen unserm Lauf.

Aug, mein Aug, was sinkst du nieder?
Goldne Träume, kommt ihr wieder?
Weg, du Traum! so gold du bist;
Hier auch Lieb und Leben ist.

Auf der Welle blinken
Tausend schwebende Sterne,
Weiche Nebel trinken
Rings die türmende Ferne;
Morgenwind umflügelt
Die beschattete Bucht,
Und im See bespiegelt
Sich die reifende Frucht.

Herbstgefühl

Fetter grüne, du Laub,
Am Rebengeländer
Hier mein Fenster herauf!
Gedrängter quellet,
Zwillingsbeeren, und reifet
Schneller und glänzend voller!
Euch brütet der Mutter Sonne
Scheideblick, euch umsäuselt
Des holden Himmels
Fruchtende Fülle,
Euch kühlet des Mondes
Freundlicher Zauberhauch,
Und euch betauen, ach!
Aus diesen Augen
Der ewig belebenden Liebe
Vollschwellende Tränen.

———

Warum gabst du uns die tiefen Blicke,
Unsre Zukunft ahnungsvoll zu schaun,
Unsrer Liebe, unserm Erdenglücke
Wähnend selig nimmer hinzutraun?
Warum gabst uns, Schicksal, die Gefühle,
Uns einander in das Herz zu sehn,
Um durch all die seltenen Gewühle
Unser wahr Verhältnis auszuspähn?

Ach, so viele tausend Menschen kennen,
Dumpf sich treibend, kaum ihr eigen Herz,
Schweben zwecklos hin und her und rennen
Hoffnungslos in unversehnem Schmerz,
Jauchzen wieder, wenn der schnellen Freuden
Unerwart'te Morgenröte tagt;
Nur uns armen liebevollen beiden
Ist das wechselseitge Glück versagt,
Uns zu lieben, ohn uns zu verstehen,
In dem andern sehn, was er nie war,
Immer frisch auf Traumglück auszugehen
Und zu schwanken auch in Traumgefahr.

Glücklich, den ein leerer Traum beschäftigt,
Glücklich, dem die Ahndung eitel wär!
Jede Gegenwart und jeder Blick bekräftigt
Traum und Ahndung leider uns noch mehr.
Sag, was will das Schicksal uns bereiten?
Sag, wie band es uns so rein genau?
Ach, du warst in abgelebten Zeiten
Meine Schwester oder meine Frau.

Kanntest jeden Zug in meinem Wesen,
Spähtest, wie die reinste Nerve klingt,
Konntest mich mit Einem Blicke lesen,
Den so schwer ein sterblich Aug durchdringt;
Tropftest Mäßigung dem heißen Blute,
Richtetest den wilden irren Lauf,
Und in deinen Engelsarmen ruhte
Die zerstörte Brust sich wieder auf;
Hieltest zauberleicht ihn angebunden
Und vergaukeltest ihm manchen Tag.
Welche Seligkeit glich jenen Wonnestunden,
Da er dankbar dir zu Füßen lag,
Fühlt' sein Herz an deinem Herzen schwellen,
Fühlte sich in deinem Auge gut,
Alle seine Sinnen sich erhellen
Und beruhigen sein brausend Blut!

Und von allem dem schwebt ein Erinnern
Nur noch um das ungewisse Herz,
Fühlt die alte Wahrheit ewig gleich im Innern,
Und der neue Zustand wird ihm Schmerz.
Und wir scheinen uns nur halb beseelet,
Dämmernd ist um uns der hellste Tag.
Glücklich, daß das Schicksal, das uns quälet
Uns doch nicht verändern mag!

Wandrers Nachtlied

Der du von dem Himmel bist,
Alles Leid und Schmerzen stillest,
Den, der doppelt elend ist,

Doppelt mit Erquickung füllest,
Ach, ich bin des Treibens müde!
Was soll all der Schmerz und Lust?
Süßer Friede,
Komm, ach komm in meine Brust!

Ein gleiches

Über allen Gipfeln
Ist Ruh,
In allen Wipfeln
Spürest du
Kaum einen Hauch;
Die Vögelein schweigen im Walde.
Warte nur, balde
Ruhest du auch.

An den Mond

Füllest wieder Busch und Tal
Still mit Nebelglanz,
Lösest endlich auch einmal
Meine Seele ganz,

Breitest über mein Gefild
Lindernd deinen Blick,
Wie des Freundes Auge mild
Über mein Geschick.

Jeden Nachklang fühlt mein Herz
Froh- und trüber Zeit,
Wandle zwischen Freud und Schmerz
In der Einsamkeit.

Fließe, fließe, lieber Fluß!
Nimmer werd ich froh,
So verrauschte Scherz und Kuß
Und die Treue so.

Ich besaß es doch einmal,
Was so köstlich ist!
Daß man doch zu seiner Qual
Nimmer es vergißt!

Rausche, Fluß, das Tal entlang,
Ohne Rast und Ruh,
Rausche, flüstre meinem Sang
Melodien zu,

Wenn du in der Winternacht
Wütend überschwillst
Oder um die Frühlingspracht
Junger Knospen quillst.

Selig, wer sich vor der Welt
Ohne Haß verschließt,
Einen Freund am Busen hält
Und mit dem genießt,

Was, von Menschen nicht gewußt
Oder nicht bedacht,
Durch das Labyrinth der Brust
Wandelt in der Nacht.

Das Göttliche

Edel sei der Mensch,
Hilfreich und gut!
Denn das allein
Unterscheidet ihn
Von allen Wesen,
Die wir kennen.

Heil den unbekannten
Höhern Wesen,
Die wir ahnen!
Ihnen gleiche der Mensch;
Sein Beispiel lehr uns
Jene glauben.

Denn unfühlend
Ist die Natur:
Es leuchtet die Sonne
Über Bös' und Gute,
Und dem Verbrecher
Glänzen wie dem Besten
Der Mond und die Sterne.

Wind und Ströme,
Donner und Hagel
Rauschen ihren Weg
Und ergreifen
Vorüber eilend
Einen um den andern.

Auch so das Glück
Tappt unter die Menge,
Faßt bald des Knaben
Lockige Unschuld,
Bald auch den kahlen
Schuldigen Scheitel.

Nach ewigen, ehrnen,
Großen Gesetzen
Müssen wir alle
Unseres Daseins
Kreise vollenden.

Nur allein der Mensch
Vermag das Unmögliche:
Er unterscheidet,
Wählet und richtet;
Er kann dem Augenblick
Dauer verleihen.

Er allein darf
Den Guten lohnen
Den Bösen strafen,
Heilen und retten,
Alles Irrende, Schweifende
Nützlich verbinden.

Und wir verehren
Die Unsterblichen,

Als wären sie Menschen,
Täten im Großen,
Was der Beste im Kleinen
Tut oder möchte.

Der edle Mensch
Sei hilfreich und gut!
Unermüdet schaff er
Das Nützliche, Rechte,
Sei uns ein Vorbild
Jener geahneten Wesen!

Römische Elegien V

Froh empfind ich mich nun auf klassischem Boden begeistert;
   Vor- und Mitwelt spricht lauter und reizender mir.
Hier befolg ich den Rat, durchblättre die Werke der Alten
   Mit geschäftiger Hand, täglich mit neuem Genuß.
Aber die Nächte hindurch hält Amor mich anders beschäftigt;
   Werd ich auch halb nur gelehrt, bin ich doch doppelt beglückt.
Und belehr ich mich nicht, indem ich des lieblichen Busens
   Formen spähe, die Hand leite die Hüften hinab?
Dann versteh ich den Marmor erst recht; ich denk und vergleiche,
   Sehe mit fühlendem Aug, fühle mit sehender Hand.
Raubt die Liebste denn gleich mir einige Stunden des Tages,
   Gibt sie Stunden der Nacht mir zur Entschädigung hin.
Wird doch nicht immer geküßt, es wird vernünftig gesprochen;
   Überfällt sie der Schlaf, lieg ich und denke mir viel.
Oftmals hab ich auch schon in ihren Armen gedichtet
   Und des Hexameters Maß leise mit fingernder Hand
Ihr auf den Rücken gezählt. Sie atmet in lieblichem Schlummer,
   Und es durchglühet ihr Hauch mir bis ins Tiefste die Brust.
Amor schüret die Lamp indes und denket der Zeiten,
   Da er den nämlichen Dienst seinen Triumvirn getan.

Dauer im Wechsel

Hielte diesen frühen Segen
Ach, nur Eine Stunde fest!

Aber vollen Blütenregen
Schüttelt schon der laue West.
Soll ich mich des Grünen freuen,
Dem ich Schatten erst verdankt?
Bald wird Sturm auch das zerstreuen,
Wenn es falb im Herbst geschwankt.

Willst du nach den Früchten greifen.
Eilig nimm dein Teil davon!
Diese fangen an zu reifen,
Und die andern keimen schon;
Gleich mit jedem Regengusse
Ändert sich dein holdes Tal,
Ach, und in demselben Flusse
Schwimmst du nicht zum zweitenmal.

Du nun selbst! Was felsenfeste
Sich vor dir hervorgetan,
Mauern siehst du, siehst Paläste
Stets mit andern Augen an.
Weggeschwunden ist die Lippe,
Die im Kusse sonst genas,
Jener Fuß, der an der Klippe
Sich mit Gemsenfreche maß,

Jene Hand, die gern und milde
Sich bewegte wohlzutun,
Das gegliederte Gebilde,
Alles ist ein andres nun.
Und was sich an jener Stelle
Nun mit deinem Namen nennt,
Kam herbei wie eine Welle,
Und so eilt's zum Element.

Laß den Anfang mit dem Ende
Sich in Eins zusammenziehn!
Schneller als die Gegenstände
Selber dich vorüberfliehn.
Danke, daß die Gunst der Musen
Unvergängliches verheißt,
Den Gehalt in deinem Busen
Und die Form in deinem Geist.

Selige Sehnsucht

Sagt es niemand, nur den Weisen,
Weil die Menge gleich verhöhnet,
Das Lebendge will ich preisen
Das nach Flammentod sich sehnet.

In der Liebesnächte Kühlung,
Die dich zeugte, wo du zeugtest,
Überfällt dich fremde Fühlung,
Wenn die stille Kerze leuchtet.

Nicht mehr bleibest du umfangen
In der Finsternis Beschattung,
Und dich reißet neu Verlangen
Auf zu höherer Begattung.

Keine Ferne macht dich schwierig,
Kommst geflogen und gebannt,
Und zuletzt, des Lichts begierig,
Bist du Schmetterling verbrannt.

Und so lang du das nicht hast,
Dieses: Stirb und werde!
Bist du nur ein trüber Gast
Auf der dunklen Erde.

Um Mitternacht

Um Mitternacht ging ich, nicht eben gerne,
Klein, kleiner Knabe, jenen Kirchhof hin
Zu Vaters Haus, des Pfarrers; Stern am Sterne,
Sie leuchteten doch alle gar zu schön;
    Um Mitternacht.

Wenn ich dann ferner in des Lebens Weite
Zur Liebsten mußte, mußte, weil sie zog,
Gestirn und Nordschein über mir im Streite,
Ich gehend, kommend Seligkeiten sog;
    Um Mitternacht.

Bis dann zuletzt des vollen Mondes Helle
So klar und deutlich mir ins Finstere drang,
Auch der Gedanke willig, sinnig, schnelle
Sich ums Vergangne wie ums Künftige schlang;
  Um Mitternacht.

Der Bräutigam

Um Mitternacht, ich schlief, im Busen wachte
Das liebevolle Herz, als wär es Tag;
Der Tag erschien, mir war, als ob es nachte,
Was ist es mir, so viel er bringen mag.

Sie fehlte ja; mein emsig Tun und Streben
Für sie allein ertrug ichs durch die Glut
Der heißen Stunde; welch erquicktes Leben
Am kühlen Abend! lohnend wars und gut.

Die Sonne sank, und Hand in Hand verpflichtet
Begrüßten wir den letzten Segensblick,
Und Auge sprach, ins Auge klar gerichtet:
Von Osten, hoffe nur, sie kommt zurück!

Um Mitternacht, der Sterne Glanz geleitet
Im holden Traum zur Schwelle, wo sie ruht.
O sei auch mir dort auszuruhn bereitet,
Wie es auch sei, das Leben, es ist gut!

———

  Nun weiß man erst, was Rosenknospe sei,
  Jetzt, da die Rosenzeit vorbei;
  Ein Spätling noch am Stocke glänzt
  Und ganz allein die Blumenwelt ergänzt.

FRIEDRICH SCHILLER

1759–1805

Die Götter Griechenlandes

Da ihr noch die schöne Welt regiertet,
An der Freude leichtem Gängelband
Glücklichere Menschenalter führtet,
Schöne Wesen aus dem Fabelland!
Ach! da euer Wonnedienst noch glänzte,
Wie ganz anders, anders war es da!
Da man deine Tempel noch bekränzte,
Venus Amathusia!

Da der Dichtkunst malerische Hülle
Sich noch lieblich um die Wahrheit wand,
Durch die Schöpfung floß da Lebensfülle,
Und was nie empfinden wird, empfand.
An der Liebe Busen sie zu drücken,
Gab man höhern Adel der Natur.
Alles wies den eingeweihten Blicken,
Alles eines Gottes Spur.

Wo jetzt nur, wie unsre Weisen sagen,
Seelenlos ein Feuerball sich dreht,
Lenkte damals seinen goldnen Wagen
Helios in stiller Majestät.
Dies Höhen füllten Oreaden,
Eine Dryas starb mit jenem Baum,
Aus den Urnen lieblicher Najaden
Sprang der Ströme Silberschaum.

Jener Lorbeer wand sich einst um Hilfe,
Tantals Tochter schweigt in diesem Stein,
Syrinx' Klage tönt' aus jenem Schilfe,
Philomelens Schmerz in diesem Hain.

Jener Bach empfing Demeters Zähre,
Die sie um Persephonen geweint,
Und von diesem Hügel rief Cythere,
Ach, vergebens! ihrem schönen Freund.

Zu Deukalions Geschlechte stiegen
Damals noch die Himmlischen herab,
Pyrrhas schöne Töchter zu besiegen,
Nahm Hyperion den Hirtenstab.
Zwischen Menschen, Göttern and Heroen
Knüpfte Amor einen schönen Bund.
Sterbliche mit Göttern und Heroen
Huldigten in Amathunt.

Betend an der Grazien Altären
Kniete da die holde Priesterin,
Sandte stille Wünsche an Cytheren
Und Gelübde an die Charitin.
Hoher Stolz, auch droben zu gebieten,
Lehrte sie den göttergleichen Rang,
Und des Reizes heilgen Gürtel hüten,
Der den *Donnrer* selbst bezwang.

Himmlisch und unsterblich war das Feuer,
Das in Pindars stolzen Hymnen floß,
Niederströmte in Arions Leier,
In den Stein des Phidias sich goß.
Bessre Wesen, edlere Gestalten
Kündigten die hohe Abkunft an.
Götter, die vom Himmel niederwallten,
Sahen *hier* ihn wieder aufgetan.

Werter war von eines Gottes Güte,
Teurer jede Gabe der Natur.
Unter Iris' schönem Bogen blühte
Reizender die perlenvolle Flur.
Prangender erschien die Morgenröte
In Himerens rosigtem Gewand,
Schmelzender erklang die Flöte
In des Hirtengottes Hand.

Liebenswerter malte sich die Jugend,
Blühender in Ganymedas Bild,
Heldenkühner, göttlicher die Tugend

Mit Tritoniens Medusenschild.
Sanfter war, da Hymen es noch knüpfte,
Heiliger der Herzen ewges Band.
Selbst des Lebens zarter Faden shlüpfte
Weicher durch der Parzen Hand.

Das Evoë muntrer Thyrusschwinger
Und der Panther prächtiges Gespann
Meldeten den großen Freudebringer.
Faun und Satyr taumeln ihm voran,
Um ihn springen rasende Mänaden,
Ihre Tänze loben seinen Wein,
Und die Wangen des Bewirters laden
Lustig zu dem Becher ein.

Höher war der Gabe Wert gestiegen,
Die der Geber freundlich *mit* genoß,
Näher war der Schöpfer dem Vergnügen,
Das im Busen des Geschöpfes floß.
Nennt der meinige sich dem Verstande?
Birgt ihn etwa der Gewölke Zelt?
Mühsam späh ich im Ideenlande,
Fruchtlos in der Sinnenwelt.

Eure Tempel lachten gleich Palästen,
Euch verherrlichte das Heldenspiel
An des Isthmus kronenreichen Festen,
Und die Wagen donnerten zum Ziel.
Schön geschlungne seelenvolle Tänze
Kreisten um den prangenden Altar,
Eure Schläfe schmückten Siegeskränze,
Kronen euer duftend Haar.

Seiner Güter schenkte man das beste,
Seiner Lämmer liebstes gab der Hirt,
Und der Freudetaumel seiner Gäste
Lohnte dem erhabnen Wirt.
Wohin tret ich? Diese traur'ge Stille,
Kündigt sie mir meinen Schöpfer an?
Finster, wie er selbst, ist seine Hülle,
Mein Entsagen − was ihn feiern kann.

Damals trat kein gräßliches Gerippe
Vor das Bett des Sterbenden. Ein Kuß

Nahm das letzte Leben von der Lippe,
Still und traurig senkt' ein Genius
Seine Fackel, Schöne, lichte Bilder
Scherzten auch um die Notwendigkeit,
Und das ernste Schicksal blickte milder
Durch den Schleier sanfter Menschlichkeit.

Nach der Geister schrecklichen Gesetzen
Richtete kein heiliger Barbar,
Dessen Augen Tränen nie benetzen,
Zarte Wesen, die ein Weib gebar.
Selbst des Orkus strenge Richterwaage
Hielt der Enkel einer Sterblichen,
Und des Thrakers seelenvolle Klage
Rührte die Erinnyen.

Seine Freuden traf der frohe Schatten
In Elysiens Hainen wieder an;
Treue Liebe fand den treuen Gatten
Und der Wagenlenker seine Bahn;
Orpheus' Spiel tönt die gewohnten Lieder,
In Alcestens Arme sinkt Admet,
Seinen Freund erkennt Orestes wieder,
Seine Waffen Philoktet.

Aber ohne Wiederkehr verloren
Bleibt, was *ich* auf dieser Welt verließ,
Jede Wonne hab ich abgeschworen,
Alle Bande, die ich selig pries.
Fremde, nie verstandene Entzücken
Schaudern mich aus jenen Welten an,
Und für Freuden, die mich jetzt beglücken,
Tausch ich neue, die ich missen kann.

Höhre Preise stärkten da den Ringer
Auf der Tugend arbeitvoller Bahn;
Großer Taten herrliche Vollbringer
Klimmten zu den Seligen hinan;
Vor dem Wiederforderer der Toten
Neigte sich der Götter stille Schar.
Durch die Fluten leuchtet dem Piloten
Vom Olymp das Zwillingspaar.

Schöne Welt, wo bist du? – Kehre wieder,
Holdes Blütenalter der Natur!
Ach! nur in dem Feenland der Lieder
Lebt noch deine goldne Spur.
Augestorben trauert das Gefilde,
Keine Gottheit zeigt sich meinem Blick,
Ach! von jenem lebenwarmen Bilde
Blieb nur das Gerippe mir zurück.

Alle jenen Blüten sind gefallen
Von des Nordes winterlichem Wehn.
Einen zu bereichern unter allen
Mußte diese Götterwelt vergehn.
Traurig such ich an dem Sternenbogen,
Dich, Selene, find ich dort nicht mehr;
Durch die Wälder ruf ich, durch die Wogen,
Ach! sie widerhallen leer!

Unbewußt der Freuden, die sie schenket,
Nie entzückt von ihrer Trefflichkeit,
Nie gewahr des Armes, der sie lenket,
Reicher nie durch meine Dankbarkeit,
Fühllos selbst für ihres Künstlers Ehre,
Gleich dem toten Schlag der Pendeluhr,
Dient sie knechtisch dem Gesetz der Schwere,
Die entgötterte Natur!

Morgen wieder neu sich zu entbinden,
Wühlt sie heute sich ihr eignes Grab,
Und an ewig gleicher Spindel winden
Sich von selbst die Monde auf und ab.
Müßig kehrten zu dem Dichterlande
Heim die Götter, unnütz einer Welt,
Die, entwachsen ihrem Gängelbande,
Sich durch eignes Schweben hält.

Freundlos, ohne Bruder, ohne Gleichen,
Keiner Göttin, keiner Irdschen Sohn,
Herrscht ein andrer in des Äthers Reichen
Auf Saturnus' umgestürztem Thron.
Selig, eh sich Wesen um ihn freuten,
Selig im entvölkerten Gefild,
Sieht er in dem langen Strom der Zeiten
Ewig nur – sein eignes Bild.

Bürger des Olymps konnt ich erreichen,
Jenem Gotte, den sein Marmor preist,
Konnte einst der hohe Bildner gleichen;
Was ist neben *dir* der höchste Geist
Derer, welche Sterbliche gebaren?
Nur der Würmer Erster, Edelster.
Da die Götter menschlicher noch waren,
Waren Menschen göttlicher.

Dessen Strahlen mich darnieder schlagen,
Werk und Schöpfer des Verstandes! dir
Nachzuringen, gib mir Flügel, Waagen,
Dich zu wägen — oder nimm von mir,
Nimm die ernste, strenge Göttin wieder,
Die den Spiegel blendend vor mir hält;
Ihre sanftre Schwester sende nieder,
Spare jene für die andre Welt.

Die Ideale

So willst du treulos von mir scheiden
Mit deinen holden Phantasien,
Mit deinen Schmerzen, deinen Freuden,
Mit allen unerbittlich fliehn?
Kann nichts dich, Fliehende, verweilen,
O meines Lebens goldne Zeit?
Vergebens, deine Wellen eilen
Hinab ins Meer der Ewigkeit.

Erloschen sind die heitern Sonnen,
Die meiner Jugend Pfad erhellt,
Die Ideale sind zerronnen,
Die einst das trunkne Herz geschwellt,
Er ist dahin, der süße Glaube
An Wesen, die mein Traum gebar,
Der rauhen Wirklichkeit zum Raube,
Was einst so schön, so göttlich war.

Wie einst mit flehendem Verlangen
Pygmalion den Stein umschloß,
Bis in des Marmors kalte Wangen

Empfindung glühend sich ergoß,
So schlang ich mich mit Liebesarmen
Um die Natur, mit Jugendlust,
Bis sie zu atmen, zu erwarmen
Begann an meiner Dichterbrust

Und, teilend meine Flammentriebe,
Die Stumme eine Sprache fand,
Mir wiedergab den Kuß der Liebe
Und meines Herzens Klang verstand;
Da lebte mir der Baum, die Rose,
Mir sang der Quellen Silberfall,
Es fühlte selbst das Seelenlose
Von meines Lebens Widerhall.

Es dehnte mit allmächtgem Streben
Die enge Brust ein kreisend All,
Herauszutreten in das Leben,
In Tat und Wort, in Bild und Schall.
Wie groß war diese Welt gestaltet,
Solang die Knospe sie noch barg,
Wie wenig, ach! hat sich entfaltet,
Dies wenige, wie klein und karg!

Wie sprang, von kühnem Mut beflügelt,
Beglückt in seines Traumes Wahn,
Von keiner Sorge noch gezügelt,
Der Jüngling in des Lebens Bahn.
Bis an des Äthers bleichste Sterne
Erhob ihn der Entwürfe Flug,
Nichts war so hoch und nichts so ferne,
Wohn ihr Flügel ihn nicht trug.

Wie leicht ward er dahingetragen,
Was war dem Glücklichen zu schwer!
Wie tanzte vor des Lebens Wagen
Die luftige Begleitung her!
Die Liebe mit dem süßen Lohne,
Das Glück mit seinem goldnen Kranz,
Der Ruhm mit seiner Sternenkrone,
Die Wahrheit in der Sonne Glanz!

Doch, ach! schon auf des Weges Mitte
Verloren die Begleiter sich,

Sie wandten treulos ihre Schritte,
Und einer nach dem andern wich.
Leichtfüßig war das Glück entflogen,
Des Wissens Durst blieb ungestillt,
Des Zweifels finstre Wetter zogen
Sich um der Wahrheit Sonnenbild.

Ich sah des Ruhmes heilge Kränze
Auf der gemeinen Stirn entweiht.
Ach, allzuschnell nach kurzem Lenze
Entfloh die schöne Liebeszeit.
Und immer stiller ward's und immer
Verlassner auf dem rauhen Steg,
Kaum warf noch einen bleichen Schimmer
Die Hoffnung auf den finstern Weg.

Von all dem rauschenden Geleite,
Wer harrte liebend bei mir aus?
Wer steht mir tröstend noch zur Seite
Und folgt mir bis zum finstern Haus?
Du, die du alle Wunden heilest,
Der Freundschaft leise, zarte Hand,
Des Lebens Bürden liebend teilest,
Du, die ich frühe sucht und fand,

Und du, die gern sich mit ihr gattet,
Wie sie der Seele Sturm beschwört,
Beschäftigung, die nie ermattet,
Die langsam schafft, doch nie zerstört,
Die zu dem Bau der Ewigkeiten
Zwar Sandkorn nur für Sandkorn reicht,
Doch von der großen Schuld der Zeiten
Minuten, Tage, Jahre streicht.

Nänie

Auch das Schöne muß sterben! Das Menschen und Götter
     bezwinget,
  Nicht die eherne Brust rührt es des stygischen Zeus.
Einmal nur erweichte die Liebe den Schattenbeherrscher,
  Und an der Schwelle noch, streng, rief er zurück sein Geschenk.

Nicht stillt Aphrodite dem schönen Knaben die Wunde,
 Die in den zierlichen Leib grausam der Eber geritzt.
Nicht errettet den göttlichen Held die unsterbliche Mutter,
 Wann er, am skäischen Tor fallend, sein Schicksal erfüllt.
Aber sie steigt aus dem Meer mit allen Töchtern des Nereus,
 Und die Klage hebt an um den verherrlichten Sohn.
Siehe! Da weinen die Götter, es weinen die Göttinnen alle,
 Daß das Schöne vergeht, daß das Vollkommene stirbt.
Auch ein Klaglied zu sein im Mund der Geliebten, ist herrlich,
 Denn das Gemeine geht klanglos zum Orkus hinab.

FRIEDRICH HÖLDERLIN

1770–1843

Hyperions Schicksalslied

Ihr wandelt droben im Licht
  Auf weichem Boden, selige Genien!
    Glänzende Götterlüfte
      Rühren euch leicht,
        Wie die Finger der Künstlerin
          Heilige Saiten.

Schicksallos, wie der schlafende
  Säugling, atmen die Himmlischen;
    Keusch bewahrt
      In bescheidener Knospe,
        Blühet ewig
          Ihnen der Geist,
            Und die seligen Augen
              Blicken in stiller
                Ewiger Klarheit.

Doch uns ist gegeben,
  Auf keiner Stätte zu ruhn,
    Es schwinden, es fallen
      Die leidenden Menschen
        Blindlings von einer
          Stunde zur andern,
            Wie Wasser von Klippe
              Zu Klippe geworfen,
                Jahrlang ins Ungewisse hinab.

An die Parzen

Nur Einen Sommer gönnt, ihr Gewaltigen!
  Und einen Herbst zu reifem Gesange mir,
    Daß williger mein Herz, vom süßen
      Spiele gesättiget, dann mir sterbe.

Die Seele, der im Leben ihr göttlich Recht
Nicht ward, sie ruht auch drunten im Orkus nicht.
    Doch ist mir einst das Heilge, das am
        Herzen mir liegt, das Gedicht gelungen,

Willkommen dann, o Stille der Schattenwelt!
Zufrieden bin ich, wenn auch mein Saitenspiel
    Mich nicht hinab geleitet; Einmal
        Lebt ich, wie Götter, und mehr bedarf's nicht.

Abendphantasie

Vor seiner Hütte ruhig im Schatten sitzt
Der Pflüger, dem Genügsamen raucht sein Herd.
    Gastfreundlich tönt dem Wanderer im
        Friedlichen Dorfe die Abendglocke.

Wohl kehren itzt die Schiffer zum Hafen auch,
In fernen Städten, fröhlich verrauscht des Markts
    Geschäfter Lärm; in stiller Laube
        Glänzt das gesellige Mahl den Freunden.

Wohin denn ich? Es leben die Sterblichen
Von Lohn und Arbeit; wechselnd in Müh und Ruh
    Ist alles freudig; warum schläft denn
        Nimmer nur mir in der Brust der Stachel?

Am Abendhimmel blühet ein Frühling auf;
Unzählig blühn die Rosen und ruhig scheint
    Die goldne Welt; o dorthin nimmt mich,
        Purpurne Wolken! Und möge droben

In Licht und Luft zerrinnen mir Lieb und Leid! –
Doch, wie verscheucht von töriger Bitte, flieht
    Der Zauber; dunkel wird's, und einsam
        Unter dem Himmmel, wie immer, bin ich –

Komm du nun, sanfter Schlummer! Zu viel begehrt
Das Herz; doch endlich, Jugend! verglühst du ja,
    Du ruhelose, träumerische!
        Friedlich und heiter ist dann das Alter.

———

Da ich ein Knabe war,
  Rettet' ein Gott mich oft
    Vom Geschrei und der Rute der Menschen,
    Da spielt ich sicher und gut
      Mit den Blumen des Hains,
        Und die Lüftchen des Himmels
          Spielten mit mir.

Und wie du das Herz
Der Pflanzen erfreust,
Wenn sie entgegen dir
Die zarten Arme strecken,
So hast du mein Herz erfreut,
Vater Helios! Und, wie Endymion,
War ich dein Liebling,
Heilige Luna!

O all ihr treuen
Freundlichen Götter!
Daß ihr wüßtet,
Wie euch meine Seele geliebt!

Zwar damals rief ich noch nicht
Euch mit Namen, auch ihr
Nanntet mich nie, wie die Menschen sich nennen,
Als kennten sie sich.

Doch kannt' ich euch besser
Als ich je die Menschen gekannt,
Ich verstand die Stille des Äthers,
Der Menschen Worte verstand ich nie.

Mich erzog der Wohllaut
Des säuselnden Hains
Und lieben lernt' ich
Unter den Blumen.

Im Arme der Götter wuchs ich groß.

Mein Eigentum

In seiner Fülle ruhet der Herbsttag nun,
  Geläutert ist die Traub, und der Hain ist rot
    Vom Obst, wenn schon der holden Blüten
      Manche der Erde zum Danke fielen.

Und rings im Felde, wo ich den Pfad hinaus,
  Den stillen, wandle, ist den Zufriedenen
    Ihr Gut gereift, und viel der frohen
      Mühe gewähret der Reichtum ihnen.

Vom Himmel blicket zu den Geschäftigen
  Durch ihre Bäume milde das Licht herab,
    Die Freude teilend, denn es wuchs durch
      Hände der Menschen allein die Frucht nicht.

Und leuchtest du, o Goldnes, auch mir, und wehst
  Auch du mir wieder, Lüftchen, als segnetest
    Du eine Freude mir wie einst und
      Irrst, wie um Glückliche, mir am Busen?

Einst war ich's, doch wie Rosen, vergänglich war
  Das fromme Leben, ach! und es mahnen noch,
    Die blühend mir geblieben sind, die
      Holden Gestirne zu oft mich dessen.

Beglückt, wer, ruhig liebend ein frommes Weib,
  Am eignen Herd in rühmlicher Heimat lebt,
    Es leuchtet über festem Boden
      Schöner dem sicheren Mann sein Himmel.

Denn wie die Pflanze, wurzelt auf eignem Grund
  Sie nicht, verglüht die Seele des Sterblichen,
    Der mit dem Tageslichte nur, ein
      Armer, auf heiliger Erde wandelt.

Zu mächtig, ach! ihr himmlischen Höhen, zieht
  Ihr mich empor, bei Stürmen, am heitern Tag
    Fühl ich verzehrend euch im Busen
      Wechseln, ihr wandelnde Götterkräfte.

Doch heute laß mich stille den trauten Pfad
  Zum Haine gehn, dem golden die Wipfel schmückt
    Sein sterbend Laub, und kränzt auch mir die
      Stirne, ihr holden Erinnerungen!

Und daß mir auch, zu retten mein sterblich Herz,
  Wie andern eine bleibende Stätte sei,
    Und heimatlos die Seele mir nicht
      Über das Leben hinweg sich sehne,

Sei du, Gesang, mein freundlich Asyl! sei du,
Beglückender! mit sorgender Liebe mir
  Gepflegt, der Garten, wo ich, wandelnd
    Unter den Blüten, den immerjungen,

In sichrer Einfalt wohne, wenn draußen mir
Mit ihren Wellen allen die mächtge Zeit,
  Die Wandelbare, fern rauscht und die
    Stillere Sonne mein Wirken fördert.

Ihr segnet gütig über den Sterblichen,
Ihr Himmelskräfte! jedem sein Eigentum,
  O segnet meines auch und daß zu
    Frühe die Parze den Traum nicht ende.

Der Abschied

Trennen wollten wir uns? Wähnten es gut und klug?
Da wir's taten, warum schröckte, wie Mord, die Tat?
  Ach? wir kennen uns wenig,
    Denn es waltet ein Gott in uns.

Den verraten? ach, ihn, welcher uns alles erst,
Sinn und Leben erschuf, ihn, den beseelenden
  Schutzgott unserer Liebe,
    Dies, dies Eine vermag ich nicht.

Aber anderen Fehl denket der Weltsinn sich,
Andern ehernen Dienst übt er und anders Recht,
  Und es listet die Seele
    Tag für Tag der Gebrauch uns ab.

Wohl! ich wußt es zuvor. Seit die gewurzelte
Ungestalte, die Furcht Götter und Menschen trennt,
  Muß, mit Blut sie zu sühnen,
    Muß der Liebenden Herz vergehn.

Laß mich schweigen! O, laß nimmer von nun an mich
Dieses Tödliche sehn, daß ich im Frieden doch
  Hin ins Einsame ziehe
    Und noch unser der Abschied sei!

Reich die Schale mir selbst, daß ich des rettenden
Heilgen Giftes genug, daß ich des Lethetranks
Mit dir trinke, daß alles,
Haß und Liebe, vergessen sei!

Hingehn will ich. Vielleicht seh ich in langer Zeit
Diotima? dich hier. Aber verblutet ist
Dann das Wünschen, und friedlich
Gleich den Seligen, fremde gehn

Wir umher, ein Gespräch führet uns ab und auf,
Sinnend, zögernd, doch itzt mahnt die Vergessenen
Hier die Stelle des Abschieds,
Es erwarmet ein Herz in uns,

Staunend seh ich dich an, Stimmen and süßen Sang,
Wie aus voriger Zeit hör ich und Saitenspiel,
Und die Lilie duftet
Golden über dem Bach uns auf.

Die Heimat

Froh kehrt der Schiffer heim an den stillen Strom,
Von Inseln fernher, wenn er geerntet hat;
So käm auch ich zur Heimat, hätt ich
Güter so viele, wie Leid, geerntet.

Ihr teuern Ufer, die mich erzogen einst,
Stillt ihr der Liebe Leiden, versprecht ihr mir,
Ihr Wälder meiner Jugend, wenn ich
Komme, die Ruhe noch einmal wieder?

Am kühlen Bache, wo ich der Wellen Spiel,
Am Strome, wo ich gleiten die Schiffe sah,
Dort bin ich bald; euch traute Berge,
Die mich behüteten einst, der Heimat

Verehrte sichre Grenzen, der Mutter Haus
Und liebender Geschwister Umarmungen
Begrüß ich bald und ihr umschließt mich,
Daß, wie in Banden, das Herz mir heile,

Ihr treugebliebnen! aber ich weiß, ich weiß,
Der Liebe Leid, dies heilet so bald mir nicht,
Dies singt kein Wiegensang, den tröstend
Sterbliche singen, mir aus dem Busen.

Denn sie, die uns das himmlische Feuer leihn,
Die Götter schenken heiliges Leid uns auch,
Drum bleibe dies. Ein Sohn der Erde
Schein ich; zu lieben gemacht, zu leiden.

Hälfte des Lebens

Mit gelben Birnen hänget
Und voll mit wilden Rosen
Das Land in den See,
Ihr holden Schwäne,
Und trunken von Küssen
Tunkt ihr das Haupt
Ins heilignüchterne Wasser.

Weh mir, wo nehm ich, wenn
Es Winter ist, die Blumen, und wo
Den Sonnenschein
Und Schatten der Erde?
Die Mauern stehn
Sprachlos und kalt, im Winde
Klirren die Fahnen.

Brot und Wein
An Heinze

1

Rings um ruhet die Stadt; still wird die erleuchtete Gasse,
Und, mit Fackeln geschmückt, rauschen die Wagen hinweg.
Satt gehn heim von Freuden des Tags zu ruhen die Menschen,
Und Gewinn und Verlust wäget ein sinniges Haupt
Wohlzufrieden zu Haus; leer steht von Trauben und Blumen,
Und von Werken der Hand ruht der geschäftige Markt.

Aber das Saitenspiel tönt fern aus Gärten; vielleicht, daß
   Dort ein Liebendes spielt oder ein einsamer Mann
Ferner Freunde gedenkt und der Jugendzeit; und die Brunnen
   Immerquillend und frisch rauschen an duftendem Beet.
Still in dämmriger Luft ertönen geläutete Glocken,
   Und der Stunden gedenk rufet ein Wächter die Zahl.
Jetzt auch kommmet ein Wehn und regt die Gipfel des Hains auf,
   Sieh! und das Schattenbild unserer Erde, der Mond
Kommet geheim nun auch; die Schwärmerische, die Nacht,
     kommt,
   Voll mit Sternen und wohl wenig bekümmert um uns,
Glänzt die Erstaunende dort, die Fremdlingin unter den Menschen,
   Über Gebirgeshöhn traurig und prächtig herauf.

2

Wunderbar ist die Gunst der Hocherhabnen und niemand
   Weiß, von wannen und was einem geschiehet von ihr.
So bewegt sie die Welt und die hoffende Seele der Menschen,
   Selbst kein Weiser versteht, was sie bereitet, denn so
Will es der oberste Gott, der sehr dich liebet, und darum
   Ist noch lieber, wie sie, dir der besonnene Tag.
Aber zuweilen liebt auch klares Auge den Schatten
   Und versuchet zu Lust, eh es die Not ist, den Schlaf,
Oder es blickt auch gern ein treuer Mann in die Nacht hin,
   Ja, es ziemet sich, ihr Kränze zu weihn und Gesang,
Weil den Irrenden sie geheiliget ist und den Toten,
   Selber aber besteht, ewig, in freiestem Geist.
Aber sie muß uns auch, daß in der zaudernden Weile,
   Daß im Finstern für uns einiges Haltbare sei,
Uns die Vergessenheit und das Heiligtrunkene gönnen,
   Gönnen das strömende Wort, das, wie die Liebenden, sei,
Schlummerlos und vollern Pokal und kühneres Leben,
   Heilig Gedächtnis auch, wachend zu bleiben bei Nacht.

3

Auch verbergen umsonst das Herz im Busen, umsonst nur
   Halten den Mut noch wir, Meister und Knaben, denn wer
Möcht es hindern, und wer möcht uns die Freude verbieten?
   Göttliches Feuer auch treibet, bei Tag und bei Nacht,
Aufzubrechen. So komm! daß wir das Offene schauen,
   Daß ein Eigenes wir suchen, so weit es auch ist.
Fest bleibt Eins; es sei um Mittag oder es gehe
   Bis in die Mitternacht, immer bestehet ein Maß,

Allen gemein, doch jeglichem auch ist eignes beschieden,
  Dahin gehet und kommt jeder, wohin er es kann.
Drum! und spotten das Spotts mag gern frohlockender Wahnsinn,
  Wenn er in heiliger Nacht plötzlich die Sänger ergreift.
Drum an den Isthmos komm! dorthin, wo das offene Meer rauscht
  Am Parnaß und der Schnee delphische Felsen umglänzt,
Dort ins Land des Olymps, dort auf die Höhe Cithärons,
  Unter die Fichten dort, unter die Trauben, von wo
Thebe drunten und Ismenos rauscht im Lande des Kadmos,
  Dorther kommt und zurück deutet der kommende Gott.

4

Seliges Griechenland! Du Haus der Himmlischen alle,
  Also ist wahr, was einst wir in der Jugend gehört?
Festlicher Saal! der Boden ist Meer! und Tische die Berge,
  Wahrlich zu einzigem Brauche vor alters gebaut!
Aber die Thronen, wo? die Tempel und wo die Gefäße,
  Wo mit Nektar gefüllt, Göttern zu Lust der Gesang?
Wo, wo leuchten sie denn, die fernhintreffenden Sprüche?
  Delphi schlummert und wo tönet das große Geschick?
Wo ist das schnelle? Wo bricht's, allgegenwärtigen Glücks voll,
  Donnernd aus heiterer Luft über die Augen herein?
Vater Aether! so rief's und flog von Zunge zu Zunge
  Tausendfach, es ertrug keiner das Leben allein;
Ausgeteilet erfreut solch Gut und getauschet, mit Fremden,
  Wird's ein Jubel, es wächst schlafend des Wortes Gewalt:
Vater! heiter! und hallt, so weit es gehet, das uralt
  Zeichen, von Eltern geerbt, treffend und schaffend hinab.
Denn so kehren die Himmlischen ein, tiefschütternd gelangt so
  Aus dem Schatten herab unter die Menschen ihr Tag.

5

Unempfunden kommen sie erst, es streben entgegen
  Ihnen die Kinder, zu hell kommet, zu blendend das Glück,
Und es scheut sie der Mensch, kaum weiß zu sagen ein Halbgott,
  Wer mit Namen sie sind, die mit den Gaben ihm nahn.
Aber der Mut von ihnen ist groß, es füllen das Herz ihm
  Ihre Freuden, und kaum weiß er zu brauchen das Gut,
Schafft, verschwendet, und fast ward ihm Unheiliges heilig,
  Das er mit segnender Hand töricht und gütig berührt.
Möglichst dulden die Himmlischen dies; dann aber in Wahrheit
  Kommen sie selbst, und gewohnt werden die Menschen des
    Glücks

Und des Tags und zu schaun die Offenbaren, das Antlitz
  Derer, welche, schon längst Eines und Alles genannt,
Tief die verschwiegene Brust mit freier Genüge gefüllet
  Und zuerst und allein alles Verlangen beglückt.
So ist der Mensch; wenn da ist das Gut, und es sorget mit Gaben
  Selber ein Gott für ihn, kennet und sieht er es nicht.
Tragen muß er, zuvor; nun aber nennt er sein Liebstes,
  Nun, nun müssen dafür Worte, wie Blumen, entstehn.

6

Und nun denkt er zu ehren in Ernst die seligen Götter,
  Wirklich und wahrhaft muß alles verkünden ihr Lob.
Nichts darf schauen das Licht, was nicht den Hohen gefället,
  Vor den Aether gebührt Müßigversuchendes nicht.
Drum in der Gegenwart der Himmlischen würdig zu stehen,
  Richten in herrlichen Ordnungen Völker sich auf
Untereinander und baun die schönen Tempel und Städte
  Fest und edel, sie gehn über Gestaden empor –
Aber wo sind sie? Wo blühn die Bekannten, die Kronen des Festes?
  Thebe welkt und Athen; rauschen die Waffen nicht mehr
In Olympia, nicht die goldnen Wagen des Kampfspiels,
  Und bekränzan sich denn nimmer die Schiffe Korinths?
Warum schweigen auch sie, die alten heilgen Theater?
  Warum freuet sich denn nicht der geweihete Tanz?
Warum zeichnet, wie sonst, die Stirne des Mannes ein Gott nicht,
  Drückt den Stempel, wie sonst, nicht dem Getroffenen auf?
Oder er kam auch selbst und nahm des Menschen Gestalt an
  Und vollendet, und schloß tröstend das himmlische Fest.

7

Aber Freund! wir kommen zu spät. Zwar leben die Götter,
  Aber über dem Haupt droben in anderer Welt.
Endlos wirken sie da und scheinen's wenig zu achten,
  Ob wir leben, so sehr schonen die Himmlischen uns.
Denn nicht immer vermag ein schwaches Gefäß sie zu fassen,
  Nur zu Zeiten erträgt göttliche Fülle der Mensch.
Traum von ihnen ist drauf das Leben. Aber da Irrsal
  Hilft, wie Schlummer, und stark machet die Not und die Nacht,
Bis daß Helden genug in der ehernen Wiege gewachsen,
  Herzen an Kraft, wie sonst, ähnlich den Himmlischen sind.
Donnernd kommen sie drauf. Indessen dünket mir öfters
  Besser zu schlafen, wie so ohne Genossen zu sein,

So zu harren, und was zu tun indes und zu sagen,
  Weiß ich nicht, und wozu Dichter in dürftiger Zeit?
Aber sie sind, sagst du, wie des Weingotts heilige Priester,
  Welche von Lande zu Land zogen in heiliger Nacht.

8

Nämlich, als vor einiger Zeit, uns dünket sie lange,
  Aufwärts stiegen sie all, welche das Leben beglückt,
Als der Vater gewandt sein Angesicht von den Menschen
  Und das Trauern mit Recht über der Erde begann,
Als erschienen zuletzt ein stiller Genius, himmlisch
  Tröstend, welcher des Tags Ende verkündet' und schwand,
Ließ zum Zeichen, daß einst er da gewesen und wieder
  Käme, der himmlische Chor einige Gaben zurück,
Derer menschlich, wie sonst, wir uns zu freuen vermöchten,
  Denn zur Freude, mit Geist, wurde das Größre zu groß
Unter den Menschen und noch, noch fehlen die Starken zu
      höchsten
  Freuden, aber es lebt stille noch einiger Dank.
Brot ist der Erde Frucht, doch ist's vom Lichte gesegnet,
  Und vom donnernden Gott kommet die Freude des Weins.
Darum denken wir auch dabei der Himmlischen, die sonst
  Da gewesen und die kehren in richtiger Zeit,
Darum singen sie auch mit Ernst, die Sänger, den Weingott,
  Und nicht eitel erdacht tönet dem Alten das Lob.

9

Ja! sie sagen mit Recht, er söhne den Tag mit der Nacht aus,
  Führe des Himmels Gestirn ewig hinunter, hinauf,
Allzeit froh, wie das Laub der immergrünenden Fichte,
  Das er liebt, und der Kranz, den er von Efeu gewählt,
Weil er bleibet und selbst die Spur der entflohenen Götter
  Götterlosen hinab unter das Finstere bringt.
Was der Alten Gesang von Kindern Gottes geweissagt,
  Siehe! wir sind es, wir; Frucht von Hesperien ist's!
Wunderbar und genau ist's als an Menschen erfüllet,
  Glaube, wer es geprüft! Aber so vieles geschieht,
Keines wirket, denn wir sind herzlos, Schatten, bis unser
  Vater Aether erkannt jeden und allen gehört.
Aber indessen kommt als Fackelschwinger des Höchsten
  Sohn, der Syrier, unter die Schatten herab.
Selige Weise sehn's; ein Lächeln aus der gefangnen
  Seele leuchtet, dem Licht tauet ihr Auge noch auf.
Sanfter träumet und schläft in Armen der Erde der Titan,
  Selbst der neidische, selbst Cerberus trinket und schläft.

NOVALIS

1772–1801

Hymnen an die Nacht II

Muß immer der Morgen wiederkommen?
Endet nie des Irrdischen Gewalt?
Unselige Geschäftigkeit verzehrt
Den himmlischen Anflug der Nacht?
Wird nie der Liebe geheimes Opfer
Ewig brennen?
Zugemessen ward
Dem Lichte seine Zeit
Und dem Wachen –
Aber zeitlos ist der Nacht Herrschaft,
Ewig ist die Dauer des Schlafs.
Heiliger Schlaf!
Beglücke zu selten nicht
Der Nacht Geweihte –
In diesem irrdischen Tagwerck.
Nur die Thoren verkennen dich
Und wissen von keinem Schlafe
Als den Schatten,
Den du mitleidig auf uns wirfst
In jener Dämmrung
Der wahrhaften Nacht.
Sie fühlen dich nicht
In der goldnen Flut der Trauben
In des Mandelbaums
Wunderöl
Und dem braunen Safte des Mohns.
Sie wissen nicht
Daß du es bist
Der des zarten Mädchens

Busen umschwebt
Und zum Himmel den Schoos macht —
Ahnden nicht
Daß aus alten Geschichten
Du himmelöffnend entgegentrittst
Und den Schlüssel trägst
Zu den Wohnungen der Seligen,
Unendlicher Geheimnisse
Schweigender Bote.

———

Wenn ich ihn nur habe,
Wenn er mein nur ist,
Wenn mein Herz bis hin zum Grabe
Seine Treue nie vergißt:
Weiß ich nichts von Leide,
Fühle nichts als Andacht, Lieb und Freude.

Wenn ich ihn nur habe,
Laß ich alles gern,
Folg an meinem Wanderstabe
Treugesinnt nur meinem Herrn;
Lasse still die andern
Breite, lichte, volle Straßen wandern.

Wenn ich ihn nur habe,
Schlaf ich fröhlich ein,
Ewig wird zu süßer Labe
Seines Herzens Flut mir sein,
Die mit sanftem Zwingen
Alles wird erweichen und durchdringen.

Wenn ich ihn nur habe,
Hab ich auch die Welt,
Selig wie ein Himmelsknabe,
Der der Jungfrau Scheier hält.
Hingesenkt im Schauen
Kann mir vor dem Irdischen nicht grauen.

Wo ich ihn nur habe,
Ist mein Vaterland;
Und es fällt mir jede Gabe

Wie ein Erbteil in die Hand;
Längst vermißte Brüder
Find ich nun in seinen Jüngern wieder.

CLEMENS BRENTANO

1778–1842

Wie sich auch die Zeit will wenden, enden
Will sich nimmer doch die Ferne,
Freude mag der Mai mir spenden, senden
Möcht Dir alles gerne, weil ich Freude mir erlerne,
Wenn Du mit gefaltnen Händen
Freudig hebst der Augen Sterne.

Alle Blumen mich nicht grüßen, süßen
Gruß nehm ich von Deinem Munde.
Was nicht blühet Dir zu Füßen, büßen
Muß es bald zur Stunde, eher ich auch nicht gesunde,
Bis Du mir mit frohen Küssen
Bringest meines Frühlings Kunde.

Wenn die Abendlüfte wehen, sehen
Mich die lieben Vöglein kleine
Traurig an der Linde stehen, spähen,
Wen ich wohl so ernstlich meine, daß ich helle Tränen weine,
Wollen auch nicht schlafen gehen,
Denn sonst wär ich ganz alleine.

Vöglein, euch mag's nicht gelingen, klingen
Darf es nur von ihrem Sange,
Wie des Maies Wonneschlingen, singen
Alles ein in neuem Zwange; aber daß ich Dein verlange
Und Du mein, mußt Du auch singen,
Ach, das ist schon ewig lange.

Der Spinnerin Nachtlied

Es sang vor langen Jahren
Wohl auch die Nachtigall,

73

Das war wohl süßer Schall,
Da wir zusammen waren.

Ich sing und kann nicht weinen
Und spinne so allein
Den Faden klar und rein,
Solang der Mond wird scheinen.

Als wir zusammen waren,
Da sang die Nachtigall;
Nun mahnet mich ihr Schall,
Daß du von mir gefahren.

So oft der Mond mag scheinen,
Denk ich wohl dein allein,
Mein Herz ist klar und rein,
Gott wolle uns vereinen.

Seit du von mir gefahren,
Singt stets die Nachtigall,
Ich denk bei ihrem Schall,
Wie wir zusammen waren.

Gott wolle uns vereinen,
Hier spinn ich so allein,
Der Mond scheint klar und rein,
Ich sing und möchte weinen.

Verzweiflung an der Liebe in der Liebe

In Liebeskampf? in Todeskampf gesunken?
Ob Atem noch von ihren Lippen fließt?
Ob ihr der Krampf den kleinen Mund verschließt?
Kein Öl die Lampe? oder keinen Funken?

Der Jüngling — betend? tot? in Liebe trunken?
Ob er der Jungfrauu höchste Gunst genießt?
Was ist's, das der gefallne Becher gießt?
Hat Gift, hat Wein, hat Balsam sie getrunken?

Des Jünglings Arme Engelsflügel werden —
Nein, Mantelsfalten — Leichentuches Falten.
Um sie strahlt Heilgenschein — zerraufte Haare.

Strahl Himmelslicht, flamm Hölle zu der Erde,
Brich der Verzweiflung rasende Gewalten,
Enthüll — verhüll — das Freudenbett — die Bahre!

Frühlingsschrei eines Knechtes aus der Tiefe

Meister, ohne dein Erbarmen
Muß im Abgrund ich verzagen,
Willst du nicht mit starken Armen
Wieder mich zum Lichte tragen?

Jährlich greifet deine Güte
In die Erde, in die Herzen,
Jährlich weckest du die Blüte,
Weckst in mir die alten Schmerzen.

Einmal nur zum Licht geboren,
Aber tausendmal gestorben,
Bin ich ohne dich verloren,
Ohne dich in mir verdorben.

Wenn sich so die Erde reget,
Wenn die Luft so sonnig wehet,
Dann wird auch die Flut beweget,
Die in Todesbanden stehet.

Und in meinem Herzen schauert
Ein betrübter bittrer Bronnen,
Wenn der Frühling draußen lauert,
Kömmt die Angstflut angeronnen.

Weh! durch giftge Erdenlagen,
Wie die Zeit so angeschwemmet,
Habe ich den Schacht geschlagen,
Und er ist nur schwach verdämmet.

Wenn nun rings die Quellen schwellen,
Wenn der Grund gebärend ringet,
Brechen her die giftgen Wellen,
Die kein Fluch, kein Witz mir zwinget.

Andern ruf ich: Schwimme, schwimme!
Mir kann solcher Ruf nicht taugen,
Denn in mir ja steigt die grimme
Sündflut, bricht aus meinen Augen.

Und dann scheinen bös Gezüchte.
Mir die bunten Lämmer alle,
Die ich grüßte, süße Früchte,
Die mir reiften, bittre Galle.

Herr, erbarme du dich meiner,
Daß mein Herz neu blühend werde!
Mein erbarmte sich noch keiner
Von den Frühlingen der Erde.

Meister, wenn dir all Hände
Nahn mit süßerfüllten Schalen,
Kann ich mit der bittern Spende
Meine Schuld dir nimmer zahlen.

Ach, wie ich auch tiefer wühle,
Wie ich schöpfe, wie ich weine,
Nimmer ich den Schwall erspüle
Zum Kristallgrund fest und reine.

Immer stürzen mir die Wände.
Jede Schicht hat mich belogen,
Und die arbeitblutgen Hände
Brennen in den bittern Wogen.

Weh! der Raum wird immer enger,
Wilder, wüster stets die Wogen,
Herr, o Herr! Ich treib's nicht länger,
Schlage deinen Regenbogen.

Herr, ich mahne dich: Verschone!
Herr, ich hört in jungen Tagen,
Wunderbare Rettung wohne,
Ach, in deinem Blute, sagen.

Und so muß ich zu dir schreien,
Schreien aus der bittern Tiefe,
Könntest du auch nicht verzeihen,
Daß dein Knecht so kühnlich riefe!

Daß des Lichtes Quelle wieder
Rein und heilig in mir flute,
Träufle einen Tropfen nieder,
Jesus, mir von deinem Blute!

———

Einsam will ich untergehn,
Keiner soll mein Leiden wissen,
Wird der Stern, den ich gesehn,
Von dem Himmel mir gerissen,
Will ich einsam untergehn
Wie ein Pilger in der Wüste.

Einsam will ich untergehn
Wie ein Pilger in der Wüste,
Wenn der Stern, den ich gesehn,
Mich zum letzten Male grüßte,
Will ich einsam untergehn
Wie ein Bettler auf der Heide.

Einsam will ich untergehn
Wie ein Bettler auf der Heide
Gibt der Stern, den ich gesehn,
Mir nicht weiter das Geleite,
Will ich einsam untergehn
Wie der Tag im Abendgrauen.

Einsam will ich untergehn
Wie der Tag im Abendgrauen,
Will der Stern, den ich gesehn,
Nicht mehr auf mich niederschauen,
Will ich einsam untergehn
Wie ein Sklave an der Kette.

Einsam will ich untergehn
Wie ein Sklave an der Kette,
Scheint der Stern, den ich gesehn,

Nicht mehr auf mein Dornenbette,
Will ich einsam untergehn
Wie ein Schwanenlied im Tode.

Einsam will ich untergehn
Wie ein Schwanenlied im Tode,
Ist der Stern, den ich gesehn,
Mir nicht mehr ein Friedensbote,
Will ich einsam untergehn
Wie ein Schiff in wüsten Meeren.

Einsam will ich untergehn
Wie ein Schiff in wüsten Meeren,
Wird der Stern, den ich gesehn,
Jemals weg von mir sich kehren,
Will ich einsam untergehn
Wie der Trost in stummen Schmerzen.

Einsam will ich untergehn
Wie der Trost in stummen Schmerzen,
Soll den Stern, den ich gesehn,
Jemals meine Schuld verscherzen,
Will ich einsam untergehn
Wie mein Herz in deinem Herzen!

25. August 1817

———

Wenn der lahme Weber träumt, er webe,
Träumt die kranke Lerche auch, sie schwebe,
Träumt die stumme Nachtigall, sie singe,
Daß das Herz des Widerhalls zerspringe,
Träumt das blinde Huhn, es zähl die Kerne,
Und der drei je zählte kaum, die Sterne,
Träumt das starre Erz, gar linde tau es,
Und das Eisenherz, ein Kind vertrau es,
Träumt die taube Nüchternheit, sie lausche,
Wie der Traube Schüchternheit berausche;
Kömmt dann Wahrheit mutternackt gelaufen,
Führt der hellen Töne Glanzgefunkel
Und der grellen Lichter Tanz durchs Dunkel,
Rennt den Traum sie schmerzlich übern Haufen,

Horch! die Fackel lacht, horch! Schmerz-Schalmeien
Der erwachten Nacht ins Herz all schreien;
Weh, ohn Opfer gehn die süßen Wunder,
Gehn die armen Herzen einsam unter!

JOSEPH FREIHERR VON EICHENDORFF

1788–1857

Wünschelrute

Schläft ein Lied in allen Dingen,
Die da träumen fort und fort,
Und die Welt hebt an zu singen,
Triffst du nur das Zauberwort.

Sehnsucht

Es schienen so golden die Sterne,
Am Fenster ich einsam stand
Und hörte aus weiter Ferne
Ein Posthorn im stillen Land.
Das Herz mir im Leib entbrennte;
Da hab ich mir heimlich gedacht:
Ach, wer da mitreisen könnte
In der prächtigen Sommernacht!

Zwei junge Gesellen gingen
Vorüber am Bergeshang,
Ich hörte im Wandern sie singen
Die stille Gegend entlang:
Von schwindelnden Felsenschlüften,
Wo die Wälder rauschen so sacht,
Von Quellen, die von den Klüften
Sich stürzen in die Waldesnacht.

Sie sangen von Marmorbildern,
Von Gärten, die überm Gestein

In dämmernden Lauben verwildern,
Palästen im Mondenschein,
Wo die Mädchen am Fenster lauschen,
Wann der Lauten Klang erwacht
Und die Brunnen verschlafen rauschen
In der prächtigen Sommernacht.

Lockung

Hörst du nicht die Bäume rauschen
Draußen durch die stille Rund?
Lockt's dich nicht, hinabzulauschen
Von dem Söller in den Grund,
Wo die vielen Bäche gehen
Wunderbar im Mondenschein
Und die stillen Schlösser sehen
In den Fluß vom hohen Stein?

Kennst du noch die irren Lieder
Aus der alten, schönen Zeit?
Sie erwachen alle wieder
Nachts in Waldeseinsamkeit,
Wenn die Bäume träumend lauschen
Und der Flieder duftet schwül
Und im Fluß die Nixen rauschen –
Komm herab, hier ist's so kühl.

Das zerbrochene Ringlein

In einem kühlen Grunde
Da geht ein Mühlenrad,
Mein' Liebste ist verschwunden,
Die dort gewohnet hat.

Sie hat mir Treu versprochen,
Gab mir ein'n Ring dabei,
Sie hat die Treu gebrochen,
Mein Ringlein sprang entzwei.

Ich möcht als Spielmann reisen
Weit in die Welt hinaus
Und singen meine Weisen
Und gehn von Haus zu Haus.

Ich möcht als Reiter fliegen
Wohl in die blutge Schlacht,
Um stille Feuer liegen
Im Feld bei dunkler Nacht.

Hör ich das Mühlrad gehen:
Ich weiß nicht, was ich will —
Ich möcht am liebsten sterben,
Da wär's auf einmal still!

Mondnacht

Es war, als hätt der Himmel
Die Erde still geküßt,
Daß sie im Blütenschimmer
Von ihm nun träumen müßt.

Die Luft ging durch die Felder,
Die Ähren wogten sacht,
Es rauschten leis die Wälder,
So sternklar war die Nacht.

Und meine Seele spannte
Weit ihre Flügel aus,
Flog durch die stillen Lande,
Als flöge sie nach Haus.

Der Einsiedler

Komm, Trost der Welt, du stille Nacht!
Wie steigst du von den Bergen sacht,
Die Lüfte alle schlafen,
Ein Schiffer nur noch, wandermüd,

Singt übers Meer sein Abendlied
Zu Gottes Lob im Hafen.

Die Jahre wie die Wolken gehn
Und lassen mich hier einsam stehn,
Die Welt hat mich vergessen,
Da trat'st du wunderbar zu mir,
Wenn ich beim Waldesrauschen hier
Gedankenvoll gesessen.

O Trost der Welt, du stille Nacht!
Der Tag hat mich so müd gemacht,
Das weite Meer schon dunkelt,
Laß ausruhn mich von Lust und Not,
Bis daß das ewge Morgenrot
Den stillen Wald durchfunkelt.

HEINRICH HEINE

1797–1856

Wahrhaftig

Wenn der Frühling kommt mit dem Sonnenschein,
Dann knospen und blühen die Blümlein auf;
Wenn der Mond beginnt seinen Strahlenlauf,
Dann schwimmen die Sternlein hintendrein;
Wenn der Sänger zwei süße Äuglein sieht,
Dann quellen ihm Lieder aus tiefem Germüt; –
Doch Lieder und Sterne und Blümelein
Und Äuglein und Mondglanz und Sonnenschein,
Wie sehr das Zeug auch gefällt,
So macht's doch noch lang keine Welt.

———

Die Welt ist dumm, die Welt ist blind,
Wird täglich abgeschmackter!
Sie spicht von dir, mein schönes Kind,
Du hast keinen guten Charakter.

Die Welt ist dumm, die Welt ist blind,
Und dich wird sie immer verkennen;
Sie weiß nicht, wie süß deine Küsse sind
Und wie sie beseligend brennen.

———

Ein Jüngling liebt ein Mädchen,
Die hat einen andern erwählt;
Der andre liebt eine andre
Und hat sich mit dieser vermählt.

Das Mädchen heiratet aus Ärger
Den ersten besten Mann,
Der ihr in den Weg gelaufen;
Der Jüngling ist übel dran.

Es ist eine alte Geschichte,
Doch bleibt sie immer neu;
Und wem sie just passieret,
Dem bricht das Herz entzwei.

————

Ich weiß nicht, was soll es bedeuten,
Daß ich so traurig bin;
Ein Märchen aus alten Zeiten,
Das kommt mir nicht aus dem Sinn.

Die Luft ist kühl und es dunkelt,
Und ruhig fließt der Rhein;
Der Gipfel des Berges funkelt
Im Abendsonnenschein.

Die schönste Jungfrau sitzet
Dort oben wunderbar;
Ihr goldnes Geschmeide blitzet,
Sie kämmt ihr goldenes Haar.

Sie kämmt es mit goldenem Kamme
Und singt ein Lied dabei;
Das hat eine wundersame,
Gewaltige Melodei.

Den Schiffer im kleinen Schiffe
Ergreift es mit wildem Weh;
Er schaut nicht die Felsenriffe,
Er schaut nur hinauf in die Höh.

Ich glaube, die Wellen verschlingen
Am Ende Schiffer und Kahn;
Und das hat mit ihrem Singen
Die Lore-Ley getan.

Seegespenst

Ich aber lag am Rande des Schiffes
Und schaute träumenden Auges
Hinab in das spiegelklare Wasser
Und schaute tiefer und tiefer —
Bis tief im Meeresgrunde,
Anfangs wie dämmernde Nebel,
Jedoch allmählich farbenbestimmter,
Kirchenkuppel und Türme sich zeigten
Und endlich, sonnenklar, eine ganze Stadt,
Altertümlich niederländisch
Und menschenbelebt.
Bedächtige Männer, schwarzbemäntelt,
Mit weißen Halskrausen und Ehrenketten
Und langen Degen und langen Gesichtern,
Schreiten über den wimmelnden Marktplatz
Nach dem treppenhohen Rathaus,
Wo steinerne Kaiserbilder
Wacht halten mit Zepter und Schwert.
Unferne, vor langen Häuserreihn,
Wo spiegelblanke Fenster
Und pyramidisch beschnittene Linden,
Wandeln seidenrauschende Jungfern,
Schlanke Leibchen, die Blumengesichter
Sittsam umschlossen von schwarzen Mützchen
Und hervorquellendem Goldhaar.
Bunte Gesellen, in spanischer Tracht,
Stolzieren vorüber und nicken.
Bejahrte Frauen
In braunen, verschollnen Gewändern,
Gesangbuch und Rosenkranz in der Hand,
Eilen trippelnden Schritts
Nach dem großen Dome,
Getrieben von Glockengeläute
Und rauschendem Orgelton.

Mich selbst ergreift des fernen Klangs
Geheimnisvoller Schauer!
Unendliches Sehnen, tiefe Wehmut
Beschleicht mein Herz,

Mein kaum geheiltes Herz; —
Mir ist, als würden seine Wunden
Von lieben Lippen aufgeküßt
Und täten wieder bluten —
Heiße, rote Tropfen,
Die lang und langsam niederfalln
Auf ein altes Haus, dort unten
In der tiefen Meerstadt,
Auf ein altes, hochgegiebeltes Haus,
Wo melancholisch einsam
Unten am Fenster ein Mädchen sitzt,
Den Kopt auf den Arm gelehnt,
Wie ein armes, vergessenes Kind —
Und ich kenne dich armes, vergessenes Kind!

So tief, meertief also
Verstecktest du dich vor mir,
Aus kindischer Laune,
Und konntest nicht mehr herauf
Und saßest fremd unter fremden Leuten,
Jahrhundertelang,
Derweilen ich, die Seele voll Gram,
Auf der ganzen Erde dich suchte
Und immer dich suchte,
Du Immergeliebte,
Du Längstverlorene,
Du Endlichgefundene —
Ich hab dich gefunden und schaue wieder
Dein süßes Gesicht,
Die klugen, treuen Augen,
Das Liebe Lächeln —
Und nimmer will ich dich wieder varlassen,
Und ich komme hinab zu dir,
Und mit ausgebreiteten Armen
Stürz ich hinab an dein Herz —

Aber zur rechten Zeit noch
Ergriff mich beim Fuß der Kapitän
Und zog mich vom Schiffsrand
Und rief, ärgerlich lachend:
Doktor, sind Sie des Teufels?

Mein Kind, wir waren Kinder

Mein Kind, wir waren Kinder,
Zwei Kinder, klein und froh;
Wir krochen ins Hühnerhäuschen,
Versteckten uns unter das Stroh.

Wir krähten wie die Hähne,
Und kamen Leute vorbei —
'Kikereküh!' sie glaubten,
Es wäre Hahnengeschrei.

Die Kisten auf unserem Hofe
Die tapezierten wir aus,
Und wohnten drin beisammen,
Und machten ein vornehmes Haus.

Des Nachbars alte Katze
Kam öfters zum Besuch;
Wir machten ihr Bückling' und Knickse
Und Komplimente genug.

Wir haben nach ihrem Befinden
Besorglich und freundlich gefragt;
Wir haben seitdem desselbe
Mancher alten Katze gesagt.

Wir saßen auch oft und sprachen
Vernünftig, wie alte Leut',
Und klagten, wie alles besser
Gewesen zu unserer Zeit;

Wie Lieb' und Treu' und Glauben
Verschwunden aus der Welt,
Und wie so teuer der Kaffee
Und wie so rar das Geld! — — —

Vorbei sind die Kinderspiele
Und alles rollt vorbei, —
Das Geld und die Welt und die Zeiten,
Und Glauben und Lieb' und Treu'.

Der Doppelgänger

Still ist die Nacht, es ruhen die Gassen,
In diesem Hause wohnte mein Schatz;
Sie hat schon längst die Stadt verlassen,
Doch steht noch das Haus auf demselben Platz.

Da steht auch ein Mensch und starrt in die Höhe,
Und ringt die Hände vor Schmerzensgewalt;
Mir graust es, wenn ich sein Antlitz sehe, –
Der Mond zeigt mir meine eigne Gestalt.

Du Doppeltgänger! du bleicher Geselle!
Was äffst du nach mein Liebesleid,
Das mich gequält auf dieser Stelle,
So manche Nacht, in alter Zeit?

———

Nun ist es Zeit, daß ich mit Verstand
Mich aller Torheit entled'ge;
Ich hab' so lang' als ein Komödiant
Mit dir gespielt die Komödie.

Die prächt'gen Kulissen, sie waren bemalt
Im hochromantischen Stile,
Mein Rittermantel hat goldig gestrahlt,
Ich fühlte die feinsten Gefühle.

Und nun ich mich gar säuberlich
Des tollen Tands entled'ge,
Noch immer elend fühl' ich mich,
Als spielt' ich noch immer Komödie.

Ach Gott! im Scherz und unbewußt
Sprach ich was ich gefühlet;
Ich hab' mit dem Tod in der eignen Brust
Den sterbenden Fechter gespielet.

Die schlesischen Weber

Im düstern Auge keine Träne,
Sie sitzen am Webstuhl und fletschen die Zähne:

Deutschland, wir weben dein Leichentuch,
Wir weben hinein den dreifachen Fluch —
    Wir weben, wir weben!

Ein Fluch dem Gotte, zu dem wir gebeten.
In Winterskälte und Hungersnöten;
Wir haben vergebens gehofft und geharrt,
Er hat uns geäfft und gefoppt und genarrt —
    Wir weben, wir weben!

Ein Fluch dem König, dem König der Reichen,
Den unser Elend nicht konnte erweichen,
Der den letzten Groschen von uns erpreßt
Und uns wie Hunde erschießen läßt —
    Wir weben, wir weben!

Ein Fluch dem falschen Vaterlande,
Wo nur gedeihen Schmach und Schande,
Wo jede Blume früh geknickt,
Wo Fäulnis und Moder den Wurm erquickt —
    Wir weben, wir weben!

Das Schiffchen fliegt, der Webstuhl kracht,
Wir weben emsig Tag und Nacht —
Altdeutschland, wir weben dein Leichentuch,
Wir weben hinein den dreifachen Fluch,
    Wir weben, und weben!

———

Es hatte mein Haupt die schwarze Frau
Zärtlich ans Herz geschlossen;
Ach! meine Haare wurden grau,
Wo ihre Tränen geflossen.

Sie küßte mich lahm, sie küßte mich krank,
Sie küßte mir blind die Augen;
Das Mark aus meinem Rückgrat trank
Ihr Mund mit wildem Saugen.

Mein Leib ist jetzt ein Leichnam, worin
Der Geist ist eingekerkert —
Manchmal wird ihm unwirsch zu Sinn,
Er tobt und rast und berserkert.

Ohnmächtige Flüche! Dein schlimmster Fluch
Wird keine Fleige töten.
Ertrage die Schickung, und versuch'
Gelinde zu flennen, zu beten.

———

Mich locken nicht die Himmelsauen
Im Paradies, im sel'gen Land;
Dort find' ich keine schönre Frauen,
Als ich bereits auf Erden fand.

Kein Engel mit den feinsten Schwingen
Könnt' mir ersetzen dort mein Weib;
Auf Wolken sitzend Psalmen singen,
Wär' auch nicht just mein Zeitvertreib.

O Herr! ich glaub', es wär' das beste,
Du ließest mich in dieser Welt;
Heil nur zuvor mein Leibgebreste,
Und sorge auch für etwas Geld.

Ich weiß, es ist voll Sünd' und Laster
Die Welt; jedoch ich bin einmal
Gewöhnt, auf diesem Erdpechpflaster
Zu schlendern durch das Jammertal.

Genieren wird das Weltgetriebe
Mich nie, denn selten geh' ich aus;
In Schlafrock und Pantoffeln bleibe
Ich gern bei meiner Frau zu Haus.

Laß mich bei ihr! Hör' ich sie schwätzen,
Trinkt meine Seele die Musik
Der holden Stimme mit Ergötzen.
So treu und ehrlich ist ihr Blick!

Gesundheit nur und Geldzulage
Verlang' ich, Herr! O laß mich froh
Hinleben noch viel schöne Tage
Bei meiner Frau im statu quo!

Miserere

Die Söhne des Glückes beneid' ich nicht
Ob ihrem Leben, beneiden
Will ich sie nur ob ihrem Tod,
Dem schmerzlos raschen Verscheiden.

Im Prachtgewand, des Haupt bekränzt
Und Lachen auf der Lippe,
Sitzen sie froh beim Lebensbankett —
Da trifft sie jählings die Hippe.

Im Festkleid und mit Rosen geschmückt,
Die noch wie lebend blühten,
Gelangen sie in das Schattenreich
Fortunas Favoriten.

Nie hatte Siechtum sie entstellt,
Sind Tote von guter Miene,
Und huldreich empfängt sie an ihrem Hof
Zarewna Proserpine.

Wie sehr muß ich beneiden ihr Los!
Schon sieben Jahre mit herben,
Qualvollen Gebresten wälz' ich mich
Am Boden, und kann nicht sterben!

O Gott, verkürze meine Qual,
Damit man mich bald begrabe;
Du weißt ja, daß ich kein Talent
Zum Martyrtume habe.

Ob deiner Inkonsequenz, o Herr,
Erlaube, daß ich staune:
Du schufest den fröhlichsten Dichter, und raubst
Ihm jetzt seine gute Laune.

Der Schmerz verdumpft den heitern Sinn
Und macht mich melancholisch,
Nimmt nicht der traurige Spaß ein End',
So werd' ich am Ende katholisch.

Ich heule dir dann die Ohren voll,
Wie andre gute Christen —
O Miserere! Verloren geht
Der beste der Humoristen!

ANNETTE VON DROSTE-HÜLSHOFF

1797–1848

Am Turme

Ich steh auf hohem Balkone am Turm,
Umstrichen vom schreienden Stare,
Und laß gleich einer Mänade den Sturm
Mir wühlen im flatternden Haare;
O wilder Geselle, o toller Fant,
Ich möchte dich kräftig umschlingen,
Und, Sehne an Sehne, zwei Schritte vom Rand
Auf Tod und Leben dann ringen!

Und drunten seh ich am Strand, so frisch
Wie spielende Doggen, die Wellen
Sich tummeln rings mit Geklaff und Gezisch
Und glänzende Flocken schnellen.
O, springen möcht ich hinein alsbald,
Recht in die tobende Meute,
Und jagen durch den korallenen Wald
Das Walroß, die lustige Beute!

Und drüben seh ich ein Wimpel wehn
So keck wie eine Standarte,
Seh auf und nieder den Kiel sich drehn
Von meiner luftigen Warte;
O, sitzen möcht ich im kämpfenden Schiff,
Das Steuerruder ergreifen
Und zischend über das brandende Riff
Wie eine Seemöwe streifen.

Wär ich ein Jäger auf freier Flur,
Ein Stück nur von einem Soldaten,
Wär ich ein Mann doch mindestens nur,

93

So würde der Himmel mir raten;
Nun muß ich sitzen so fein und klar,
Gleich einem artigen Kinde,
Und darf nur heimlich lösen mein Haar
Und lassen es flattern im Winde!

Das Spiegelbild

Schaust du mich an aus dem Kristall
Mit deiner Augen Nebelball,
Kometen gleich, die im Verbleichen;
Mit Zügen worin wunderlich
Zwei Seelen wie Spione sich
Umschleichen, ja, dann flüstre ich:
Phantom, du bist nicht meinesgleichen!

Bist nur entschlüpft der Träume Hut,
Zu eisen mir das warme Blut,
Die dunkle Locke mir zu blassen;
Und dennoch, dämmerndes Gesicht,
Drin seltsam spielt ein Doppellicht,
Trätest du vor, ich weiß es nicht,
Würd ich dich lieben oder hassen?

Zu deiner Stirne Herrscherthron,
Wo die Gedanken leisten Fron
Wie Knechte, würd ich schüchtern blicken;
Doch von des Auges kaltem Glast,
Voll toten Lichts, gebrochen fast,
Gespenstig, würd, ein scheuer Gast,
Weit, weit ich meinen Schemel rücken.

Und was den Mund umspielt so lind,
So weich und hülflos wie ein Kind,
Das möcht in treue Hut ich bergen;
Und wieder, wenn er höhnend spielt,
Wie von gespanntem Bogen zielt,
Wenn leis es durch die Züge wühlt,
Dann möcht ich fliehen wie vor Schergen.

Es ist gewiß, du bist nicht Ich,
Ein fremdes Dasein, dem ich mich

Wie Moses nahe, unbeschuhet,
Voll Kräfte, die mir nicht bewußt,
Voll fremden Leides, fremder Lust;
Gnade mir Gott, wenn in der Brust
Mir schlummernd deine Seele ruhet!

Und dennoch fühl ich, wie verwandt,
Zu deinen Schauern mich gebannt,
Und Liebe muß der Furcht sich einen.
Ja, trätest aus Kristalles Rund,
Phantom, du lebend auf den Grund,
Nur leise zittern würd ich, und
Mich dünkt — ich würde um dich weinen!

Mondesaufgang

An des Balkones Gitter lehnte ich
Und wartete, du mildes Licht, auf dich.
Hoch über mir, gleich trübem Eiskristalle,
Zerschmolzen schwamm des Firmamentes Halle;
Der See verschimmerte mit leisem Dehnen,
Zerflossne Perlen order Wolkentränen?
Es rieselte, es dämmerte um mich,
Ich wartete, du mildes Licht, auf dich.

Hoch stand ich, neben mir der Linden Kamm,
Tief unter mir Gezweige, Ast und Stamm;
Im Laube summte der Phalänen* Reigen,
Die Feuerfliege sah ich glimmend steigen,
Und Blüten taumelten wie halb entschlafen;
Mir war, als treibe hier ein Herz zum Hafen,
Ein Herz, das übervoll von Glück und Leid
Und Bildern seliger Vergangenheit.

Das Dunkel stieg, die Schatten drangen ein —
Wo weilst du, weilst du denn, mein milder Schein? —
Sie drangen ein wie sündige Gedanken,
Des Firmamentes Woge schien zu schwanken,
Verzittert war der Feuerfliege Funken,
Längst die Phaläne an den Grund gesunken,

Nur Bergeshäupter standen hart und nah,
Ein düstrer Richterkreis, im Düster da.

Und Zweige zischelten an meinen Fuß
Wie Warnungsflüstern oder Todesgruß,
Ein Summen stieg im weiten Wassertale
Wie Volksgemurmel vor dem Tribunale;
Mir war, als müsse etwas Rechnung geben,
Als stehe zagend ein verlornes Leben,
Als stehe ein verkümmert Herz allein,
Einsam mit seiner Schuld und seiner Pein.

Da auf die Wellen sank ein Silberflor,
Und langsam stiegst du, frommes Licht, empor;
Der Alpen finstre Stirnen strichst du leise,
Und aus den Richtern wurden sanfte Greise;
Der Wellen Zucken ward ein lächelnd Winken,
An jedem Zweige sah ich Tropfen blinken,
Und jeder Tropfen schien ein Kämmerlein,
Drin flimmerte der Heimatlampe Schein.

O Mond, du bist mir wie ein später Freund,
Der seine Jugend dem Verarmten eint,
Um seine sterbenden Erinnerungen
Des Lebens zarten Widerschein geschlungen,
Bist keine Sonne, die entzückt und blendet,
In Feuerströmen lebt, im Blute endet —
Bist, was dem kranken Sänger sein Gedicht,
Ein fremdes, aber o! ein mildes Licht.

[Phaläne: moth]

Im Grase

Süße Ruh, süßer Taumel im Gras,
Von des Krautes Arome umhaucht,
Tiefe Flut, tief tief trunkne Flut,
Wenn die Wolk am Azure verraucht,
Wenn aufs müde, schwimmende Haupt
Süßes Lachen gaukelt herab,
Liebe Stimme säuselt und träuft
Wie die Lindenblüt auf ein Grab.

Wenn im Busen die Toten dann,
Jede Leiche sich streckt und regt,
Leise, leise den Odem zieht,
Die geschlossne Wimper bewegt,
Tote Lieb, tote Lust, tote Zeit,
All die Schätze, im Schutt verwühlt,
Sich berühren mit schüchternem Klang
Gleich den Glöckchen, vom Winde umspielt.

Stunden, flüchtger ihr als der Kuß
Eines Strahls auf den trauernden See,
Als des ziehenden Vogels Lied,
Das mir nieder perlt aus der Höh,
Als des schillernden Käfers Blitz,
Wenn den Sonnenpfad er durcheilt,
Als der heiße Druck einer Hand,
Die zum letzten Male verweilt.

Dennoch, Himmel, immer mir nur
Dieses eine mir: für das Lied
Jedes freien Vogels im Blau
Eine Seele, die mit ihm zieht,
Nur für jeden kärglichen Strahl
Meinen farbig schillernden Saum,
Jeder warmen Hand meinen Druck
Und für jedes Glück meinen Traum.

Am letzten Tag des Jahres (Silvester)

Das Jahr geht um,
Der Faden rollt sich sausend ab.
Ein Stündchen noch, das letzte heut,
Und stäubend rieselt in sein Grab,
Was einstens war lebendge Zeit.
Ich harre stumm.

's ist tiefe Nacht!
Ob wohl ein Auge offen noch?
In diesen Mauern rüttelt dein
Verrinnen, Zeit! Mir schaudert, doch

Es will die letzte Stunde sein
Einsam durchwacht,

Gesehen all,
Was ich begangen und gedacht.
Was mir aus Haupt und Herzen stieg,
Das steht nun eine ernste Wacht
Am Himmelstor. O halber Sieg!
O schwerer Fall!

Wie reißt der Wind
Am Fensterkrueze! Ja, es will
Auf Sturmesfittichen das Jahr
Zerstäuben, nicht ein Schatten still
Verhauchen unterm Sternenklar.
Du Sündenkind,

War nicht ein hohl
Und heimlich Sausen jeder Tag
In deiner wüsten Brust Verließ,
Wo langsam Stein an Stein zerbrach,
Wenn es den kalten Odem stieß
Vom starren Pol?

Mein Lämpchen will
Verlöschen, und begierig saugt
Der Docht den letzten Tropfen Öl.
Ist so mein Leben auch verraucht?
Eröffnet sich des Grabes Höhl
Mir schwarz und still?

Wohl in dem Kreis,
Den dieses Jahres Lauf umzieht,
Mein Leben bricht. Ich wußt es lang!
Und dennoch hat dies Herz geglüht
In eitler Leidenschaften Drang!
Mir brüht der Schweiß

Der tiefsten Angst
Auf Stirn und Hand. — Wie? dämmert feucht
Ein Stern dort durch die Wolken nicht?
Wär es der Liebe Stern vielleicht,
Dir zürnend mit dem trüben Licht,
Daß du so bangst?

Horch, welch Gesumm?
Und wieder? Sterbemelodie!
Die Glocke regt den ehrnen Mund.
O Herr, ich falle auf das Knie:
Sei gnädig meiner letzten Stund!
Das Jahr ist um!

EDUARD MÖRIKE

1804–1875

Mein Fluß

O Fluß, mein Fluß im Morgenstrahl!
Empfange nun, empfange
Den sehnsuchtsvollen Leib einmal
Und küsse Brust und Wange!
— Er fühlt mir schon herauf die Brust,
Er kühlt mit Liebesschauerlust
Und jauchzendem Gesange.

Es schlüpft der goldne Sonnenschein
In Tropfen an mir nieder,
Die Woge wieget aus und ein
Die hingegebnen Glieder;
Die Arme hab ich ausgespannt,
Sie kommt auf mich herzugerannt,
Sie faßt und läßt mich wieder.

Du murmelst so, mein Fluß, warum?
Du trägst seit alten Tagen
Ein seltsam Märchen mit dir um
Und mühst dich, es zu sagen;
Du eilst so sehr und läufst so sehr,
Als müßtest du im Land umher,
Man weiß nicht wen, drum fragen.

Der Himmel, blau und kinderrein,
Worin die Wellen singen,
Der Himmel ist die Seele dein:
O laß mich ihn durchdringen!
Ich tauche mich mit Geist und Sinn
Durch die vertiefte Bläue hin
Und kann sie nicht erschwingen!

Was ist so tief, so tief wie sie?
Die Liebe nur alleine.
Sie wird nicht satt und sättigt nie
Mit ihrem Wechselscheine.
 — Schwill an, mein Fluß, und hebe dich!
Mit Grausen übergieße mich!
Mein Leben um das deine!

Du weisest schmeichelnd mich zurück
Zu deiner Blumenschwelle.
So trage denn allein dein Glück
Und wieg auf deiner Welle
Der Sonne Pracht, des Mondes Ruh.
Nach tausend Irren kehrest du
Zur ewgen Mutterquelle!

Im Frühling

Hier lieg ich auf dem Frühlingshügel:
Die Wolke wird mein Flügel,
Ein Vogel fliegt mir voraus.
Ach, sag mir, alleinzige Liebe,
Wo du bleibst, daß ich bei dir bliebe!
Doch du und die Lüfte, ihr habt kein Haus.

Der Sonnenblume gleich steht mein Gemüte offen,
Sehnend,
Sich dehnend
In Lieben und Hoffen.
Frühling, was bist du gewillt?
Wann werd ich gestillt?

Die Wolke seh ich wandeln und den Fluß,
Es dringt der Sonne goldner Kuß
Mir tief bis ins Geblüt hinein;
Die Augen, wunderbar berauschet,
Tun, als schliefen sie ein,
Nur noch das Ohr dem Ton der Biene lauschet.
Ich denke dies und denke das,
Ich sehne mich und weiß nicht recht, nach was:
Halb ist es Lust, halb ist es Klage;

Mein Herz, o sage,
Was webst du für Erinnerung
In golden grüner Zweige Dämmerung?
— Alte unnennbare Tage!

Das verlassene Mägdlein

Früh, wann die Hähne krähn,
Eh die Sternlein verschwinden,
Muß ich am Herde stehn,
Muß Feuer zünden.

Schön ist der Flammen Schein,
Es springen die Funken;
Ich schaue so drein,
In Leid versunken.

Plötzlich, da kommt es mir,
Treuloser Knabe,
Daß ich die Nacht von dir
Geträumet habe.

Träne auf Träne dann
Stürzet hernieder;
So kommt der Tag heran —
O ging er wieder!

Die schöne Buche

Ganz verborgen im Wald kenn' ich ein Plätzchen, da stehet
    Eine Buche: man sieht schöner im Bilde sie nicht.
Rein und glatt, in gediegenem Wuchs erhebt sie sich einzeln,
    Keiner der Nachbarn rührt ihr an den seidenen Schmuck.
Rings, so weit sein Gezweig der stattliche Baum ausbreitet,
    Grünet der Rasen, das Aug' still zu erquicken, umher.
Gleich nach allen Seiten umzirkt er den Stamm in der Mitte;
    Kunstlos schuf die Natur selber dies liebliche Rund.
Zartes Gebüsch umkränzet es erst, hochstämmige Bäume,
    Folgend in dichtem Gedräng', wehren dem himmlischen Blau.

Neben der dunkleren Fülle des Eichbaums wieget die Birke
    Ihr jungfräuliches Haupt schüchtern im goldenen Licht.
Nur wo, verdeckt vom Felsen, der Fußsteig jäh sich hinabschlingt,
    Lässet die Hellung mich ahnen das offene Feld. —
Als ich unlängst einsam, von neuen Gestalten des Sommers
    Ab dem Pfade gelockt, dort im Gebüsch mich verlor,
Führt' ein freundlicher Geist, des Hains auflauschende Gottheit,
    Hier mich zum erstenmal plötzlich, den Staunenden, ein.
Welch Entzücken! Es war um die hohe Stunde des Mittags:
    Lautlos alles, es schwieg selber der Vogel im Laub.
Und ich zauderte noch, auf den zierlichen Teppich zu treten;
    Festlich empfing er den Fuß, leise beschritt ich ihn nur.
Jetzo, gelehnt an den Stamm (er trägt sein breites Gewölbe
    Nicht zu hoch), ließ ich rundum die Augen ergehn,
Wo den beschatteten Kreis die feurig strahlende Sonne,
    Fast gleich messend umher, säumte mit blendendem Rand.
Aber ich stand und rührte mich nicht, dämonischer Stille,
    Unergründlicher Ruh' lauschte mein innerer Sinn.
Eingeschlossen mit dir in diesem sonnigen Zauber —
    Gürtel, o Einsamkeit, fühlt' ich und dachte nur dich.

Auf eine Lampe

Noch unverrückt, o schöne Lampe, schmückest du,
An leichten Ketten zierlich aufgehangen hier,
Die Decke des nun fast vergessnen Lustgemachs.
Auf deiner weißen Marmorschale, deren Rand
Der Efeukranz von goldengrünem Erz umflicht,
Schlingt fröhlich eine Kinderschar den Ringelreihn.
Wie reizend alles! lachend, und ein sanfter Geist
Des Ernstes doch ergossen um die ganze Form —
Ein Kunstgebild der echten Art. Wer achtet sein?
Was aber schön ist, selig scheint es in ihm selbst.

Denk es, o Seele!

Ein Tännlein grünet wo,
Wer weiß, im Walde,

Ein Rosenstrauch, wer sagt,
In welchem Garten?
Sie sind erlesen schon,
Denk es, o Seele!
Auf deinem Grab zu wurzeln
Und zu wachsen.

Zwei schwarze Rößlein weiden
Auf der Wiese,
Sie kehren heim zur Stadt
In muntern Sprüngen.
Sie werden schrittweis gehn
Mit deiner Leiche;
Vielleicht, vielleicht noch eh
An ihren Hufen
Das Eisen los wird,
Das ich blitzen sehe!

Um Mitternacht

Gelassen stieg die Nacht ans Land,
Lehnt träumend an der Berge Wand,
Ihr Auge sieht die goldne Wage nun
Der Zeit in gleichen Schalen stille ruhn;
    Und kecker rauschen die Quellen hervor,
    Sie singen der Mutter, der Nacht, ins Ohr
        Vom Tage,
Vom heute gewesenen Tage.

Das uralt alte Schlummerlied,
Sie achtet's nicht, sie ist es müd;
Ihr klingt des Himmels Bläue süßer noch,
Der flüchtgen Stunden gleichgeschwungnes Joch.
    Doch immer behalten die Quellen das Wort,
    Es singen die Wasser im Schlafe noch fort
        Vom Tage,
Vom heute gewesenen Tage.

HUGO VON HOFMANNSTHAL

1874–1929

Vorfrühling

Es läuft der Frühlingswind
Durch kahle Alleen,
Seltsame Dinge sind
In seinem Wehn.

Er hat sich gewiegt,
Wo Weinen war,
Und hat sich geschmiegt
In zerrüttetes Haar.

Er schüttelte nieder
Akazienblüten
Und kühlte die Glieder,
Die atmend glühten.

Lippen im Lachen
Hat er berührt,
Die weichen und wachen
Fluren durchspürt.

Er glitt durch die Flöte
Als schluchzender Schrei,
An dämmernder Röte
Flog er vorbei.

Er flog mit Schweigen
Durch flüsternde Zimmer
Und löschte im Neigen
Der Ampel Schimmer.

Es läuft der Frühlingswind
Durch kahle Alleen,
Seltsame Dinge sind
In seinem Wehn.

Durch die glatten
Kahlen Alleen
Treibt sein Wehn
Blasse Schatten.

Und den Duft,
Den er gebracht,
Von wo er gekommen
Seit gestern Nacht.

Erlebnis

Mit silbergrauem Dufte war das Tal
Der Dämmerung erfüllt, wie wenn der Mond
Durch Wolken sickert. Doch es war nicht Nacht.
Mit silbergrauem Duft des dunklen Tales
Verschwammen meine dämmernden Gedanken,
Und still versank ich in dem webenden,
Durchsichtgen Meere und verließ das Leben.
Wie wunderbare Blumen waren da
Mit Kelchen dunkelglühend! Pflanzendickicht,
Durch das ein gelbrot Licht wie von Topasen
In warmen Strömen drang und glomm. Das Ganze
War angefüllt mit einem tiefen Schwellen
Schwermütiger Musik. Und dieses wußt ich,
Obgleich ichs nicht begreife, doch ich wußt es:
Das ist der Tod. Der ist Musik geworden,
Gewaltig sehnend, süß und dunkelglühend,
Verwandt der tiefsten Schwermut.

                         Aber seltsam!
Ein namenloses Heimweh weinte lautlos
In meiner Seele nach dem Leben, weinte,
Wie einer weint, wenn er auf großem Seeschiff
Mit gelben Riesensegeln gegen Abend
Auf dunkelblauem Wasser an der Stadt,
Der Vaterstadt, vorüberfährt. Da sieht er
Die Gassen, hört die Brunnen rauschen, riecht
Den Duft der Fliederbüsche, sieht sich selber,
Ein Kind, am Ufer stehn, mit Kindesaugen,

Die ängstlich sind und weinen wollen, sieht
Durchs offne Fenster Licht in seinem Zimmer —
Das große Seeschiff aber trägt ihn weiter
Auf dunkelblauem Wasser lautlos gleitend
Mit gelben fremdgeformten Riesensegeln.

Die Beiden

Sie trug den Becher in der Hand
— Ihr Kinn und Mund glich seinem Rand —,
So leicht und sicher war ihr Gang,
Kein Tropfen aus dem Becher sprang.

So leicht und fest war seine Hand:
Er ritt auf einem jungen Pferde,
Und mit nachlässiger Gebärde
Erzwang er, daß es zitternd stand.

Jedoch, wenn er aus ihrer Hand
Den leichten Becher nehmen sollte,
So war es beiden allzu schwer:
Denn beide bebten sie so sehr,
Daß keine Hand die andre fand
Und dunkler Wein am Boden rollte.

Weltgeheimnis

Der tiefe Brunnen weiß es wohl,
Einst waren alle tief und stumm,
Und alle wußten drum.

Wie Zauberworte, nachgelallt
Und nicht begriffen in den Grund
So geht es jetzt von Mund zu Mund.

Der tiefe Brunnen weiß es wohl;
In den gebückt, begriffs ein Mann,
Begriff es und verlor es dann.

Und redet' irr und sang ein Lied —
Auf dessen dunklen Spiegel bückt
Sich einst ein Kind und wird entrückt.

Und wächst und weiß nichts von sich selbst
Und wird ein Weib, das einer liebt
Und — wunderbar wie Liebe gibt!

Wie Liebe tiefe Kunde gibt! —
Da wird an Dinge, dumpf geahnt,
In ihren Küssen tief gemahnt . . .

In unsern Worten liegt es drin,
So tritt des Bettlers Fuß den Kies,
Der eines Edelsteins Verlies.

Der tiefe Brunnen weiß es wohl,
Einst aber wußten alle drum,
Nun zuckt im Kreis ein Traum herum.

Ballade des äußeren Lebens

Und Kinder wachsen auf mit tiefen Augen,
Die von nichts wissen, wachsen auf und sterben,
Und alle Menschen gehen ihre Wege.

Und süße Früchte werden aus den herben
Und fallen nachts wie tote Vögel nieder
Und liegen wenig Tage und verderben.

Und immer weht der Wind, und immer wieder
Vernehmen wir und reden viele Worte
Und spüren Lust und Müdigkeit der Glieder.

Und Straßen laufen durch das Gras, und Orte
Sind da und dort, voll Fackeln, Bäumen, Teichen,
Und drohende, und totenhaft verdorrte . . .

Wozu sind diese aufgebaut? und gleichen
Einander nie? und sind unzählig viele?
Was wechselt Lachen, Weinen und Erbleichen?

Was frommt das alles uns und diese Spiele,
Die wir doch groß und ewig einsam sind
Und wandernd nimmer suchen irgend Ziele?

Was frommts, dergleichen viel gesehen haben?
Und dennoch sagt der viel, der ,,Abend'' sagt,
Ein Wort, daraus Tiefsinn und Trauer rinnt

Wie schwerer Honig aus den hohlen Waben.

Terzinen über Vergänglichkeit I

Noch spür ich ihren Atem auf den Wangen:
Wie kann das sein, daß diese nahen Tage
Fort sind, für immer fort, und ganz vergangen?

Dies ist ein Ding, das keiner voll aussinnt,
Und viel zu grauenvoll, als daß man klage:
Daß alles gleitet und vorüberrinnt.

Und daß mein eignes Ich, durch nichts gehemmt,
Herüberglitt aus einem kleinen Kind
Mir wie ein Hund unheimlich stumm und fremd.

Dann: daß ich auch vor hundert Jahren war
Und meine Ahnen, die im Totenhemd,
Mit mir verwandt sind wie mein eignes Haar,

So eins mit mir als wie mein eignes Haar.

Manche freilich . . .

Manche freilich müssen drunten sterben,
Wo die schweren Ruder der Schiffe streifen,
Andre wohnen bei dem Steuer droben,
Kennen Vogelflug und die Länder der Sterne.

Manche liegen immer mit schweren Gliedern
Bei den Wurzeln des verworrenen Lebens,
Andern sind die Stühle gerichtet
Bei den Sibyllen, den Königinnen,

Und da sitzen sie wie zu Hause,
Leichten Hauptes und leichter Hände.

Doch ein Schatten fällt von jenen Leben
In die anderen Leben hinüber,
Und die leichten sind an die schweren
Wie an Luft und Erde gebunden:

Ganz vergessener Völker Müdigkeiten
Kann ich nicht abtun von meinen Lidern,
Noch weghalten von der erschrockenen Seele
Stummes Niederfallen ferner Sterne.

Viele Geschicke weben neben dem meinen,
Durcheinander spielt sie alle das Dasein,
Und mein Teil ist mehr als dieses Lebens
Schlanke Flamme oder schmale Leier.

RAINER MARIA RILKE

1875–1926

Ich fürchte mich so vor der Menschen Wort.
Sie sprechen alles so deutlich aus:
Und dieses heißt Hund und jenes heißt Haus,
und hier ist Beginn und das Ende ist dort.

Mich bangt auch ihr Sinn, ihr Spiel mit dem Spott,
sie wissen alles, was wird und war;
kein Berg ist ihnen mehr wunderbar;
ihr Garten und Gut grenzt grade an Gott.

Ich will immer warnen und wehren: Bleibt fern.
Die Dinge singen hör ich so gern.
Ihr rührt sie an: sie sind starr und stumm.
Ihr bringt mir alle die Dinge um.

Herbsttag

Herr: es ist Zeit. Der Sommer war sehr groß.
Leg deinen Schatten auf die Sonnenuhren,
und auf den Fluren laß die Winde los.

Befiehl den letzten Früchten voll zu sein;
gieb ihnen noch zwei südlichere Tage,
dränge sie zur Vollendung hin und jage
die letzte Süße in den schweren Wein.

Wer jetzt kein Haus hat, baut sich keines mehr.
Wer jetzt allein ist, wird es lange bleiben,
wird wachen, lesen, lange Briefe schreiben
und wird in den Alleen hin und her
unruhig wandern, wenn die Blätter treiben.

111

Fortschritt

Und wieder rauscht mein tiefes Leben lauter,
als ob es jetzt in breitern Ufern ginge.
Immer verwandter werden mir die Dinge
und alle Bilder immer angeschauter.
Dem Namenlosen fühl ich mich vertrauter:
Mit meinen Sinnen, wie mit Vögeln, reiche
ich in die windigen Himmel aus der Eiche,
und in den abgebrochnen Tag der Teiche
sinkt, wie auf Fischen stehend, mein Gefühl.

Der Panther
Im Jardin des Plantes, Paris

Sein Blick ist vom Vorübergehn der Stäbe
so müd geworden, daß er nichts mehr hält.
Ihm ist, als ob es tausend Stäbe gäbe
und hinter tausend Stäben keine Welt.

Der weiche Gang geschmeidig starker Schritte,
der sich im allerkleinsten Kreise dreht,
ist wie ein Tanz von Kraft um eine Mitte,
in der betäubt ein großer Wille steht.

Nur manchmal schiebt der Vorhang der Pupille
sich lautlos auf −. Dann geht ein Bild hinein,
geht durch der Glieder angespannte Stille −
und hört im Herzen auf zu sein.

Die Gazelle
Gazella Dorcas

Verzauberte: wie kann der Einklang zweier
erwählter Worte je den Reim erreichen,

der in dir kommt und geht, wie auf ein Zeichen.
Aus deiner Stirne steigen Laub und Leier,

und alles Deine geht schon im Vergleich
durch Liebeslieder, deren Worte, weich
wie Rosenblätter, dem, der nicht mehr liest,
sich auf die Augen legen, die er schließt:

um dich zu sehen: hingetragen, als
wäre mit Sprüngen jeder Lauf geladen
und schösse nur nicht ab, solang der Hals

das Haupt ins Horchen hält: wir wenn beim Baden
im Wald die Badende sich unterbricht:
den Waldsee im gewendeten Gesicht.

Römische Fontäne
Borghese

Zwei Becken, ein das andre übersteigend
aus einem alten runden Marmorrand,
und aus dem oberen Wasser leis sich neigend
zum Wasser, welches unten wartend stand,

dem leise redenden entgegenschweigend
und heimlich, gleichsam in der hohlen Hand,
ihm Himmel hinter Grün und Dunkel zeigend
wie einen unbekannten Gegenstand;

sich selber ruhig in der schönen Schale
verbreitend ohne Heimweh, Kreis aus Kreis,
nur manchmal träumerisch und tropfenweis

sich niederlassend an den Moosbehängen
zum letzten Spiegel, der sein Becken leis
von unten lächeln macht mit Übergängen.

Das Karussell
Jardin du Luxembourg

Mit einem Dach und seinem Schatten dreht
sich eine kleine Weile der Bestand
von bunten Pferden, alle aus dem Land,
das lange zögert, eh es untergeht.
Zwar manche sind an Wagen angespannt,
doch alle haben Mut in ihren Mienen;
ein böser roter Löwe geht mit ihnen
und dann und wann ein weißer Elefant.

Sogar ein Hirsch ist da, ganz wie im Wald,
nur daß er einen Sattel trägt und drüber
ein kleines blaues Mädchen aufgeschnallt.

Und auf dem Löwen reitet weiß ein Junge
und hält sich mit der kleinen heißen Hand,
dieweil der Löwe Zähne zeigt und Zunge.

Und dann und wann ein weißer Elefant.

Und auf den Pferden kommen sie vorüber,
auch Mädchen, helle, diesem Pferdesprunge
fast schon entwachsen; mitten in dem Schwunge
schauen sie auf, irgendwohin, herüber —

Und dann und wann ein weißer Elefant.

Und das geht hin und eilt sich, daß es endet,
und kreist und dreht sich nur und hat kein Ziel.
Ein Rot, ein Grün, ein Grau vorbeigesendet,
ein kleines kaum begonnenes Profil —.
Und manchesmal ein Lächeln, hergewendet,
ein seliges, das blendet und verschwendet
an dieses atemlose blinde Spiel . . .

Archaïscher Torso Apollos

Wir kannten nicht sein unerhörtes Haupt,
darin die Augenäpfel reiften. Aber

sein Torso glüht noch wie ein Kandelaber,
in dem sein Schauen, nur zurückgeschraubt,

sich hält und glänzt. Sonst könnte nicht der Bug
der Brust dich blenden, und im leisen Drehen
der Lenden könnte nicht ein Lächeln gehen
zu jener Mitte, die die Zeugung trug.

Sonst stünde dieser Stein entstellt und kurz
unter der Schultern durchsichtigem Sturz
und flimmerte nicht so wie Raubtierfelle;

und bräche nicht aus allen seinen Rändern
aus wie ein Stern: denn da ist keine Stelle,
die dich nicht sieht. Du mußt dein Leben ändern.

DUINESER ELEGIEN
Elegy 1

Wer, wenn ich schriee, hörte mich denn aus der Engel
Ordnungen? und gesetzt selbst, es nähme
einer mich plötzlich ans Herz: ich verginge von seinem
stärkeren Dasein. Denn das Schöne ist nichts
als des Schrecklichen Anfang, den wir noch grade ertragen,
und wir bewundern es so, weil es gelassen verschmäht,
uns zu zerstören. Ein jeder Engel ist schrecklich.

Und so verhalt ich mich denn und verschlucke den Lockruf
dunkelen Schluchzens. Ach, wen vermögen
wir denn zu brauchen? Engel nicht, Menschen nicht,
und die findigen Tiere merken es schon,
daß wir nicht sehr verläßlich zu Haus sind
in der gedeuteten Welt. [. . .]

Elegy 9

Warum, wenn es angeht, also die Frist des Daseins
hinzubringen, als Lorbeer, ein wenig dunkler als alles
andere Grün, mit kleinen Wellen an jedem

Blattrand (wie eines Windes Lächeln) − : warum dann
Menschliches müssen − und, Schicksal vermeidend,
sich sehnen nach Schicksal? . . .

　　　　　　　　　　　Oh, *nicht*, weil Glück *ist*,
dieser voreilige Vorteil eines nahen Verlusts.
Nicht aus Neugier, oder zur Übung des Herzens,
das auch im Lorbeer *wäre*. . . .

Aber weil Hiersein viel ist, und weil uns scheinbar
alles das Hiesige braucht, dieses Schwindende, das
seltsam uns angeht. Uns, die Schwindendsten. *Ein* Mal
jedes, nur *ein* Mal. *Ein* Mal und nichtmehr. Und wir auch
ein Mal. Nie wieder. Aber dieses
ein Mal gewesen zu sein, wenn auch nur *ein* Mal:
irdisch gewesen zu sein, scheint nicht widerrufbar.

Und so drängen wir uns und wollen es leisten,
wollens enthalten in unsern einfachen Händen,
im überfüllteren Blick und im sprachlosen Herzen.
Wollen es werden. − Wem es geben? Am liebsten
alles behalten für immer . . . Ach, in den andern Bezug,
wehe, was nimmt man hinüber? Nicht das Anschaun, das hier
langsam erlernte, und kein hier Ereignetes. Keins.
Also die Schmerzen. Also vor allem das Schwersein,
also der Liebe lange Erfahrung, − also
lauter Unsägliches. Aber später,
unter den Sternen, was solls: *die* sind *besser* unsäglich.
Bringt doch der Wanderer auch vom Hange des Bergrands
nicht eine Hand voll Erde ins Tal, die Allen unsägliche, sondern
ein erworbenes Wort, reines, den gelben und blaun
Enzian. Sind wir vielleicht *hier*, um zu sagen: Haus,
Brücke, Brunnen, Tor, Krug, Obstbaum, Fenster, −
höchstens: Säule, Turm . . . . aber zu *sagen*, verstehs,
oh zu sagen *so*, wie selber die Dinge niemals
innig meinten zu sein. Ist nicht die heimliche List
dieser verschwiegenen Erde, wenn sie die Liebenden drängt,
daß sich in ihrem Gefühl jedes und jedes entzückt?
Schwelle: was ists für zwei
Liebende, daß sie die eigne ältere Schwelle der Tür
ein wenig verbrauchen, auch sie, nach den vielen vorher
und vor den Künftigen . . . . ., leicht.

Hier ist des *Säglichen* Zeit, *hier* seine Heimat.
Sprich und bekenn. Mehr als je
fallen die Dinge dahin, die erlebbaren, denn,
was sie verdrängend ersetzt, ist ein Tun ohne Bild.
Tun unter Krusten, die willig zerspringen, sobald
innen das Handeln entwächst und sich anders begrenzt.
Zwischen den Hämmern besteht
unser Herz, wie die Zunge
zwischen den Zähnen, die doch,
dennoch, die preisende bleibt.

Preise dem Engel die Welt, nicht die unsägliche, *ihm*
kannst du nicht großtun mit herrlich Erfühltem; im Weltall,
wo er fühlender fühlt, bist du ein Neuling. Drum zeig
ihm das Einfache, das, von Geschlecht zu Geschlechtern gestaltet,
als ein Unsriges lebt, neben der Hand und im Blick.
Sag ihm die Dinge. Er wird staunender stehn; wie du standest
bei dem Seiler in Rom, oder beim Töpfer am Nil.
Zeig ihm, wie glücklich ein Ding sein kann, wie schuldlos und
        unser,
wie selbst das klagende Leid rein zur Gestalt sich entschließt,
dient als ein Ding, oder stirbt in ein Ding —, und jenseits
selig der Geige entgeht. — Und diese, von Hingang
lebenden Dinge verstehn, daß du sie rühmst; vergänglich,
traun sie ein Rettendes uns, den Vergänglichsten, zu.
Wollen, wir sollen sie ganz im unsichtbarn Herzen verwandeln
in — o unendlich — in uns! Wer wir am Ende auch seien.

    Erde, ist es nicht dies, was du willst: *unsichtbar*
in uns erstehn? — Ist es dein Traum nicht,
einmal unsichtbar zu sein? — Erde! unsichtbar!
Was, wenn Verwandlung nicht, ist dein drängender Auftrag?
Erde, du liebe, ich will. Oh glaub, es bedürfte
nicht deiner Frühlinge mehr, mich die zu gewinnen —, *einer*,
ach, ein einziger ist schon dem Blute zu viel.
Namenlos bin ich zu dir entschlossen, von weit her.
Immer warst du im Recht, und dein heiliger Einfall
ist der vertrauliche Tod.

Siehe, ich lebe. Woraus? Weder Kindheit noch Zukunft
werden weniger . . . . Überzähliges Dasein
entspringt mir im Herzen.

Die Sonette an Orpheus

Part One: III

Ein Gott vermags. Wie aber, sag mir, soll
ein Mann ihm folgen durch die schmale Leier?
Sein Sinn ist Zwiespalt. An der Kreuzung zweier
Herzwege steht kein Tempel für Apoll.

Gesang, wie du ihn lehrst, ist nicht Begehr,
nicht Werbung um ein endlich noch Erreichtes;
Gesang ist Dasein. Für den Gott ein Leichtes.
Wann aber *sind* wir? Und wann wendet *er*

an unser Sein die Erde und die Sterne?
Dies *ists* nicht, Jüngling, daß du liebst, wenn auch
die Stimme dann den Mund dir aufstößt, – lerne

vergessen, daß du aufsangst. Das verrinnt.
In Wahrheit singen, ist ein andrer Hauch.
Ein Hauch um Nichts. Ein Wehn im Gott. Ein Wind.

Part Two: XV

O Brunnen-Mund, du gebender, du Mund,
der unerschöpflich Eines, Reines, spricht, –
du, vor des Wassers fließendem Gesicht,
marmorne Maske. Und im Hintergrund

der Aquädukte Herkunft. Weither an
Gräbern vorbei, vom Hang des Apennins
tragen sie dir dein Sagen zu, das dann
am schwarzen Altern deines Kinns

vorüberfällt in das Gefäß davor.
Dies ist das schlafend hingelegte Ohr,
das Marmorohr, in das du immer sprichst.

Ein Ohr der Erde. Nur mit sich allein
redet sie also. Schiebt ein Krug sich ein,
so scheint es ihr, daß du sie unterbrichst.

GEORG TRAKL

1887–1914

Die Bauern

Vorm Fenster tönendes Grün und Rot.
Im schwarzverräucherten, niederen Saal
Sitzen die Knechte und Mägde beim Mahl;
Und sie schenken den Wein und sie brechen das Brot.

Im tiefen Schweigen der Mittagszeit
Fällt bisweilen ein karges Wort.
Die Äcker flimmern in einem fort
Und der Himmel bleiern und weit.

Fratzenhaft flackert im Herd die Glut
Und ein Schwarm von Fliegen summt.
Die Mägde lauschen blöd und verstummt
Und ihre Schläfen hämmert das Blut.

Und manchmal treffen sich Blicke voll Gier,
Wenn tierischer Dunst die Stube durchweht.
Eintönig spricht ein Knecht das Gebet
Und ein Hahn kräht unter der Tür.

Und wieder ins Feld. Ein Grauen packt
Sie oft im tosenden Ährengebraus
Und klirrend schwingen ein und aus
Die Sensen geisterhaft im Takt.

Verklärter Herbst

Gewaltig endet so das Jahr
Mit goldnem Wein und Frucht der Gärten.

Rund schweigen Wälder wunderbar
Und sind des Einsamen Gefährten.

Da sagt der Landmann: Es ist gut.
Ihr Abendglocken lang und leise
Gebt noch zum Ende frohen Mut.
Ein Vogelzug grüßt auf der Reise.

Es ist der Liebe milde Zeit.
Im Kahn den blauen Fluß hinunter
Wie schön sich Bild an Bildchen reiht –
Das geht in Ruh und Schweigen unter.

De profundis

Es ist ein Stoppelfeld, in das ein schwarzer Regen fällt.
Es ist ein brauner Baum, der einsam dasteht.
Es ist ein Zischelwind, der leere Hütten umkreist.
Wie traurig dieser Abend.

Am Weiler vorbei
Sammelt die sanfte Waise noch spärliche Ähren ein.
Ihre Augen weiden rund und goldig in der Dämmerung
Und ihr Schoß harrt des himmlischen Bräutigams.

Bei der Heimkehr
Fanden die Hirten den süßen Leib
Verwest im Dornenbusch.

Ein Schatten bin ich ferne finsteren Dörfern.
Gottes Schweigen
Trank ich aus dem Brunnen des Hains.

Auf meine Stirne tritt kaltes Metall
Spinnen suchen mein Herz.
Es ist ein Licht, das in meinem Mund erlöscht.

Nachts fand ich mich auf einer Heide,
Starrend von Unrat und Staub der Sterne.
Im Haselgebüsch
Klangen wieder kristallne Engel.

Der Herbst des Einsamen

Der dunkle Herbst kehrt ein voll Frucht und Fülle,
Vergilbter Glanz von schönen Sommertagen.
Ein reines Blau tritt aus verfallener Hülle;
Der Flug der Vögel tönt von alten Sagen.
Gekeltert ist der Wein, die milde Stille
Erfüllt von leiser Antwort dunkler Fragen.

Und hier und dort ein Kreuz auf ödem Hügel;
Im roten Wald verliert sich eine Herde.
Die Wolke wandert übern Weiherspiegel;
Es ruht des Landmanns ruhige Geberde.
Sehr leise rührt des Abends blauer Flügel
Ein Dach von dürrem Stroh, die schwarze Erde.

Bald nisten Sterne in des Müden Brauen;
In kühle Stuben kehrt ein still Bescheiden
Und Engel treten leise aus den blauen
Augen der Liebenden, die sanfter leiden.
Es rauscht das Rohr; anfällt ein knöchern Grauen,
Wenn schwarz der Tau tropft von den kahlen Weiden.

Ein Winterabend

Wenn der Schnee ans Fenster fällt,
Lang die Abendglocke läutet,
Vielen ist der Tisch bereitet
Und das Haus ist wohlbestellt.

Mancher auf der Wanderschaft
Kommt ans Tor auf dunklen Pfaden.
Golden blüht der Baum der Gnaden
Aus der Erde kühlem Saft.

Wanderer tritt still herein;
Schmerz versteinerte die Schwelle.
Da erglänzt in reiner Helle
Auf dem Tische Brot und Wein.

Grodek

Am Abend tönen die herbstlichen Wälder
Von tödlichen Waffen, die goldnen Ebenen
Und blauen Seen, darüber die Sonne
Düstrer hinrollt; umfängt die Nacht
Sterbende Krieger, die wilde Klage
Ihrer zerbrochenen Münder.
Doch stille sammelt im Weidengrund
Rotes Gewölk, darin ein zürnender Gott wohnt
Das vergoßne Blut sich, mondne Kühle;
Alle Straßen münden in schwarze Verwesung.
Unter goldnem Gezweig der Nacht und Sternen
Es schwankt der Schwester Schatten durch den schweigenden Hain,
Zu grüßen die Geister der Helden, die blutenden Häupter;
Und leise tönen im Rohr die dunkeln Flöten des Herbstes.
O stolzere Trauer! ihr ehernen Altäre
Die heiße Flamme des Geistes nährt heute ein gewaltiger Schmerz,
Die ungebornen Enkel.

GOTTFRIED BENN

1886–1956

Mann und Frau gehn durch die Krebsbaracke

Der Mann:
Hier diese Reihe sind zerfallene Schöße
und diese Reihe ist zerfallene Brust.
Bett stinkt bei Bett. Die Schwestern wechseln stündlich.

Komm, hebe ruhig diese Decke auf.
Sieh, dieser Klumpen Fett und faule Säfte,
das war einst irgendeinem Mann groß
und hieß auch Rausch und Heimat.

Komm, sieh auf diese Narbe an der Brust.
Fühlst du den Rosenkranz von weichen Knoten?
Fühl ruhig hin. Das Fleisch ist weich und schmerzt nicht.

Hier diese blutet wie aus dreißig Leibern.
Kein Mensch hat so viel Blut.
Hier dieser schnitt man
erst noch ein Kind aus dem verkrebsten Schoß.

Man läßt sie schlafen. Tag und Nacht. – Den Neuen
sagt man: hier schläft man sich gesund. – Nur sonntags
für den Besuch läßt man sie etwas wacher.

Nahrung wird wenig noch verzehrt. Die Rücken
sind wund. Du siehst die Fliegen. Manchmal
wäscht sie die Schwester. Wie man Bänke wäscht.

Hier schwillt der Acker schon um jedes Bett.
Fleisch ebnet sich zu Land. Glut gibt sich fort.
Saft schickt sich an zu rinnen. Erde ruft.

Wer allein ist —

Wer allein ist, ist auch im Geheimnis,
immer steht er in der Bilder Flut,
ihrer Zeugung, ihrer Keimnis,
selbst die Schatten tragen ihre Glut.

Trächtig ist er jeder Schichtung
denkerisch erfüllt und aufgespart,
mächtig ist er der Vernichtung
allem Menschlichen, das nährt und paart.

Ohne Rührung sieht er, wie die Erde
eine andere ward, als ihm begann,
nicht mehr Stirb und nicht mehr Werde:
formstill sieht ihn die Vollendung an.

Einsamer nie —

Einsamer nie als im August:
Erfüllungsstunde — im Gelände
die roten und die goldenen Brände,
doch wo ist deiner Gärten Lust?

Die Seen hell, die Himmel weich,
die Äcker rein und glänzen leise,
doch wo sind Sieg und Siegsbeweise
aus dem von dir vertretenen Reich?

Wo alles sich durch Glück beweist
und tauscht den Blick und tauscht die Ringe
im Weingeruch, im Rausch der Dinge —:
dienst du dem Gegenglück, dem Geist.

Gedichte

Im Namen dessen, der die Stunden spendet,
im Schicksal des Geschlechts, dem du gehört,

hast du fraglosen Aug's den Blich gewendet
in eine Stunde, die den Blick zerstört,
die Dinge dringen kalt in die Gesichte
und reißen sich der alten Bindung fort,
es gibt nur ein Begegnen: im Gedichte
die Dinge mystisch bannen durch das Wort.

Am Steingeröll der großen Weltruine,
dem Ölberg, wo die tiefste Seele litt,
vorbei am Posilip der Anjouine,
dem Stauferblut und ihrem Racheschritt:
ein neues Kreuz, ein neues Hochgerichte,
doch eine Stätte ohne Blut und Strang,
sie schwört in Strophen, urteilt im Gedichte,
die Spindeln drehen still: die Parze sang.

Im Namen dessen, der die Stunden spendet,
erahnbar nur, wenn er vorüberzieht
an einem Schatten, der das Jahr vollendet,
doch unausdeutbar bleibt das Stundenlied —
ein Jahr am Steingeröll der Weltgeschichte,
Geröll der Himmel und Geröll der Macht,
und nun die Stunde, deine: im Gedichte
das Selbstgespräch des Leides und der Nacht.

Verlorenes Ich

Verlorenes Ich, zersprengt von Stratosphären,
Opfer des Ion — : Gamma-Strahlen-Lamm —
Teilchen und Feld — : Unendlichkeitschimären
auf deinem grauen Stein von Notre-Dame.

Die Tage gehn dir ohne Nacht und Morgen,
die Jahre halten ohne Schnee und Frucht
bedrohend das Unendliche verborgen —
die Welt als Flucht.

Wo endest du, we lagerst du, wo breiten
sich deine Sphären an — Verlust, Gewinn — :

ein Spiel von Bestien: Ewigkeiten,
an ihren Gittern fliehst du hin.

Der Bestienblick: die Sterne als Kaldaunen,
der Dschungeltod als Seins- und Schöpfungsgrund,
Mensch, Völkerschlachten, Katalaunen
hinab den Bestienschlund.

Die Welt zerdacht. Und Raum und Zeiten
und was die Menschheit wob und wog,
Funktion nur von Unendlichkeiten –
die Mythe log.

Woher, wohin – nicht Nacht, nicht Morgen,
kein Evoë, kein Requiem,
du möchtest dir ein Stichwort borgen –
allein bei wem?

Ach, als sich alle einer Mitte neigten
und auch die Denker nur den Gott gedacht,
sie sich den Hirten und dem Lamm verzweigten,
wenn aus dem Kelch das Blut sie rein gemacht,

und alle rannen aus der einen Wunde,
brachen das Brot, das jeglicher genoß –
o ferne zwingende erfüllte Stunde,
die einst auch das verlorne Ich umschloß.

Was schlimm ist

Wenn man kein Englisch kann,
von einem guten englischen Kriminalroman zu hören,
der nicht ins Deutsche übersetzt ist.

Bei Hitze ein Bier sehn,
das man nicht bezahlen kann.

Einen neuen Gedanken haben,
den man nicht in einen Hölderlinvers einwickeln kann,
wie es die Professoren tun.

Nachts auf Reisen Wellen schlagen hören
und sich sagen, daß sie das immer tun.

Sehr schlimm: eingeladen sein,
wenn zu Hause die Räume stiller,
der Café besser
und keine Unterhaltung nötig ist.

Am schlimmsten:
nicht im Sommer sterben,
wenn alles hell ist
und die Erde für Spaten leicht.

Leben — niederer Wahn

Leben — niederer Wahn!
Traum für Knaben und Knechte,
doch du von altem Geschlechte,
Rasse am Ende der Bahn,

was erwartest du hier?
immer noch eine Berauschung,
eine Studenvertauschung
von Welt und dir?

Suchst du noch Frau und Mann?
ward dir nicht alles bereitet,
Glauben und wie es entgleitet
und die Zerstörung dann?

Form nur ist Glaube und Tat,
die erst von Händen berührten,
doch dann den Händen entführten
Statuen bergen die Saat.

BERTOLT BRECHT

1898–1956

Vom ertrunkenen Mädchen

1

Als sie ertrunken war und hinunterschwamm
Von den Bächen in die größeren Flüsse
Schien der Opal des Himmels sehr wundersam
Als ob er die Leiche begütigen müsse.

2

Tang und Algen hielten sich an ihr ein
So daß sie langsam viel schwerer ward.
Kühl die Fische schwammen an ihrem Bein
Pflanzen und Tiere beschwerten noch ihre letzte Fahrt.

3

Und der Himmel ward abends dunkel wie Rauch
Und hielt nachts mit den Sternen das Licht in Schwebe.
Aber früh ward er hell, daß es auch
Noch für sie Morgen und Abend gebe.

4

Als ihr bleicher Leib im Wasser verfaulet war
Geschah es (sehr langsam), daß Gott sie allmählich vergaß
Erst ihr Gesicht, dann die Hände und ganz zuletzt erst ihr Haar.
Dann ward sie Aas in Flüssen mit vielem Aas.

Erinnerung an die Marie A.

1

An jenem Tag im blauen Mond September
Still unter einem jungen Pflaumenbaum
Da hielt ich sie, die stille bleiche Liebe

128

In meinem Arm wie einen holden Traum.
Und über uns im schönen Sommerhimmel
War eine Wolke, die ich lange sah
Sie war sehr weiß und ungeheuer oben
Und als ich aufsah, war sie nimmer da.

2

Seit jenem Tag sind viele, viele Monde
Geschwommen still hinunter und vorbei.
Die Pflaumenbäume sind wohl abgehauen
Und fragst du mich, was mit der Liebe sei?
So sag ich dir: ich kann mich nicht erinnern
Und doch, gewiß, ich weiß schon, was du meinst.
Doch ihr Gesicht, das weiß ich wirklich nimmer
Ich weiß nur mehr: ich küßte es dereinst.

3

Und auch den Kuß, ich hätt ihn längst vergessen
Wenn nicht die Wolke dagewesen wär
Die weiß ich noch und werd ich immer wissen
Sie war sehr weiß und kam von oben her.
Die Pflaumenbäume blühn vielleicht noch immer
Und jene Frau hat jetzt vielleicht das siebte Kind
Doch jene Wolke blühte nur Minuten
Und als ich aufsah, schwand sie schon im Wind.

Liturgie vom Hauch

1

Einst kam ein altes Weib einher

2

Die hatte kein Brot zum Essen mehr

3

Das Brot, das fraß das Militär

4

Da fiel sie in die Goss', die war kalte

5

Da hatte sie keinen Hunger mehr.

6

Darauf schwiegen die Vöglein im Walde
Über allen Wipfeln ist Ruh
In allen Gipfeln spürest du
Kaum einen Hauch.

7

Da kam einmal ein Totenarzt einher

8

Der sagte: Die Alte besteht auf ihrem Schein

9

Da grub man die hungrige Alte ein

10

So sagte das alte Weib nichts mehr

11

Nur der Arzt lachte noch über die Alte.

12

Auch die Vöglein schwiegen im Walde
Über allen Wipfeln ist Ruh
In allen Gipfeln spürest du
Kaum einen Hauch.

13

Da kam einmal ein einziger Mann einher

14

Der hatte für die Ordnung keinen Sinn

15

Der fand in der Sache einen Haken drin

16

Der war eine Art Freund für die Alte

17

Der sagte, ein Mensch müsse essen können, bitte sehr –

18

Darauf schwiegen die Vöglein im Walde
Über allen Wipfeln ist Ruh
In allen Gipfeln spürest du
Kaum einen Hauch.

19

Da kam mit einemmal ein Kommissar einher

20

Der hatte einen Gummiknüppel dabei

21

Und zerklopfte dem Mann seinen Hinterkopf zu Brei

22

Und da sagte auch dieser Mann nichts mehr

23

Doch der Kommissar sagte, daß es schallte:

24

Und jetzt schweigen die Vöglein im Walde
Über allen Wipfeln ist Ruh
In allen Gipfeln spürest du
Kaum einen Hauch.

25

Da kamen einmal drei bärtige Männer einher

26

Die sagten, das sei nicht eines einzigen Mannes Sache allein.

27

Und sie sagten es so lang, bis es knallte

28

Aber dann krochen Maden durch ihr Fleisch in ihr Bein

29

Da sagten die bärtigen Männer nichts mehr.

30

Darauf schwiegen die Vöglein im Walde
Über allen Wipfeln ist Ruh
In allen Gipfeln spürest du
Kaum einen Hauch.

31

Da kamen mit einemmal viele Männer einher

32

Die wollten einmal reden mit dem Militär

33

Doch das Militär redete mit dem Maschinengewehr

34

Und da sagten alle die Männer nichts mehr.

35

Doch sie hatten auf der Stirn noch eine Falte.

36

Darauf schwiegen die Vöglein im Walde
Über allen Wipfeln ist Ruh
In allen Gipfeln spürest du
Kaum einen Hauch.

37

Da kam einmal ein großer roter Bär einher

38

Der wußte nichts von den Bräuchen hier, das brauchte er nicht als
    Bär.

39

Doch er war nicht von gestern und ging nicht auf jeden Teer

40

Und der fraß die Vöglein im Walde.

41

Da schwiegen die Vöglein nicht mehr
Über allen Wipfeln ist Unruh
In allen Gipfeln spürest du
Jetzt einen Hauch.

Fragen eines lesenden Arbeiters

Wer baute das siebentorige Theben?
In den Büchern stehen die Namen von Königen.
Haben die Könige die Felsbrocken herbeigeschleppt?
Und das mehrmals zerstörte Babylon —
Wer baute es so viele Male auf? In welchen Häusern
Des goldstrahlenden Lima wohnten die Bauleute?

Wohin gingen an dem Abend, wo die Chinesische Mauer fertig war
Die Maurer? Das große Rom
Ist voll von Triumphbögen. Wer errichtete sie? Über wen
Triumphierten die Cäsaren? Hatte das vielbesungene Byzanz
Nur Paläste für seine Bewohner? Selbst in dem sagenhaften
      Atlantis
Brüllten in der Nacht, wo das Meer es verschlang
Die Ersaufenden nach ihren Sklaven.

Der junge Alexander eroberte Indien.
Er allein?
Cäsar schlug die Gallier.
Hatte er nicht wenigstens einen Koch bei sich?
Philipp von Spanein weinte, als seine Flotte
Untergegangen war. Weinte sonst niemand?
Friedrich der Zweite siegte im Siebenjährigen Krieg. Wer
Siegte außer ihm?

Jede Seite ein Sieg.
Wer kochte den Siegesschmaus?
Alle zehn Jahre ein großer Mann.
Wer bezahlte die Spesen?

So viele Berichte.
So viele Fragen.

An die Nachgeborenen

I

Wirklich, ich lebe in finsteren Zeiten!
Das arglose Wort ist töricht. Eine glatte Stirn
Deutet auf Unempfindlichkeit hin. Der Lachende
Hat die furchtbare Nachricht
Nur noch nicht empfangen.

Was sind das für Zeiten, wo
Ein Gespräch über Bäume fast ein Verbrechen ist
Weil es ein Schweigen über so viele Untaten einschließt!
Der dort ruhig über die Straße geht
Ist wohl nicht mehr erreichbar für seine Freunde
Die in Not sind?

Es ist wahr: ich verdiene noch meinen Unterhalt
Aber glaubt mir: das ist nur ein Zufall. Nichts
Von dem, was ich tue, berechtigt mich dazu, mich sattzuessen.
Zufällig bin ich verschont. (Wenn mein Glück aussetzt, bin ich
     verloren.)

Man sagt mir: Iß und trink du! Sei froh, daß du hast!
Aber wie kann ich essen und trinken, wenn
Ich dem Hungernden entreiße, was ich esse, und
Mein Glas Wasser einem Verdurstenden fehlt?
Und doch esse und trinke ich.

Ich wäre gerne auch weise.
In den alten Büchern steht, was weise ist:
Sich aus dem Streit der Welt halten und die kurze Zeit
Ohne Furcht verbringen
Auch ohne Gewalt auskommen
Böses mit Gutem vergelten
Seine Wünsche nicht erfüllen, sondern vergessen
Gilt für weise.
Alles das kann ich nicht:
Wirklich, ich lebe in finsteren Zeien!

II

In die Städte kam ich zur Zeit der Unordnung
Als da Hunger herrschte.
Unter die Menschen kam ich zu der Zeit des Aufruhrs
Und ich empörte mich mit ihnen.
So verging meine Zeit
Die auf Erden mir gegeben war.

Mein Essen aß ich zwischen den Schlachten
Schlafen legte ich mich unter die Mörder
Der Liebe pflegte ich achtlos
Und die Natur sah ich ohne Geduld.
So verging meine Zeit
Die auf Erden mir gegeben war.

Die Straßen führten in den Sumpf zu meiner Zeit.
Die Sprache verriet mich dem Schlächter.
Ich vermochte nur wenig. Aber die Herrschenden
Saßen ohne mich sicherer, das hoffte ich.

So verging meine Zeit
Die auf Erden mir gegeben war.

Die Kräfte waren gering. Das Ziel
Lag in großer Ferne
Es war deutlich sichtbar, wenn auch für mich
Kaum zu erreichen.
So verging meine Zeit
Die auf Erden mir gegeben war.

III

Ihr, die ihr auftauchen werdet aus der Flut
In der wir untergegangen sind
Gedenkt
Wenn ihr von unseren Schwächen sprecht
Auch der finsteren Zeit
Der ihr entronnen seid.

Gingen wir doch, öfter als die Schuhe die Länder wechselnd
Durch die Kriege der Klassen, verzweifelt
Wenn da nur Unrecht war und keine Empörung.

Dabei wissen wir doch:
Auch der Haß gegen die Niedrigkeit
Verzerrt die Züge.
Auch der Zorn über das Unrecht
Macht die Stimme heiser. Ach, wir
Die wir den Boden bereiten wollten für Freundlichkeit
Konnten selber nicht freundlich sein.

Ihr aber, wenn es so weit sein wird
Daß der Mensch dem Menschen ein Helfer ist
Gedenkt unsrer
Mit Nachsicht.

Schlechte Zeit für Lyrik

Ich weiß doch: nur der Glückliche
Ist beliebt. Seine Stimme
Hört man gern. Sein Gesicht ist schön.

Der verkrüppelte Baum im Hof
Zeigt auf den schlechten Boden, aber
Die Vorübergehenden schimpfen ihn einen Krüppel
Doch mit Recht.

Die grünen Boote und die lustigen Segel des Sundes
Sehe ich nicht. Von allem
Sehe ich nur der Fischer rissiges Garnnetz.
Warum rede ich nur davon
Daß die vierzigjährige Häuslerin gekrümmt geht?
Die Brüste der Mädchen
Sind warm wie ehedem.

In meinem Lied ein Reim
Käme mir fast vor wie Übermut.

In mir streiten sich
Die Begeisterung über den blühenden Apfelbaum
Und das Entsetzen über die Reden des Anstreichers.
Aber nur das zweite
Drängt mich zum Schreibtisch.

Der Radwechsel

Ich sitze am Straßenrand
Der Fahrer wechselt das Rad.
Ich bin nicht gern, wo ich herkomme.
Ich bin nicht gern, wo ich hinfahre.
Warum sehe ich den Radwechsel
Mit Ungeduld?

Der Rauch

Das kleine Haus unter Bäumen am See.
Vom Dach steigt Rauch.
Fehlte er
Wie trostlos dann wären
Haus, Bäume und See.

PAUL CELAN

1920–1970

Espenbaum, dein Laub blickt weiß ins Dunkel.
Meiner Mutter Haar ward nimmer weiß.

Löwenzahn, so grün ist die Ukraine.
Meine blonde Mutter kam nicht heim.

Regenwolke, säumst du an den Brunnen?
Meine leise Mutter weint für alle.

Runder Stern, du schlingst die goldne Schleife.
Meiner Mutter Herz ward wund von Blei.

Eichne Tür, wer hob dich aus den Angeln?
Meine sanfte Mutter kann nicht kommen.

Todesfuge

Schwarze Milch der Frühe wir trinken sie abends
wir trinken sie mittags und morgens wir trinken sie nachts
wir trinken und trinken
wir schaufeln ein Grab in den Lüften da liegt man nicht eng
Ein Mann wohnt im Haus der spielt mit den Schlangen der schreibt
der schreibt wenn es dunkelt nach Deutschland dein goldenes Haar
      Margarete
er schreibt es und tritt vor das Haus und es blitzen die Sterne er
      pfeift seine Rüden herbei
er pfeift seine Juden hervor läßt schaufeln ein Grab in der Erde
er befiehlt uns spielt auf nun zum Tanz

Schwarze Milch der Frühe wir trinken dich nachts
wir trinken dich morgens und mittags wir trinken dich abends
wir trinken und trinken
Ein Mann wohnt im Haus der spielt mit den Schlangen der schreibt

der schreibt wenn es dunkelt nach Deutschland dein goldenes Haar
    Margarete
Dein aschenes Haar Sulamith wir schaufeln ein Grab in den Lüften
    da liegt man nicht eng

Er ruft stecht tiefer ins Erdreich ihr einen ihr andern singet und
    spielt
er greift nach dem Eisen im Gurt er schwingts seine Augen sind
    blau
stecht tiefer die Spaten ihr einen ihr andern spielt weiter zum Tanz
    auf

Schwarze Milch der Frühe wir trinken dich nachts
wir trinken dich mittags und morgens wir trinken dich abends
wir trinken und trinken
ein Mann wohnt im Haus dein goldenes Haar Margarete
dein aschenes Haar Sulamith er spielt mit den Schlangen

Er ruft spielt süßer den Tod der Tod ist ein Meister aus
    Deutschland
er ruft streicht dunkler die Geigen dann steigt ihr als Rauch in die
    Luft
dann habt ihr ein Grab in den Wolken da liegt man nicht eng

Schwarze Milch der Frühe wir trinken dich nachts
wir trinken dich mittags der Tod ist ein Meister aus Deutschland
wir trinken dich abends und morgens wir trinken und trinken
der Tod ist ein Meister aus Deutschland sein Auge ist blau
er trifft dich mit bleierner Kugel er trifft dich genau
ein Mann wohnt im Haus dein goldenes Haar Margarete
er hetzt seine Rüden auf uns er schenkt uns ein Grab in her Luft
er spielt mit den Schlangen und träumet der Tod ist ein Meister aus
    Deutschland

dein goldenes Haar Margarete
dein aschenes Haar Sulamith

Sprich auch du

    Sprich auch du,
    sprich als letzter,
    sag deinen Spruch.

Sprich —
Doch scheide das Nein nicht vom Ja.
Gib deinem Spruch auch den Sinn:
gib ihm den Schatten.

Gib ihm Schatten genug,
gib ihm so viel,
als du um dich verteilt weißt zwischen
Mittnacht und Mittag und Mittnacht.

Blicke umher:
sieh, wie's lebendig wird rings —
Beim Tode! Lebendig!
Wahr spricht, wer Schatten spricht.

Nun aber schrumpft der Ort, wo du stehst:
Wohin jetzt, Schattenentblößter, wohin?
Steige. Taste empor.
Dünner wirst du, unkenntlicher, feiner!
Feiner: ein Faden,
an dem er herabwill, der Stern:
un unten zu schwimmen, unten,
wo er sich schimmern sieht: in der Dünung
wandernder Worte.

Tenebrae

Nah sind wir, Herr,
nahe und greifbar.

Gegriffen schon, Herr,
ineinander verkrallt, als wär
der Leib eines jeden von uns
dein Leib, Herr.

Bete, Herr,
bete zu uns,
wir sind nah.

Windschief gingen wir hin,
gingen wir hin, uns zu bücken
nach Mulde und Maar.

Zur Tränke gingen wir, Herr.
Es war Blut, es war,
was du vergossen, Herr.

Es glänzte.

Es warf uns dein Bild in die Augen, Herr.
Augen und Mund stehn so offen und leer, Herr.

Wir haben getrunken, Herr.
Das Blut und das Bild, das im Blut war, Herr.

Bete, Herr.
Wir sind nah.

———

Weggebeizt vom
Strahlenwind deiner Sprache
das bunte Gerede des An-
erlebten — das hundert-
züngige Mein-
gedicht, das Genicht.

Aus-
gewirbelt,
frei
der Weg durch den menschen-
gestaltigen Schnee,
den Büßerschnee, zu
den gastlichen
Gletscherstuben und -tischen.

Tief
in der Zeitenschrunde,
beim
Webeneis
wartet, ein Atemkristall,
dein unumstößliches
Zeugnis.

———

Ich kann dich noch sehn: ein Echo,
ertastbar mit Fühl-

wörtern, am Abschieds-
grat.

Dein Gesicht scheut leise,
wenn es auf einmal
lampenhaft hell wird
in mir, an der Stelle,
wo man am schmerzlichsten Nie sagt.

———

Ein Blatt, baumlos
für Bertolt Brecht:

Was sind das für Zeiten,
wo ein Gespräch
beinah ein Verbrechen ist,
weil es soviel Gesagtes
mit einschließt?

HANS MAGNUS ENZENSBERGER

1929–

Geburtsanzeige

Wenn dieses Bündel auf die Welt geworfen wird
die Windeln sind noch nicht einmal gesäumt
der Pfarrer nimmt das Trinkgeld eh ers tauft
doch seine Träume sind längst ausgeträumt
es ist verraten und verkauft

wenn es die Zange noch am Schädel packt
verzehrt der Arzt bereits das Huhn das es bezahlt
der Händler zieht die Tratte und es trieft
von Tinte und von Blut der Stempel prahlt
es ist verzettelt und verbrieft

wenn es im süßlichen Gestank der Klinik plärrt
beziffern die Strategen schon den Tag
der Musterung des Mords der Scharlatan
drückt seinen Daumen unter den Vertrag
es ist versichert und vertan

noch wiegt es wenig häßlich rot und zart
wieviel es netto abwirft welcher Richtsatz gilt
was man es lehrt und was man ihm verbirgt
die Zukunft ist vergriffen und gedrillt
es ist verworfen und verwirkt

wenn es mit krummer Hand die Luft noch fremd begreift
steht fest was es bezahlt für Milch und Telefon
der Gastarif wenn es im grauen Bett erstickt
und für das Weib das es dann wäscht der Lohn
es ist verbucht verhängt verstrickt

wenn nicht das Bündel das da jault und greint
die Grube überhäuft den Groll vertreibt
was wir ihm zugerichtet kalt zerrauft
mit unerhörter Schrift die schiere Zeit beschreibt
ist es verraten und verkauft.

Ins Lesebuch für die Oberstufe

Lies keine Oden, mein Sohn, lies die Fahrpläne:
sie sind genauer. Roll die Seekarten auf,
eh es zu spät ist. Sei wachsam, sing nicht.
Der Tag kommt, wo sie wieder Listen ans Tor
schlagen und malen den Neinsagern auf die Brust
Zinken. Lern unerkannt gehn, lern mehr als ich:
das Viertel wechseln, den Paß, das Gesicht.
Versteh dich auf den kleinen Verrat,
die tägliche schmutzige Rettung. Nützlich
sind die Enzykliken zum Feueranzünden,
die Manifeste: Butter einzuwickeln und Salz
für die Wehrlosen. Wut und Geduld sind nötig,
in die Lungen der Macht zu blasen
den feinen tödlichen Staub, gemahlen
von denen, die viel gelernt haben,
die genau sind, von dir.

Küchenzettel

An einem müßigen Nachmittag, heute
seh ich in meinem Haus
durch die offene Küchentür
eine Milchkanne   ein Zwiebelbrett
einen Katzenteller.
Auf dem Tisch liegt ein Telegramm.
Ich habe es nicht gelesen.

In einem Museum zu Amsterdam
sah ich auf einem altern Bild

durch die offene Küchentür
eine Milchkanne   einen Brotkorb
einen Katzenteller.
Auf dem Tisch lag ein Brief.
Ich habe ihn nicht gelesen.

In einem Sommerhaus an der Moskwa
sah ich vor wenig Wochen
durch die offene Küchentür
einen Brotkorb   ein Zwiebelbrett
einen Katzenteller.
Auf dem Tisch lag die Zeitung.
Ich habe sie nicht gelesen.

Durch die offene Küchentür
seh ich vergossene Milch
Dreißigjährige Kriege
Tränen auf Zwiebelbrettern
Anti-Raketen-Raketen
Brotkörbe
Klassenkämpfe.

Links unten ganz in der Ecke
seh ich einen Katzenteller.

Weiterung

Wer soll da noch auftauchen aus der Flut,
wenn wir darin untergehen?

Noch ein paar Fortschritte,
und wir werden weitersehen.

Wer soll da unsrer gedenken
mit Nachsicht?

Das wird sich finden,
wenn es erst soweit ist.

Und so fortan
bis auf weiteres

und ohne weiteres
so weiter und so

weiter nichts

keine Nachgeborenen
keine Nachsicht

nichts weiter

Zwei Fehler

Ich gebe zu, seinerzeit
habe ich mit Spatzen auf Kanonen geschossen.

Daß das keine Volltreffer gab,
sehe ich ein.

Dagegen habe ich nie behauptet,
nun gelte es ganz zu schweigen.

Schlafen, Luftholen, Dichten:
das ist fast kein Verbrechen.

Ganz zu schweigen
von dem berühmten Gespräch über Bäume.

Kanonen auf Spatzen, das hieße doch
in den umgekehrten Fehler verfallen.

Nicht Zutreffendes streichen

Was deine Stimme so flach macht
so dünn und so blechern
das ist die Angst
etwas Falsches zu sagen

oder immer dasselbe
oder das zu sagen was alle sagen
oder etwas Unwichtiges

oder Wehrloses
oder etwas das mißverstanden werden könnte
oder den falschen Leuten gefiele
oder etwas Dummes
oder etwas schon Dagewesenes
etwas Altes

Hast du es denn nicht satt
aus lauter Angst
aus lauter Angst vor der Angst
etwas Falsches zu sagen

immer das Falsche zu sagen?

NOTES ON THE POEMS

Friedrich Gottlieb Klopstock (1724–1803) plays an absolutely crucial role in that release of the imagination which revolutionizes German literature from the mid eighteenth century on. For the young writers and critics of the time, Klopstock's voice came as a revelation. They saw in his poetry above all a language of untrammelled feeling, a liberation from artifice and convention in the name of personally experienced emotion. For us nowadays this is only part of Klopstock's achievement. For the ecstatic, exclamatory mode coexists with an ability to exploit the full syntactical possibilities of German as an inflected language.

Native English speakers are quick to notice — and often to resent — the demands of German syntax. They bemoan the fact that in subordinate clauses the verb is placed at the end, that inflections can allow for the grammatical argument of a sentence to defy the familiar linear sequence of subject–verb–predicate. In the hands of the great German writers, this weighty arsenal of architectonic effects can be used with an expressive force that is simply untranslatable into a non-inflected language (such as English). Klopstock is fond of the extended sentence pattern which allows him to suspend meaning over several lines. Indeed, often he breaks off the main argument of his sentence in order to interpolate an expression of emotion, only then to resume the grand syntactic argument of the main sentence. The style is the incarnation of his theme: Klopstock combines the grand manner of sublimity, apotheosis, allegory with the voice of unmistakably personal feeling and reaction. Nature emerges both as a deity and as a particular landscape which evokes an immediate, sensuous response. The overall effect is one of pent-up energy as stammering, well-nigh incoherent emotion delays — yet also thereby emphasizes — the overall sentence statement. The architectonic intensity of the verse looks forward to Hölderlin, Goethe, to the Expressionist poets, to

Rilke and Celan. All such poets have in common an energy of syntactical innovation: intransitive verbs are suddenly used transitively, an unexpected accusative imparts a dynamic to a static statement, present participles are made to work with verbal (rather than simply adjectival) force.

Der Zürchersee names a particular place, a particular journey undertaken with a small group of friends. The specificity of time and place is unmistakable: in stanza six there are, for example, references to contemporary poets, Gleim, Hagedorn, Ewald von Kleist, to a poem by Albrecht von Haller entitled *Doris* (1730), to Hans Kaspar Hirzel (who arranged the outing) and to his wife — under the anacreontic name of Daphne. Stanzas four to seven convey the specific journey. But these particularities are embedded in an ecstatic hymn in praise of nature, joy (the delayed subject of stanzas two and three), companionship, the immortality of poetic utterance. The last two stanzas express the wish that the community of friends should be larger: the fragmentation of Germany means that the longed-for Elysium is a promise that has to contend with distance and separation. The poem speaks of kinship, relatedness between spirit and world (in stanza one reference is made to man re-thinking the thought of nature's creation). One should note the expressions of likeness, of creative interdependence 'wie du', 'gleich', 'selber', 'selbst', 'durch dich'. Immortality, like nature, is a 'großer Gedanke'. And the 'great thoughts' coexist with intimacy of feeling and utterance — the following stanza is remarkable for its combination of colloquial and rhetorical registers:

> Dann ihr sanfteres Herz bilden und, Liebe, dich,
> Fromme Tugend, dich auch gießen ins sanfte Herz,
> Ist, beim Himmel, nicht wenig,
> Ist des Schweißes der Edlen wert!

Die Frühlingsfeier is the poem that is invoked in Goethe's novel *Werther* at a moment of intense emotion when Werther and Lotte experience a thunderstorm. The name 'Klopstock' is enough to unite them in a community of response (such as is envisaged at the end of *Der Zürchersee*). *Die Frühlingsfeier* is not mentioned by name at that moment; but Werther's and Lotte's intense openness to nature is made explicit (and articulate) by the name of 'Klopstock'. The poem begins with a celebration of the earth as a minuscule part of Creation, God's handiwork. And that sense of smallness of scale recurs throughout the poem as the poet observes the small grub, the 'Frühlingswürmchen'. The creature's smallness bespeaks vulnerability – and mortality. This produces a moment of colloquial self-observation, which comes with particular force after the grandiose vision of the Almighty Creator –

> Ich bin herausgegangen, anzubeten,
> Und ich weine?

The grief is overcome as the poet affirms his reverence for the Creator. And in the final section of the poem (the last fourteen stanzas) the Creator manifests Himself through the storm. The description of the storm is justly famous, mingling as it does the drama of precise physical details (the eerie calm of 'kaum atmen sie, / Die Morgensonne wird schwül! / Wolken strömen herauf!'; the monolithic violence of the gusting minds – 'Wie sie mit lauter Woge den Wald durchströmen!') with expressions of awe at the self-manifestation of the Almighty. The poet *thirsts* to praise God (stanza twenty-one), the earth *thirsts* for rain ('Nun ist, wie dürstete sie! die Erd' erquickt'): the lowly grub heeds the coming of the storm and of the Creator – 'ist es vielleicht nicht seelenlos?' Both visual and visionary experiences interlock.

Dem Unendlichen concerns the heart's relationship to God. The first two stanzas develop the key notion of the heart thinking God. The verb 'think' is here used transitively: what is entailed is not thinking of God, but a thinking that is active, creatively implicated in His being. Yet human thought is incommensurable with God's being. Even the thoughts that man thinks fully are only human thoughts about God ('Dann denk ich es ganz, daß du ewig mich schufst'), no human consciousness ('denken'), no human or natural utterance ('Preis', 'Jubel', 'Harfengetön', 'Chor') is 'genug', is equal to the totality of God. This yields the impassioned repetition in the final stanza as the full orchestra of the universe sounds and is, nevertheless, 'nie es ganz'. The repeated negation is pitted against the fourfold saying of 'Gott', as the object of praise and thanks. The poem works with a sense of its own (finite) linguistic utterance challenged by the infinity of what it should say and know, and the syntax beats against the very limits of the sayable (particularly in the second and fourth stanzas).

Die Sommernacht unites intimations of nature and death. The key verb in all three stanzas is 'wehen'. The smells of a summer night waft ('wehn'); as do the winds of death, supplanting the images of the natural world in the first stanza (note the extraordinary stress patterns of 'ich seh in dem Walde / *Nur es* dämmern, und es weht mir / Von der Blüte *nicht her*': the emphasis falls on the simplest of monosyllables). Yet the final stanza fuses the savouring of death ('Ich genoß einst, o ihr Toten, es mit euch!') with the wafting ('umwehen') 'Duft' and 'Kühlung' (repeated from the first stanza) of nature. The last line has a heavy break after 'Du': the 'Du' of death is also the 'Du' of 'schöne Natur' with which the poem began.

Johann Wolfgang von Goethe (1749–1832). By virtue of his sheer range of theme and form, and of his amazing linguistic skill, Goethe inevitably comes to dominate anthologies of German lyric poetry. Moreover, in his long creative life he participated in a great many of the currents and movements which in a few brief decades (from about 1770 to 1820) saw the emergence of modern German literature and culture to full European status. Goethe partakes of and contributes to the reverence for nature of the 'Sturm und Drang', the liberation from dogma brought by the 'Aufklärung', the veneration for tradition, for the values of order and containment that are central to Classicism, as well as the sense of mystery that characterizes Romanticism. Yet all these perceptions of the nature and destiny of man coexist within an intense belief in the dynamic wholeness of the manifold interactions of self and world that constitute man's life. Goethe's linguistic and technical range is staggering. Time and time again the language seems right for its theme: carefully wrought argument and complexity of thought and feeling goes hand in hand with a kind of casualness, a nonchalant linking of language and experience in the tight compass of lyrical utterance. Many of Goethe's poems move from darkness to light, from obscurity to clarity. One has the sense that the poetry is the means whereby experience is shaped, comprehended in all its urgency, rendered articulate.

Willkommen und Abschied begins with an exultantly weighty heartbeat — 'Es schlug mein Herz'. The embarking on the journey follows instantly: the doing follows upon the feeling. We note the urgency in the repeated 'schon' of the first stanza. The pace never slackens throughout the poem: for that same temporal adverb brings the parting 'schon mit der Morgensonne' in the final stanza. The meeting of the lovers is swiftly followed by the coming of day, and with it their separation. The experience, then, is one of arrival and departure as the poem moves from night to morning. But the contradictions are welcomed − as in the repeated 'doch' (of stanza two, occurring twice in the last stanza). The poem ends in the present tense − 'geliebt zu werden' and 'lieben'. And that *present* affirmation of the experience of meeting and parting is prefigured in the parallel exclamations of stanza two ('In meinen Adern welches Feuer! / In meinem Herzen welche Glut!') and stanza four ('In deinen Küssen welche Wonne! / In deinem Auge welcher Schmerz!') The exclamations have *present* force, and that presence (and present-ness) of 'Feuer', 'Glut', 'Wonne', and 'Schmerz' is affirmed in the final two lines of the poem.

Mailied expresses an ecstatic union of man, nature, love in the eruptive abundance of spring. For all its exclamatory intensity, however, there is a formal coherence to the poem which both recognizes and links different orders of being. The poem begins with the natural world, but this is nature already endowed with human properties ('Wie lacht die Flur!') The next stanza initiates a long, flowing sentence: it begins with a verb that celebrates the thrusting energy of spring − 'Es dringen'. And this thrust is present in the blossoms, the birds ('Stimmen / Aus dem Gesträuch'), in man ('Freud und Wonne / Aus jeder Brust'). But the poem, having now arrived at man, travels back along the chain of being to nature ('Wie Morgenwolken'), to the fresh field with its haze of blossoms. Stanza six addresses specifically human love ('O Mädchen, Mädchen') which is celebrated in its reciprocity − and is then linked to nature (birds, flowers), only to return again to man ('Wie ich dich liebe'). The first and last lines of the poem begin with 'wie'. The word has two meanings, both of which are invoked here: there is the 'wie' of intensity and exclamation, there is the 'wie' of similarity and kinship (meaning 'like'). Ultimately, the two meanings interlock: intensity of feeling is inseparable from kinship of feeling.

Ganymed is similar to *Mailied* in the ecstasy which it expresses. The syntax largely dissolves into an irresistible, associatively expressed movement. The intimacy and the abandon of the surrender to nature (the assonance of 'Ach' and 'schmachte') acquires a new dimension ('Ach, wohin?') as the clouds float down to meet the yearning love in perfect reciprocity. That inter-relationship is expressed in the line 'umfangend umfangen', where only one consonant differentiates the two parties to this union.

Prometheus, often seen as a companion piece to *Ganymed*, offers a very different view of both man and the divinity, and of the relationship between them. Where Ganymed finds fulfilment in surrendering the self, Promethus magnificently asserts his selfhood as the only source and medium of human achievement. The divinity embraced in *Ganymed* is immanent in the intense experience of nature, of the here and now. The divinity rejected in *Prometheus* is divorced from man and his world. *Prometheus* is dominated by the fierce opposition of personal pronouns (ich/du) and adjectives (mein/dein). The opposition is announced in the first stanza – 'deinen Himmel', 'meine Erde'; 'meine Hütte', 'meinen Herd'. Moreover, the poem also argues in terms of an opposition between maturity and immaturity. Zeus is scornfully compared to a petulant boy: and it is only 'Kinder und Bettler' who are deceived by the confidence trick of transcendental promises. Prometheus has, as stanza three tells us, grown out of such fantasies. The poem ends with the defiance being extended to a whole race of men. Prometheus is himself a creator: he makes men after his own image, men for whom worldly experience is enough on its own (anything but comfortable) terms – as the assonance tells us, 'nach *mei*nem Bilde / Ein Geschlecht, das mir *glei*ch *sei*, Zu *lei*den, zu *wei*nen, . . .' The reference to Prometheus making men in his own image clearly brings the Judaeo–Christian tradition into association with the realm of Classical mythology. In consequence, *Prometheus* becomes a proud assertion of man's independence from deities of whatever cultural tradition.

An Belinden is a love poem that sustains a complex irony. The opening stanza, in the assonance that unites 'Ach' with 'Pracht', expresses the poet's regret at being drawn so irresistibly into that 'splendour'. The next two lines express a backward glance to the poet's state before he has met the girl. And the next two stanzas are in the past tense and continue the memories. Again we note the ambivalence – the former self knew only the happiness of immaturity ('guter Junge', 'Zimmerchen'): he was 'selig' in what the present self now recognizes as the 'öden Nacht'. For the last two stanzas, the poem returns to the present. With incredulity the poet registers his way of life, spending time at the gaming tables (the 'Pracht' of the first stanza referring, then, to a very worldly splendour). The last stanza deepens the ambivalence of the poem: the ('unnatural') world of the gaming tables to which his beloved entices him is more appealing than the meadows (of which Goethe had spoken so ecstatically in *Mailied*): and, to compound the ironies, nature is where the beloved is, even if that beloved is not a 'natural' beauty. The 'Pracht', then, is the glitter of the gaming tables: *and* it is also the splendour of love. The rhythm of the final stanza is masterly, as in the surprised − and weighty − negation achieved by the enjambement between lines one and two:

> Reizender ist mir des Frühlings Blüte
> *Nun nicht* auf der Flur.

Auf dem See describes a journey across a lake. The first stanza expresses a closeness to − and dependence on − nature which is that of a child − 'saug ich', 'am Busen hält', 'wieget'. The middle stanza interrupts the energetic rhythm of the first stanza. The journey is arrested: dreams threaten to supplant the present experiences. But the present is affirmed; and the journey is resumed in the third stanza. Nature is perceived now with greater clarity and objectivity. The 'ich' is no longer mentioned. In grammatical terms, nature provides the subject of the clauses in the third stanza. The poem ends with the perception of a 'reifende Frucht'. Here surely we feel a metaphoric comment on the growth of the 'ich' from immaturity to maturity. Part of that growth is a movement away from nature − but not, in any sense, a break with nature. The natural world is seen both in its otherness, its separateness from man, and as the object of man's reflection (in both senses, that is − thinking and mirroring). As so often in Goethe, the relationship between man and nature is not a simple oneness, an unreflective (and unreflected) unity. The commerce between man and nature is, rather, a complex interchange, one that entails both similarity and dissimilarity.

Herbstgefühl is one of Goethe's supreme nature poems. Autumn is urged to attain its last fullness and sweetness − the metaphors all speak of ripeness and abundance. Yet part of autumn's loveliness is the fruition before parting: the 'Scheideblick' of the sun is linked with the pain suggested ('ach') in the tears of love.

Warum gabst du uns die tiefen Blicke is one of Goethe's richest love poems. It both celebrates and regrets a love that is too clear-sighted, too knowing to amount to a total surrender to passion. The poem moves through contrasts and uncertainty. The clarity of which it speaks in insistent metaphors of seeing ('Blicke', 'schaun', 'sehn', 'auszuspähn', 'unversehen', 'lesen') is part of the profound fusion of discomfort and love that characterizes the poem. The poet pits the 'wechselseitiges Glück' that comes from not knowing, from not questioning, against the 'Glück' of present uncertainty (as validated in the last two lines of the poem). The poem moves from an uncertain (and, initially, undirected) question in the opening lines to memories of the past (the section beginning 'Kanntest jeden Zug in meinem Wesen') in which, so distant is that past emotionally that it becomes an imagined previous incarnation, and the poet refers to his former self as 'er'. The return to the present is a return to the 'wir', and the poem ends by balancing experiential loss ('wir scheinen uns nur halb beseelet') against an affirmation of the 'Schicksal, das uns quälet'.

The two *Wandrers Nachtlieder* are justly famous: they are remarkable for their reverberant simplicity. The very sound and movement of the language incarnates and deepens the sense beyond the reach of any simple paraphrase. 'Der du von dem Himmel bist' is a prayer for peace which seeks release from emotional turmoil (captured powerfully in the grammatical telescoping of 'all der Schmerz und Lust'). The tormented syntax of the multiple relative clauses enacts the feeling of constriction of which the poet speaks. 'Über allen Gipfeln' depicts peace gradually hushing the landscape, moving from high and distant places (the mountain tops) downwards and ever closer until it finally reaches man, the most unquiet of living beings. As E. M. Wilkinson shows in her masterly analysis (*Goethe Poet and Thinker*, London, 1967, pp. 28 ff.), the order of the details evoked in the poem embodies the evolutionary progression in nature, from mineral to vegetable to animal to man. The formal organization of the poem (and this is so often true of Goethe's lyrics) is the expression of a coherent mental picture: emotion and perception become one and the same.

An den Mond sustains a complex interplay between a present moment of contemplation 'zwischen Freud und Schmerz' and memories of past experience that is now finished, but not forgotten. The river is the agency and symbol of transience, yet is also the melodious accompaniment to the song that reflects on − and distills − experience.

Das Göttliche is one of Goethe's central pronouncements on the position of man within the order of the natural world. Stanzas three to six express the perception of nature as a realm of organic processes, a realm which obeys the laws of its material organization. But stanza seven offers us the supreme paradox − 'Nur allein der Mensch / Vermag das Unmögliche'. Man has the capacity for ethical choice, he lives in a freedom unknown to other orders of nature. And this freedom is expressed in the verbs of discriminating, choosing, in the modal verbs 'vermag', 'kann', 'darf'. The poem begins with commands to man − 'Edel sei der Mensch', 'ihnen gleiche der Mensch'. And the poem returns to the mode of subjunctive imperative at the end − 'sei', 'schaff', 'sei'. The language embodies the vital difference which the poem expresses: man lives not only in the realm of facts and events but also in the realm of the possible, of ethical imperatives. Man lives, as it were, both in the indicative and the subjunctive mode.

Römische Elegien V expresses the poet's delight in the sensuousness of his experiences 'auf klassischem Boden'. The poem speaks of the joy known by both mind and senses: the shapes of the girl's body are cognate with the shapes of classical statuary. It seems no accident that 'Roma' and 'Amor' are the same word read in different directions. The 'triumvirate' referred to in the last line is a triumvirate of erotic poets (probably Catullus, Tibullus, Propertius). The poem's eros extends to its own mode. Geothe here employs the classical form of the elegiac couplet (with alternating hexameter and pentameter lines) to express his sensuous delight in the forms and shapes of ancient and modern Rome.

Dauer im Wechsel is a rumination on transience as the ineluctable law of organic life. Yet the poem ends with an affirmation of the very agency, consciousness, that makes man more transient than the rest of organic nature because he knows himself to be transient. For man, every beginning necessarily implies a known, or imagined, end. Yet beginning and end are the precondition of 'die Form in deinem Geist': an end, known in advance, can be a goal, a purpose, a projected pattern. So transience does not have the last word. For all the speed with which living matter changes, the forms renew themselves as a constant within the flux. 'Gleich' (stanza two) is used to mean 'instantly', 'immediately', invoking the dizzying pace of change. Yet the poem invites us to reflect that 'gleich' can also mean 'like', 'akin': and likeness provides the stability of pattern in the midst of change.

Selige Sehnsucht announces in its opening stanza a mystery to which only few people (the 'wise') will be party. And that mystery is a paradox: the praise of living entities that long for death in flames. Stanzas two, three, and four explore this mystery through patterns of lightness and darkness, lightness and heaviness. The consistent presence of erotic metaphors speaks of intense experience in which weighty, physical craving becomes a craving for light and lightness. The argument culminates in the image of the butterfly and the candle flame. And the final stanza puts words to the mystery with which the poem began: 'Stirb und werde!', a doctrine that all living entails constant transformation, a dying and becoming. (The butterfly is the most spectacular example in the natural world of a creature whose growth cycle produces profound transformations of physical shape.) The poem ends with a praise of man's knowingness: nothing prevents man from being but a guest on the earth; but if he knows and affirms the sequence of dying and becoming, he lives abundantly ('trüb' implies both melancholy and resistant to light, i.e. uncomprehending).

Um Mitternacht concerns three experiences: one in childhood, one in early manhood, one in old age. All three experiences are 'midnight experiences': that is, they are experiences of transitions, of moments when the self finds itself reflecting, questioning. The little boy (in stanza one) finds himself suddenly and insistently aware of experiences beyond the familiar world of home: the churchyard and the stars impinge on his consciousness, and with them the presence of death, of the universe. The young man (in stanza two) finds himself in the grip of an experience that he can neither control nor comprehend: and the stars offer contradictory pictures of both pattern ('Gestirn') and diffuse, distant glow ('Nordschein'). In old age (stanza three) thought, the life of the mind, embraces the present moment as one poised between 'Vergangnes' and 'Künftiges'. The syntax of the poem is loose: one has the sense of a mind groping for clarity amidst the flux of experience.

Der Bräutigam speaks, through the perceptions of the young man – the fiancé of the title – of the experience of a life poised at the threshold of fulfilment. The poem moves from midnight to midnight. The night hours are precious because the poet dreams of his beloved. And he resents the coming of day as something alien, whatever it brings ('so viel er bringen mag'). Stanzas two and three describe the lovers being together in the evening. The setting sun separates them, and they hope for the coming of a new day – and a new evening. In the first stanza day was rejected: yet in stanza three it is hoped for. The final stanza (in the present tense) depicts the poet again dreaming of his beloved, advancing to the threshold of her room. And the last two lines express both the wish for future fulfilment, 'O sei auch mir', and an unconditional acceptance of life even as it is now, poised on the brink of fulfilment. The 'auch' of the penultimate line ('let it be granted to me *too* to lie there') modulates into the concessive use – 'however it may be' – 'wie es auch sei'. The conditions that had been established which alone made life worth living have now been withdrawn. The total process – of both night *and* day – is affirmed.

Nun weiß man erst, was Rosenknospe sei has the brevity of an aphorism. The discovery of the isolated, last rose, the 'Spätling', is the joyous discovery of the perfect idea of the rosebud. But not as an abstraction, not as a platonic universal: but as a physical fact, perceivable to the senses, and producing a cognition that was never there before ('nun weiß man *erst* . . .'). In the briefest compass, this little poem expresses Goethe's belief in the unity of matter and mind, of sensuous experience and spiritual cognition.

Friedrich Schiller (1759–1805) is a poet who takes as his great theme the insufficiency of the modern world. The grand manner, the stately rhythms and exalted diction of his verse are intimately related to its theme. For the grand manner also expresses the matter – the insistent presence of the classical world, of concepts and ideals which enable modern man to know the extent of his own impoverishment. This kind of cultural–historical theme interlocks with many of the more immediate psychological concerns of Schiller's poetry, such as the passing of childhood, the sense of being emotionally and morally betrayed.

Die Götter Griechenlandes is a lament for a world from which the immanent deities of classical civilization have been banished. Time and time again the poem speaks of the difference between the classical past and the impoverished present (as in the 'wie ganz anders, anders war es da!' of stanza one; as in the repeated comparatives of stanza eight — 'werter', 'teurer', 'reizender'; and the alternation between past and present tense throughout the second half of the poem). Nature and man have lost the radiance that once was evident in the classical world. The poem ends with an urgent lament for the divided condition of the poet himself, and a longing for the cessation of the conflict that haunts his consciousness. Schiller is fond of an aphoristic style (which makes him an eminently quotable poet). Where, out of context, the aphorisms can sound like sententious generalization, in (poetic) context the accent of grief is unmistakable:

> Da die Götter menschlicher noch waren,
> Waren Menschen göttlicher.

Die Ideale laments the loss of youth, and the loss of the ideals that were part of youthful elation. That deprivation is attended by a sense of isolation; the 'Begleiter', the 'rauschendes Geleit' have all melted away. But the poem ends on a note of affirmation. The 'ich' finds solace in the insistently apostrophized 'du' of friendship and activity. The last two stanzas run as one sense unit: the hammering sequence of personal and relative pronouns ('Du, die du . . .', 'du, die ich . . .', 'Und du, die') carries the sentence over the stanza division in a determined evocation of the agencies that can redeem present isolation and distress. That the evocation sounds more like a vision than an attained condition give a particular poignancy to the end of the poem.

Nänie. A poem that laments that not even beauty is immortal. And all the grief of men and gods cannot touch Zeus. Only once did he relent (Orpheus and Eurydice): but even then he summoned her back. Yet the poem closes with a validation of the lament for beauty destroyed. The octet is dominated by the negation ('Nicht die eherne Brust rührt es', 'Nicht stillt Aphrodite', 'Nicht errettet den göttlichen Held die unsterbliche Mutter'). The sestet begins with the pivotal conjunction 'Aber' and goes on to affirm the 'Klagelied' as 'herrlich'. The son is 'verherrlicht', and the near assonance of 'Klaglied' and 'klanglos' suggests that the lament is a thing of beauty. 'Das Schöne' does, perhaps, know a modest victory.

Friedrich Hölderlin (1770–1843). Perhaps no poet has ever equalled Hölderlin in his mastery of the full resources of German as an inflected language. Time and time again his poetry has spiritual and cultural history as its theme: the present (i.e. modern) world is judged by the intimations of fuller, richer experience and found wanting. That fuller life is embodied in the visionary architecture of the language. Against all the odds, the tension at the heart of Hölderlin's poetry is contained, on occasion even exorcized. Perhaps one can feel the full span of Hölderlin's spiritual landscape if one juxtaposes two quotations:

> Wozu Dichter in dürftiger Zeit?   (*Brot und Wein*)
> Was bleibet aber, stiften die Dichter.   (*Andenken*)

The sense of all the resistances that, in the modern world, militate against poetry generates a supremely poignant, because threatened, awareness of the value of poetry.

Hyperions Schicksalslied works with the contrast between the divine and the human spheres. The deities live in a fateless condition, in uninterrupted oneness (the repeated adjectives of 'selig' and 'ewig' in stanzas one and two). The contrast with man is as sudden as it is brutal; and the cascading rhythm of the final stanza enacts the anchorlessness of man, his living a process of dwindling and falling.

An die Parzen. A poem in which everything is offered as a sacrifice in exchange for the 'reifer Gesang' which alone would complete (in both senses: render perfect and terminate) the poet's existence. Indeed, the poem makes clear that the achieved song would occasion the death of the heart ('vom süßen / Spiele gesättigt'). Throughout, the language insists on the 'once and for all' character of the consummation 'Nur einen Sommer', 'Und einen Herbst', 'ist mir einst', 'Einmal / Lebt ich'.

Abendphantasie. The poem contrasts the peace felt at the end of the day by ordinary mortals with the unquiet heart of the poet. The attempted escape (the apostrophe to the 'purpurne Wolken') comes to nothing. Which leaves the prospect of relief in the arms of sleep — and of old age. The poem comes to rest in the promise of peace. Yet behind the comforting promise of serene old age there vibrates the darker possibility that only death could provide release. The accents of pain in the poem are unforgettable:

> Warum schläft denn
> Nimmer nur mir in der Brust der Stachel?

The assonance and alliteration of 'nimmer nur mir' conjoins the 'never' with this particular selfhood. The promise of extinction charges the line:

> In Licht und Luft zerrinnen mir Lieb und Leid!

and that extinction informs the promise 'doch endlich, Jugend, verglühst du ja'. The conciliatory ending is a promise that cannot, we feel, be redeemed in the form in which it is put.

Da ich ein Knabe war depicts a condition of youthful oneness between self and world. The boy plays amidst the flow of breezes (stanza one). In stanza two the boy's heart rejoices with the hearts of the plants. But the third stanza shatters that harmony —

> Daß ihr wüßtet
> Wie euch meine Seele geliebt!

The unreal mode of the verb — 'wüßtet' — makes it clear that the gods do not know what once was the case (the simple past participle vibrates with finality). This cry to the gods indicates that the paradisal unity is over: youth has faded. That harmony was, as the last three stanzas make clear, pre-verbal. There was no need to name the gods: because the name indicates separateness: human language ('der Menschen Worte', 'wie die Menschen sich nennen') is symptomatic of estrangement. The boy knew only the language of nature. But now, inevitably, he has grown up. He has become a user of human language, he names the gods ('Vater Helios', 'Endymion', 'heilige Luna'). And the poet can only use language to invoke the unity that, in the very act of being named, is banished once and for all.

Mein Eigentum. The poem meditates on the many ways in which being is linked to owning (and being owned). Time and time again, the possessive adjective or the dative (of attribution and possession) is used — 'In seiner Fülle', 'den Zufriedenen', 'ihrer', 'ihre Bäume', 'am eignen Herd', 'dem sicheren Mann seine Himmel', 'auf eignem Grund', 'jedem sein Eigentum'. Yet from this security of being and belonging the 'ich' of the poet is excluded. Stanza four vibrates with the anguish of selfhood — 'auch mir', 'auch du mir', 'eine Freude mir', 'mir am Busen'. The doubts are heard again in stanzas nine

and ten − 'Kränz auch mir', 'und daß doch mir zu retten'. Stanzas
ten, eleven, and twelve run together in one long sense unit as the
'ich' cries out for the only home it may truly find − the song itself.
The wish is uttered for a dwelling where the 'ich' may be 'in sichrer
Einfalt'. But the poem movingly pays tribute to the lack of
simplicity and security which informs the poetic self.

Der Abschied. A poem which seeks to assuage the pain of parting by
arguing that a rightness and purpose informs and demands the parting,
monstrous though it is. The poem pits the needs of the self against those
external, other agencies that decree the separation. The first two lines
express the paradox: the lovers imagined it right to part, but the actual-
ity of parting felt like murder. Then come the extraordinary lines:

> Ach! wir kennen us wenig,
> Denn es waltet ein Gott in uns.

One cannot be sure what it is that the god dictates: does he require the
love − or the parting? The second stanza still leaves the ambivalence
unresolved. Which act − the loving, or the separation − would be the
betrayal of the god? Then comes the true culprit − the 'Weltsinn'. The
world's mind demands other − and alien (the thrice-named adjective
'ander') − things. The tragedy of the lovers' parting, above all the not
knowing what is right − all this is no merely personal catastrophe.
Rather, it is grounded in the world's disunity (the monster fear has
sundered gods and men, stanza four). The poet longs for the peace that
will come after the pain of separation, after, literally, walking away
from himself ('Hin . . . ziehe', 'hingehn will ich'). The poem closes with
a vision of a possible future meeting ('vielleicht') beyond the pain, with
gentle, warming memories in place of the 'Wünschen'. But the peace
envisaged is the peace of strangeness − 'fremde' − of having heeded
alien voices, served the alien purposes of the world. The peace beyond
individuation may be enticing. But it does not assuage that grief at losing the only true self one has which sounds in the paradoxical final line
of the fifth stanza:

> O laß nimmer von nun an mich
> Dieses Tödliche sehn, daß ich im Frieden doch
> Hin ins Einsame ziehe,
> Und noch unser der Abschied sei!

Die Heimat. As so often in Hölderlin, the poem contrasts the
vulnerable, unanchored existence of the 'ich' with images of

security and contentment. The pictures of home promise solace and peace: and so intense is the longing that the pulse of the poem quickens − 'Dort bin ich bald'. The 'bald' unleashes a sentence that flows over the next seven lines, crossing two stanza divisions. Only then to be brought up short by the fierce resistance of 'aber ich weiß, ich weiß'. The fusion of 'Liebe' and 'Leid', which has been invoked in stanzas one and two as constitutive of the poet's experience, recurs as something immovable, something that will not be (in Hölderlin's unforgettable phrase) 'sung out of my heart'. And the poem closes with an affirmation of the grief as 'heilig', as a sign of the will of the gods.

Hälfte des Lebens. A poem that is inexhaustible in its simplicity. Its two stanzas offer two pictures of nature: the first is one of autumnal richness (the sense of yellow pears and abundant wild roses bending the land, like a laden bough, into the water); the second is of a dead winter landscape. The first stanza invokes specific features of nature − yellow pears, wild roses, swans. The second mentions general properties of nature − flowers, sunshine, shadow − and concludes by invoking man-made objects (walls and weathervanes − 'Fahnen' stands for 'Wetterfahnen'). The 'ich' appears only implicitly in the first stanza (in the repeated address to the swans as 'ihr'); explicitly in the second, 'weh mir, wo nehm ich'. The first stanza describes a scene: the second portrays a counter-image to that scene. The title is hauntingly ambiguous: implying perhaps the middle point of life, implying the separateness of one face of life from the other. It is important to note the insistent presence of the human agent in the second stanza. If the first stanza acknowledges the abundance of the world in its palpable presence, the second is a vision, made by the poet, of what is not there but of what will be or can be. Man's consciousness enables him to transform ('Mauern') and measure ('Fahnen') the natural world. But his consciousness blights the world − and with it the capacity for vitality and creativity ('sprachlos').

Brot und Wein. The dedication 'An Heinze' refers to Hölderlin's friend Wilhelm Heinse. The great seventh section of this supreme elegy laments the fact that gods no longer dwell on the earth; and the poet writes 'Traum von ihnen ist drauf das Leben'. The 'wir' of this section associates that dream with the generality of modern man (and it is characteristic of Hölderlin's elegies that 'wir' dominates, rather than 'ich': the poet is concerned with deprivation as a general, rather than particular, condition). Men now can only dream of the gods, and this dream is the closest they come to that abundance of being that was once vouchsafed by the indwelling gods. The poem consists of three sections of three stanzas each. It begins by describing night spreading over the city. That night then becomes, in the second stanza, the night of an age from which the gods have departed. In that darkness there is still 'einiges Haltbare', intimations of the departed divinity. The third stanza takes us back to classical Greece. The next unit of three stanzas depicts the growth and flowering of Greek culture, a process in which men emerge from intuitive closeness to the divine presence into consciousness, reflection, into the giving of names. Stanza six depicts the final perfection of Greece, the building of temples, followed by the waning of the culture — we note the questions 'Aber wo sind sie?', 'wo blühn . . . ?', 'Warum schweigen auch sie . . . ?', 'Warum freut sich denn nicht . . . ?', and the weighty displacement of the negation in 'Warum zeichnet, wie sonst, die Stirne des Mannes ein Gott nicht . . . ?' But stanza six ends with the intimation of another kind of divinity, one who takes on human form and is 'tröstend'. The promise is that of Christ's mediation. Stanza seven — the shortest in the poem — returns us to a present in which divinity has withdrawn from men's lives. The lament for this condition begins in the 'wir' form, but the note of personal grief breaks in with the address to the friend, a kindred spirit. And the 'wir' contracts to 'ich' for the heartbreaking lines of almost colloquial listlessness:

> So zu harren, und was zu tun indes und zu sagen,
>> Weiß ich nicht, und wozu Dichter in dürftiger Zeit?

Yet the lament which initiates the final sequence of three stanzas is tempered by a tentative promise. The friend replies that poets are priests of the wine god. Stanza eight depicts the withdrawal of the gods, but one of their number, 'ein stiller Genius, himmlisch / Tröstend' leaves gifts behind as a sign that he will come again: bread and wine. Here the poet fuses the pagan deities of Greece with the Christian symbols of bread and wine. The poem ends with the vision of a coming that will redeem men from being husks:

> denn wir sind herzlos, Schatten, bis unser
> Vater Aether erkannt jeden und allen gehört.

In the figure of 'des Höchsten / Sohn, der Syrier' the poet conceives a divinity who is both Dionysos and Christ.

Hölderlin's great elegy mingles cultural history with intense emotion, and speaks of both deprivation and promise.

The Romantic poets express a sense of the insufficiency of the material world, a need for transcendence, a quest for experiences that point beyond the limitations of the here and now.

Novalis (1772–1801) gives powerful expression to this longing in his *Hymnen an die Nacht*. The *Hymnen* begin by asking 'Welcher Lebendige, / Sinnbegabte, / Liebt nicht vor allen / Wundererscheinungen / Des verbreiteten Raumes um ihn / Das allerfreuliche Licht?' We are told that light alone reveals 'die Wunderherrlichkeit / Des Irrdischen Reichs'. But abruptly the poet turns his back on these affirmations. And the first appearance of the 'ich' in the poem brings a profound challenge to the common indications and assumptions by which the generality of 'lebendig, sinnbegabt' men live: 'Abwärts wend ich mich / Zu der heiligen, unaussprechlichen / Geheimnißvollen Nacht'. In place of the realms (and significance) of the world we are offered the unsayable — and holy — mystery of night. The second hymn (*Muß immer der Morgen wiederkommen?*) extends the import of night beyond its everyday significance as part of the familiar, alternating rhythm of time. *That* night is but a 'shadow' of 'der wahrhaften Nacht'. True night, then, is a metaphysical realm. It is the primary realm which was interrupted by day (in the story of the creation of the world). The 'Herrschaft' of night contrasts with 'des Irrdischen Gewalt', the tyranny of earthly things which are subsumed under the categories of day and light. Night is 'himmlisch', 'heilig', 'himmelöffnend': it is the realm that harbours all intense experience — wine, love. The poem begins with four terse questions. And the answers offered flow with a rapt, expansive inevitability. The final sentence encompasses twelve lines as ever more experiential realms are associated with the beneficent glory of night. The impulses from Novalis's visionary poetry extend through the nineteenth century to Wagner and beyond.

Wenn ich ihn nur habe, from the *Geistliche Lieder* shows Novalis working with more traditional verse forms. With the exception of the first line of the final stanza, all the opening lines are the same — 'Wenn ich ihn nur habe'. The refrain comes as the first statement in each stanza, and is, then, the precondition for everything that follows. The love of God dissolves ('erweichen und durch-dringen') and replaces the world (stanzas four and five).

Clemens Brentano (1778–1842). With this poet the fissures in the experiential and poetic universe of Romanticism become bitterly apparent. The lament for lost faith, for lost love, for a lost integrity and value to experience recurs with a regularity as menacingly monotonous as the folk song refrains of which Brentano is so fond. There is an unsettling disjunction between the formal patterns of Brentano's verse, which seem to intimate containment and unity, and the catastrophic disintegration of self and world of which the poetry speaks.

Wie sich auch die Zeit will wenden is a strange poem. In terms of formal control, it is a virtuoso piece with its complex patterns of internal rhymes (in lines one, three, and four of each stanza). Thematically, the poem depicts – and laments – the poet's dependence on his beloved. Yet, perhaps because some phrases seem to be dictated more by the necessity of the rhyme than by the sense ('eher ich auch nicht gesunde', 'in neuem Zwange'), the poem remains curiously detached – and this impression is underpinned by the last line: 'Ach, das ist schon ewig lange'. It is almost as though the linguistic virtuosity is more central to the poet's consciousness than the girl, the doomed love, of which the lines speak.

Der Spinnerin Nachtlied. A poem of claustrophobic listlessness as the woman at the spinning wheel laments the loss of her beloved. The whole poem is sustained by three sound patterns which rhyme – 'Jahren/waren/gefahren', 'Nachtigall/Schall', 'weinen/allein/rein/scheinen'. There is an inescapable circularity to the poem as the sense units are reshuffled, achieving little more than the confirmation of the bitter pattern which contrasts past and present. The poem evokes numbness rather than pain – 'Ich sing und möchte weinen'.

Verzweiflung an der Liebe in der Liebe. The poem is in sonnet form. By tradition this is a compact, highly wrought form, one often used to express containment, control, a certain shapeliness of experience. Brentano's poem, however, expresses bewilderment and despair. The octet consists of nothing but questions, hardly any of them being complete sentences. The sestet sees the reduction of love and beauty to chaos and anguish: the 'Engelsflügel' become 'Mantelsfalten', which become 'Leichentuches Falten'; the 'Heilgenschein' is but 'zerraufte Haare'; the 'Freudenbett' is transformed into 'Bahre'.

Frühlingsschrei eines Knechtes aus der Tiefe. A cry of despair in which the 'ich' prays to God for release from torment. Part of that torment is a sense of spiritual and emotional sickness: the references to nature provide an ominously inverted kind of pathetic fallacy: 'Blüte' is answered by 'Schmerzen', 'Quellen' by 'giftge Wellen', 'die bunten Lämmer alle' by 'bittre Galle'. The anguish mounts in pitch in the last four stanzas, in the repeated cry of 'Herr', in the 'ich mahne dich' which is then excused by the notion of compulsion − 'Und so muß ich schrein' − in the 'kühnlich' address to God. And there is the modulation of the term 'Knecht': invoked in stanza thirteen (in the reference to the bloodied hands of the labourer), it becomes the 'dein Knecht' − 'your servant' − of stanza sixteen.

Einsam will ich untergehn works with the incantatory patterning of three sense units: the notion of 'Einsam untergehen' constitutes lines one and five of the stanzas; the star as the only comfort for a blighted life occupies lines three and four of each stanza; the similes of solitariness constitute the last line of the stanza and the second one of the subsequent stanza. The final stanza brings the poem to a concluding cadence by rhyming 'Herzen' with lines two and four. The intense patterning gives a claustrophobic quality to the notion of a self threatened by the possibility of losing its one and only companion − the 'Stern, den ich gesehen'. The claustrophobia is underpinned by the tautology of the sentences − 'I will go under alone if the star is taken from me I will go under alone'. The concluding line brings a hint (but no more) of another person whose presence could have breached the isolation of the 'ich'.

Wenn der lahme Weber träumt. The poem consists of one enormous sentence. The first ten lines catalogue examples of self-delusion in man and nature. In line eleven we are told that truth comes to put all the dreams to flight. The night resounds with grief as hearts are broken. The poem is balanced between an irony that mocks the dreams of the first ten lines and a compassion for the deluded hearts that are the casualties of truth's coming. The poem seems to cherish the experiences it devalues: dreams might, after all, be preferable to truth.

Joseph Freiherr von Eichendorff (1788–1857) is a poet who both shares in and is critical of the Romantic enchantment with the mysterious and the uncanny.

Wünschelrute expresses in brief compass the notion of a harmony in nature which the (poetic) magic word can release. That the 'Dinge' should 'träumen fort und fort' implies that nature will awaken to its full life when its song has been liberated from its dreamy absorption into mere matter.

Sehnsucht opens in the narrative mode of the past tense: the poet stands by his window, moved by the notes of the posthorn. The narrative argument continues into the first half of the second stanza as two young journeymen are described passing through the gentle landscape. The poem then changes to the present tense: their song is incorporated as a present imaginative possibility into the statement of the poem. Not only does the tense change: the world of the reported song is different from the one in which we began. The 'stille Gegend' is replaced by rocky gorges, plunging waters, and (in stanza three) by images of both man-made beauty (the marble statues) and neglect ('verwildern'). The final stanza maintains the temporal distinction between narrative past ('sie sangen') and dream-like present ('verwildern', 'lauschen'). But the two pictures of 'der prächtigen Sommernacht' overlap (the final line of the poem repeats the last line of stanza one). Both the narrative section and the reported song contain a figure standing by a window attending to music (the poet in stanza one, the girls in stanza three). The poem captures the infinite regression of longing ('Sehnsucht'): in his song the poet at his window hears a song in which girls at their window hear music . . .

Lockung gives voice to – and warns of – the enticement that emanates from the depths of nature. The warning note can be heard in the reference to 'die irren Lieder', to the oppressive scents of flowers ('der Flieder duftet schwül'). Yet even the mad songs are 'aus der alten, schönen Zeit': and the urgency of the call can be heard in the onward flow of the last four lines of both stanzas as the subordinate clause (which describes the enticing realm) simply takes over the whole sentence statement.

Das zerbrochene Ringlein is a lament for the betrayal of love. In terms of tense sequence, the poem moves from present to past, to a possible future ('Ich möcht als Spielmann reisen'), then back to the present, and ends with a statement of the only future that promises release from present turmoil − 'Ich möcht am liebsten sterben'. The key experience in (and of) the present is the mill wheel turning. The wheel symbolizes the fact that life goes on, even though, for the 'ich', it has lost its emotional centre and purpose. The mill wheel contrasts with that other symbol of continuity in the poem − the ring. Both are circular, without beginning or end. But the symbol the poet values fractures − as does what it represents. Which leaves the other symbol dominant: the mill wheel that reminds the poet both of what was and what is.

Mondnacht expresses the rapturous perception of a moonlit night in which sky and earth meet in blissful union. And that union enters the soul of the poet: the sky is also Heaven, and beckons the soul to it. The middle stanza is concerned with nature alone. The first and third stanzas (the metaphors of kissing and dreaming, the wings of the soul) invoke human feeling and responses. Delicately, the status of metaphor as metaphor − as going beyond physical facts − is pointed up in the repeated 'als' construction with the subjunctive ('als hätt . . . müßt', 'als flöge').

Der Einsiedler. The hermit sings of night's coming and bringing peace. The second and third stanzas move the poem beyond a concern with one particular night: in the past (stanza two) night has brought comfort, and the third stanza envisages a comfort that is linked with an eternal dawn. Night, then, is both part of the temporal order of things − and the promise of a world beyond time.

Heinrich Heine (1797–1856) is one of the most prolific of German poets. His extraordinary creativity coexists with an insistent knowingness whereby he makes an issue of the lyric mode at which he is so adept. The danger with Heine is that the facility can become merely facile: but this does not diminish his achievement, for he makes poetry out of a sense of living in unpoetic times.

Wahrhaftig is perhaps a good starting point. It is not, by any stretch of the imagination, a subtle poem. But then it is − precisely − distrustful of the kind of complex mood, the kind of linguistic subtlety that has often been held to be the *sine qua non* of lyric poetry. The first six lines itemize in a series of 'wenn' clauses features of a poetic landscape. The last four lines ruthlessly telescope all these features into a list (the diminutives, ending in '—lein', compound the sense of jingling triviality), and reject them all as simply untruthful. The final two lines are brutally colloquial: rhythmically − the hammering monosyllables of 'doch noch lang' − we are firmly in prosaic territory. The truth, it would seem, is not greeted with any affirmation other than that it is so. The destruction of poetic language gives an accent of pain to what otherwise could be but a simple exercise in debunking.

Die Welt ist dumm turns the irony on the poet himself. At the level of surface statement, the poem attacks the stupidity of the world: people claim that the poet's beloved is of questionable character, whereas he insists on the wonder of her kisses. The poem clearly denounces conventional worldly wisdom − as in the outrageous rhyme 'abgeschmackter / Charakter'. Yet there is a disturbing undercurrent to the poem. If the world's judgment on the girl is worth reporting in the poem, it is (presumably) also worth repudiating. And that, precisely, is what the poem does not do. The fact that her kisses are sweet and burning does not address the question of her moral character. The 'mein schönes Kind' might constitute a defence − if the girl is but a child, she must be proof against the world's calumny. But, if she is but a child (or as innocent as a child) it is slightly surprising that her kisses should be so adult. The inadmissible truth is, perhaps, that the world is right − and the poet simply does not care.

Ein Jüngling liebt ein Mädchen. The poem offers, in the first two stanzas, a jingle which loftily makes fun of the roundabout of love. But the superiority begins to drain from the poet's stance when he concedes that the old story remains ever new. And the last two lines make the point that, however clichéd the process is, to those experiencing it, it is both real and devastating. Behind the last two lines there vibrates the unacknowledged possibility that the poet is not exempt from the process he summarizes in this poem. The colloquial 'just' expresses considerable exasperation and irritation:

it is difficult not to sense the wounded self behind the 'wem'. Moreover, the poem ends with an uneasy rhyme. The effect is to point up the sound value of the 'ei' in 'entzwei'. And the 'ei' sound is a cry of anguish: an anguish, perhaps, that consists both of emotional vulnerability and of the sense that it is absurd to be vulnerable to a mechanism that one has long ago seen through.

Ich weiß nicht, was soll es bedeuten. The legend of the Lorelei, the siren who lures sailors to their doom, is a favourite subject of German poets. (Both Brentano and Eichendorff produced versions of the legend: the comparisons are instructive, not least because this kind of material raises acutely the question of a poet's relationship to folk poetry, local legend etc.) Stanzas two, three, four, and five recount the legend. The opening and closing stanzas function as a kind of frame in which we are alerted to the process whereby 'Ein Märchen aus alten Zeiten' is told by a modern poet. At the end of the poem a measure of doubt is, it seems, cast on the legend:

> Ich glaube, die Wellen verschlingen
> Am Ende Schiffer und Kahn.

Yet the poem ends with an affirmation of the legend ('Und das hat mit ihrem Singen / Die Lore-Ley getan'). The events may be doubted: but not the essential truth, a truth that haunts − and saddens − the poet (stanza one). That truth has, we may surmise, to do with the fatal power of sexuality. And the attraction is felt even by the modern poet. The evenly stressed, three beat lines suddenly shift in stanza four. 'Das hat eine wundersame, / Gewaltige Melodei' must be read against the regular metre: for a brief moment the power of the melody (and of its attendant associations) is recognized even by the poet who at the end will doubt the events of the legend.

Seegespenst deals with a similar theme. The poet, leaning over the edge of a ship, looks dreamily down into the water, and sees a vision of an old-fashioned town as in a Dutch painting. One particular house shelters the poet's long-lost beloved. He is about to plunge into the water to join her when, 'zur rechten Zeit noch', he is grabbed by the foot. The ship's captain returns him to the bourgeois world, addressing him by his academic title 'Herr Doktor'. The discomfiture of the poet is complete. The longing for escape is as preposterous as is the return to the bourgeois world.

The poem begins and ends with the ship: the poet is, it would seem, isolated from his fellow passengers — 'Ich *aber* lag'. Gradually the past tense of the narrative mode gives place to the present — 'schreiten' (line fifteen) — as the vision takes hold of the poet's consciousness. Initially the vision is perceived as a dream, a stylized picture of Atlantis, the men with 'langen Degen und langen Gesichtern' — but the sound of the bells and the sight of the girl obliterate the present altogether. The girl is a projection of the poet's own situation; she is 'fremd unter fremden Leuten', she is the perfect beloved. The awakening is as rude as it is timely. The return to the imperfect tense with which the poem opened, and the words of the captain, put the dream to flight.

Mein Kind, wir waren Kinder concerns the relationship between the worlds of childhood and adulthood. The poem begins by looking back to a distant childhood idyll. We learn of the games that were played. Central to those games (stanzas three to seven) is the children's desire to imitate adults — even down to the adult lament for their lost childhood when the world was a better place. The poem ends with the adult lament for the passing of time. Children fantasize about being grown up: and adults regret the loss of the childhood paradise in which they fantasized about being grown up and lamenting the loss of childhood. Both conditions — childhood and adulthood — are sustained by wishful thinking about the other state. The implications of this seemingly simple poem are devastating.

In *Der Doppelgänger* the poet begins by describing a scene at night. Unemotionally he registers the factual truth of this particular place: the beloved has left, but her house still stands. The second stanza brings a quickening of the emotions: but initially, the emotion is confined to the other figure who is also there. But finally emotion invades the 'ich': that other figure, going through all the postures of grief, is none other than himself. In the final stanza the 'ich' hurls imprecations at his ghostly companion. He resents what he can only see as a caricature of that grief which he went through 'so manche Nacht in alter Zeit'. Unspoken behind the anguish and impotence of that last stanza is the unacceptable fact that the love is not over and done with. The caricature hurts because of the affront to present feeling. The poem is a magnificent study in unacknowledged emotion. From the scrupulously maintained dispassion of the first stanza to the painful assonance of 'äffen' with 'gequält', from the detached view of 'doch steht noch das Haus' and 'da steht auch ein Mensch' to the revealing admission 'Was äffst du nach mein Liebesleid,' (the comma arrests the sense at the end of the line, and means that the 'Liebesleid' is suddenly admitted as a present experience), this poem attempts to state, and prove one thing, and dismantles the very case it wishes to make. Seldom has Heine's irony been so rich — or so uncomfortable.

Nun ist es Zeit works with a similar recognition of the poet's own entrapment. Here the grand moment of putting aside the masks, the props, the stage set of the posturing Romantic poet is under-cut by the dreadful realization that 'im Scherz und unbewußt' the pose was the truth. The irony is mounted at the proudly debunking certitude of the cynical poet — 'mit Verstand', 'Torheit', 'gar säuberlich'. But the promised 'cleanliness' of critical understanding is a delusion: the moment of truth is but a recognition of the truth of the masks. Or, to put the matter another way, perhaps there is no poetic truth that is not mask.

Die schlesischen Weber is justly one of Heine's most famous poems. It takes us entirely away from the problematic condition of the self-conscious poet. The 'ich' has been replaced by the 'wir' of the Silesian weavers (the poem was written soon after the revolt of the Silesian weavers in 1844). Rhythmically, the poem has the regular beat of a work song, and it also has the incantatory flavour of a curse. The particular work — weaving — functions superbly both as a social fact and as a metaphor for the weaving of destiny. The assonance of the 'tsch' sound in 'fletschen' and 'Deutschland' links the bared teeth with the name of the hated country. The threefold curse announced in the first stanza is spelt out in the three stanzas that follow, each of which begins 'Ein Fluch . . .'. The pain and outrage become manifest in the cascading past participles 'gehofft', 'geharrt', 'geäfft', 'gefoppt', 'genarrt' of the second stanza. The repeated sound patterns make it clear that the virtues, preached by religion, of 'hoping and waiting' are but delusions. The menace that runs throughout the poem is intensified in the final stanza where the alternating sequence of feminine and masculine rhymes give place to the hammering line ends of four masculine rhymes. The 'Deutschland' of the first stanza becomes 'Altdeutschland', and the implacable refrain is intensified by the 'und' of the final line.

Heine's last years were darkened by the appalling suffering caused by spinal tuberculosis which left him paralysed and confined to his sick bed − or, as he called it, the 'Matratzengruft'. The poems of these years are a remarkable mixture of accents of pain, courage, irony, and self-mockery.

Es hatte mein Haupt die schwarze Frau is the second poem from the *Zum Lazarus* cycle. The figure of death is a woman in black who, in a grotesque parody of acts of physical desire, has destroyed the poet's body. The physical details − the sucking of the marrow from the spine − undercut any grandiose Romantic notion of a 'Liebestod'. The full horror is explored in the final two stanzas. The destruction of the body has not brought death, but an imprisonment of the mind. The ugly polysyllabic rhyme of 'eingekerkert' with 'berserkert' links the imprisonment and the rage in a picture of terrible impotence. In the final stanza the poet urges himself to moderate his grief into quiet blubbering and prayer. The final two verbs, which are parallel infinitives, exist on the same level: prayer, it seems, is another version of blubbering. Even in a poem such as this which explores the extremity of physical and emotional suffering, there is an onlooking self which registers the indignity of the wasting body and the frantic mind.

Mich locken nicht die Himmelsauen is the eleventh poem in the *Zum Lazarus* group. The poem opens with a rejection of Paradise as being 'nicht just mein Zeitvertreib'. The colloquial tone is sustained throughout the poem, and the poet asserts his allegiance to unmistakably ordinary pleasures. Hence the plea, twice uttered, for health and a little financial assistance. Hence the invocation of 'Schlafrock und Pantoffeln', hence the rhymes in the final two stanzas which unite 'schwätzen' with 'Ergötzen', and 'froh' with 'status quo'. The colloquial register means that little is claimed for the earthly life that is preferred to Paradise: the poet invokes not grandiose or strenuous experience but modest bourgeois comforts (which Heine often mocked mercilessly). What makes the poem particularly poignant is the fact that, as the context of the *Zum Lazarus* poems makes clear, even these little preconditions of banal well-being are beyond the reach of the self who speaks.

Miserere opens in a grandiose manner by invoking the 'Söhne des Glückes'. But, as the rhyme of 'beneiden' with 'Verscheiden' makes clear, the 'Glück' for which they are most envied is that of a swift and painless end. The contrast with the poet's torment is powerfully expressed in stanza five as the ailments ('Gebresten') are mentioned which have him writhing on the floor. Yet the pain which sounds twice in three lines ('qualvolle Gebresten', 'verkürze meine Qual') merges with the mocking tone with which the prayer, which is announced in the title of the poem, is spoken. God is accused of inconsistency in that He is destroying the most humorous of His poets. The last four stanzas are, in context, both quizzical and defiant, for they suggest that the humorist is not yet beaten. He disclaims having the 'talent' for martyrdom, and fears that his melancholy might make him Catholic. In the third line of the penultimate stanza he writes: 'nimmt nicht der traurige Spaß ein End'. The poet who in stanzas five and six spoke of his 'Qual' now sees that 'Qual' as a 'Spaß'. The words are linked by the same long 'a' sound. The link serves to confirm that God has still not yet managed to destroy His chosen mirth-maker.

Annette von Droste-Hülshoff (1797–1848) was an almost exact contemporary of Heine's. Her poetry lacks the vitriol of his. But she too expressed a sense of the insufficiency of experience – and this theme acquires particular poignancy because she is a woman. Often she writes poems in celebration of the days within the Christian (or secular) calendar. As with Tennyson, one has the sense that Droste's feelings are not happily subsumed under the public rhythms of the preordained year.

Am Turme depicts in its first three stanzas an 'ich' standing on the balcony of a tower and looking out into a natural landscape. Each time a sensation (the feel of the wind in stanza one) or a perception (seeing the waves in stanza two, the ship in stanza three) produces the wish to partake of the physical energy of nature (the 'möchte' of line six in the first three stanzas). But the final stanza brings a drastic modification of what has gone before: the 'ich' is explicitly defined as a woman. And in the last four lines the constraints ('muß', 'darf nur') of a woman's life are spelt out. The wishes of the first three stanzas emerge as mere wishful thinking. Even the proud opening 'Ich steh auf hohem Balkone am Turm' is fanciful: the reality of the woman's life is 'Nun muß ich *sitzen*'.

Das Spiegelbild shows us the 'ich' confronting her mirror image, and disturbed by what she sees. That other figure – 'nicht meines-gleichen' – is passionate, vulnerable, awe-inspiring. Yet the final stanza acknowledges kinship with, and compassion for, the phantom figure. The mirror image is, then, the inadmissible self, the self that is, in normal, self-censoring living, suppressed. The 'ich' feels profoundly ambivalent towards this foreign, yet familiar self (note the repeated 'fremd' of stanza five and the admission – in an 'if' clause – of the possibility that the other self is not, in fact, other). The 'ich' confronts experiences that are 'entschlüpft der Träume Hut', a double that is both unwelcome and yet also inalienably part of the self (compare Heine's *Der Doppelgänger*).

Mondesaufgang. The poet waits for the moon to rise, and in the darkness before the coming of moonlight, terror holds sway. The shadows close in 'wie sündige Gedanken', the voices of nature are oppressive, accusing. Finally the moon rises and brings comfort – the comfort of domestic shelter and security:

> Und jeder Tropfen schien ein Kämmerlein,
> Drin flimmerte der Heimatlampe Schein.

The poem celebrates the calm of moonlight, contrasting it with the sun of passion, fire, and blood. The final couplet likens the moon to the poem of comfort: both are outside, and foreign to the ailing self, both bring an aura of mildness to the vulnerable sensibility. The containment which the poem praises is the more moving for its acknowledged limitation and fragility.

Im Grase is a strange, intensely atmospheric poem. The sense of absorbed, associative musing derives from the fact that none of the sentences that constitute each of the four stanzas is syntactically complete. The poem opens by expressing rapturous surrender to the enveloping haze and sweetness of the natural world. The 'tief tief trunkne Flut' of line three links with the grave mentioned in the final line of the stanza. The notion of death brings us to the second stanza in which 'Leichen' take over from the 'süßes Lachen' of the first stanza. Stanza three laments the transience of experience. And the final stanza, opening with 'dennoch', suggests that to each of the fleeting experiences enumerated in the third stanza the 'ich' brings a special kind of response to bear – a soul for the birdsong, colourful fabric (presumably the worked, lasting colours of poetry) for the fleeting ray of light, an answering pressure for a hand, a dream for the happiness. The poem moves hauntingly between erotic surrender to experience and an awareness of the death that inheres in all experience. The first stanza highlights sweetness and abundance, the second sounds the death knell (line five) for the treasures that are brought to rubble. Just as stanzas one and two juxtapose abundance and transience, so the lament of stanza three is answered by the affirmation of stanza four. But the affirmation is prefaced by 'immer mir nur / Dieses eine mir'. We sense an undercurrent of grief: the poetic sensibility may answer transience, but it does so by forfeiting full involvement with immediate experience: the 'nur' is a lament for a life made of 'Seele', 'Saum' (the woven pattern), and 'Traum' − rather than 'Glück'.

Am letzten Tag des Jahres (Silvester). The poet lives through the last hour of the old year. The sense of finality brings with it insistent images of death. Yet there is a kind of comfort won from that very finality. The reckoning with the past life is uncomfortable − the saga of 'der wüsten Brust', of 'eitler Leidenschaften Drang', the reproach from the star of love. From all this the last hour promises release. Unforgettably, the poem expresses the dignity and the pain of this final reckoning:

> Mir schaudert, doch
> Es will die letzte Stunde sein
> Einsam durchwacht

Rhythmically, the poem is particularly impressive: the containment of the stanza form is twice broken as enjambement links stanzas four and five and stanzas seven and eight. The sense of sin and terror provides the momentum for both occasions.

Eduard Mörike (1804–1875) shares with the Parnassian poets in France (Leconte de Lisle, Théophile Gautier) a questioning of Romantic subjectivism, a love affair with the poem as a completed artefact, as cipher for the perfect condition of balanced, contained being that is denied to man. Mörike's art is, however, remarkable for the precariousness of the equipoise which it expresses and enacts. The threats and subversive counter-currents are rarely far below the limpid surface of his verse.

Mein Fluß opens with two stanzas which describe the poet blissfully entering, and surrendering to the waters of the river. The sensuousness of these stanzas is linked with the strange 'Märchen' which the river carries with it. The secret which the river bears is something unattainable: the blue of its water contains the blue of the heavens. The poet plunges deeper. The changing nature of the water reminds him of the flux − and elusiveness − of love. The poet urges the water to engulf him, but the river pushes him ashore. The final stanza juxtaposes the river, at one with itself for all its wanderings, and the poet who is necessarily but an onlooker. The impassioned surrender of the opening stanzas contrasts with the separation of the closing stanza. The commerce between men and nature is, then, a complex one: and the responses of the poet are finely balanced − the voluptuousness of the act of surrender is answered by a recognition of the necessary otherness of unreflective nature.

Im Frühling similarly addresses the relationship between man and nature. Again we have an 'ich' who surrenders to nature in rapturous oneness. But love between men and women does not partake of the innocence, the unreflectivity of the natural landscape. Even as the poet surrenders himself, the questing inner voice makes itself heard:

> Ich denke dies und denke das,
> Ich sehne mich und weiß nicht recht, nach was.

The longing is, we discover, for an unobtainable object − for an immeasurably distant past. The poem is called 'Im Frühling': but man and nature are not at one in their springtime. The lines that express oneness cannot silence the unquiet spirit of man. The first six lines of the final stanza give a superbly concentrated expression of the theme − the sun's kiss penetrates the poet, his ear is given over to the bee's humming, the eyes are intoxicated. Yet in the midst of this rapture and unity, one line constitutes − and expresses − the disturbance: we read of the poet's eyes that they

> Tun, als schliefen sie ein.

The doing is separated from the consciousness, now, and (it would seem) for ever.

Das verlassene Mägdlein begins with the weariness of the maid in the early morning. The tired rhythms, the weighty repetition of the 'muß' gives the sense of constriction and dullness of spirit. With the depiction of the fire, a measure of vitality comes into the poem. But the vitality is immediately linked with the memory of loss and betrayal; the awakening to consciousness is an awakening to grief. And the girl wishes that the day which has just begun would soon end. The poem is devastating in its simplicity. It is couched in the present tense throughout. In the last two lines the girl stands back from the immediate pain and sees the day as one of a sequence. Yet the night, like those before it, will only serve to confirm her emotional dependence on her betrayer. The bitter throw-away of the final line but confirms the dreadful imprisonment. (It is worth comparing this poem with Brentano's *Der Spinnerin Nachtlied*.)

Die schöne Buche. In its metrical interplay of hexameter and pentameter lines, the poem displays great technical artistry. The formal control echoes the containment of the experience evoked, and it also links with the reflections on beauty in nature ('kunstlos') and in art which the discovery of the beech tree occasions. The first fourteen lines celebrate the beauty of the beech tree, the sense in which it constitutes a protected enclave. Metaphors of roundness and encircling predominate – 'rings', 'umzirkt', 'das liebliche Rund', 'umkränzet'. The tense changes from the present to the past in line fifteen as a narrative element is introduced: 'Als ich unlängst . . .'. The poet describes his discovery of the beech tree, his entry into its charmed circle ('rundum', 'Kreis', 'umher', 'säumte', 'Zauber- / Gürtel'). The experience is one of intense beauty, of being welcomed into a sanctuary by the benevolent deity: yet there is also the hint that the experience, in its very intensity, is threatening. It is incommensurable with human society ('einsam' in line fifteen, 'Einsamkeit' in the final line): the isolation is all-embracing, 'dämonisch', 'unergründlich'. The poem balances the sense of threat and loveliness, as in the penultimate line which combines the sense of enclosure and imprisonment ('eingeschlossen') with light and radiance ('in diesem sonnigen Zauber- / Gürtel'). The poem ends in the past tense of its narrative. The present tense of the opening section clearly implies the poet has left the charmed circle, but that he still knows of the beauty and intense isolation which the beech tree made (and makes) possible.

Auf eine Lampe celebrates the beauty of a (presumably rococo) lamp which is 'Ein Kunstgebild der echten Art'. The lamp combines grace, lightness ('zierlich', 'fröhlich', 'lachend') and nobility ('auf deiner weißen Marmorschale', 'ein sanfter Geist / Des Ernstes'). Yet the lamp is part of a largely forgotten house ('des nun fast vergessnen Lustgemachs'). The first eight lines are conceived as a direct address to the lamp. The last four generalize from the particular object to works of art as such. Again the neglectful world is mentioned — 'Wer achtet sein?' But the indifference is brushed aside in the 'aber' of the final stanza, as beauty is celebrated in and for itself. But this affirmation takes us back to the specific object with which we began. 'Scheinen' can mean both 'to seem' and 'to shine'. Presumably the lamp in its forgotten place is not lit: it only seems to shine, therefore. Or perhaps Mörike wishes us to reflect that in artistic semblance is to be found the true radiance of art (and not in its possible practical function). The 'schön' of the first and last lines is radiance enough.

Denk es, o Seele! The poem begins with strangely dislocated, yet urgent, questions. The assonance of the initial 'w' in 'wo', 'wer weiß', 'Walde', 'wer sagt', 'welchem' imparts a troubled character to the barrage of questions with which the poem opens. The final four lines of the first stanza account for the weightiness of the opening: the soul is urged to think the unthinkable thought — somewhere, in the midst of the beauty and energy of growing things, are the emblems of death — moreover, not just of death as a generality, but of the particular death ('auf deinem Grab'). The second stanza maintains the linking of liveliness and death: the two horses (presumably ponies) return home 'in muntern Sprüngen'. But that liveliness will accompany the coffin. And in the final lines the unknowable catastrophe moves a step closer. The glinting of the sun on the horseshoe suddenly has the menace of immediacy. The assonance of 'ei' sounds in 'deiner Leiche' is transferred to the repeated 'vielleicht'. The poem captures the uncertainty yet inevitability of the individual death, the hideous combination of 'vielleicht' and 'erlesen schon'.

Um Mitternacht depicts midnight as a moment of balance between the forces of day and the forces of night. The poem begins in the past, with the metaphor of night coming ashore like a floodtide and conquering the land. Night now ('lehnt') leans dreaming at the high point of the land ('Berge'). Time is finely balanced in the scales. But not for long: the springs sing insistently of the day that has been (and will soon be), and they, the children, sing a lullaby to their mother. They sing night to sleep with their song of the day. Mother night does not heed the ancient lullaby (although, in a

wonderful moment of ambivalence the poem suggests, with the notion of night being *tired*, that soon night's conquest will be over,
the tide will flow the other way). Night hears a sweeter blueness of
the sky: the notion, presumably, is that of the harmony of the
spheres, of a cosmic time beyond the alternations of earthly time,
a 'gleichgeschwungnes Joch' in which night and day could be per-
manently in balance. But that harmony is not to be known; the
'Doch immer' brings in the voice of the springs and rivers with their
song of the day. The poem magically captures the mysterious moment between two temporal divisions: and it sees that it is a moment and no more. Lines three and four of the first stanza rhyme
'nun' with 'ruhn': but the 'now' of a moment of rest cannot halt
the enjambement of 'die goldne Wage nun / Der Zeit'. For 'Zeit'
does indeed decree that the moment of stasis cannot be prolonged.

Hugo von Hofmannsthal (1874–1929) produced only a small lyric
oeuvre which comes right at the beginning of his literary career. He
was acutely aware of the fragmentation of the modern world, and
his poetry often celebrates those particular moments of privileged
being and insight when unity is again possible. With Verlaine and
Mallarmé he shares the ability to escape the substantial world in the
non-referential music of poetry. But in later life he came to distrust
this unity of incantatory magic – because it represented an impoverishment both of the self and of literature.

Vorfrühling speaks of the wind of spring whispering through the
still bare avenues of the early year. Stanzas seven and eight return
us to the opening of the poem. The intervening strophes tell of the
'seltsame Dinge' which the wind has experienced. We have glimpses
of experience – impressions of grief, love, laughter, music, and
silence. Yet these disparate experiences come together in the waft-
ting of the wind: as the poem tells us in its closing stanza which
forms a coda, the wind is heavy with the scent of its journey.

Erlebnis is reminiscent of a dramatic monologue. The 'ich' falls
into a dream which leads away from life into a sensuous landscape
of death and music. But the poem breaks this mood with the cry
'Aber seltsam': the longing for life is felt. We move into an
extended simile which likens the poet to the sailor passing his home
town, with all the familiar sights and sounds of his life, including

himself as a child. But the ship does not stop, the sailor cannot go ashore. The sails of his ship are, we are told, large and yellow: in the final line those sails are in addition, 'fremdgeformt' — they belong to a different country, they are designed for a different wind. The extended simile is in the present tense: it is the present (and presence) of death — 'Das ist der Tod' — from which there is no way back. Yet paradoxically, death heightens life, produces longing for what has been left behind.

Die Beiden expresses a moment of meeting. Two figures are described: a woman carrying a beaker of wine, a man on horseback. Both are at one with themselves, at one with their activity, as is suggested by the assurance of the 'Hand' in both cases. She is 'leicht und sicher', he is 'leicht und fest', casually in command of the horse, as expressed in the ease of the enjambement:

> Und mit nachlässiger Gebärde
> Erzwang er, daß es zitternd stand.

The final word 'stand' partakes of the rhyme pattern that links with the 'Hand' and binds the first two stanzas together to form the octave of a sonnet. Yet the trembling of the animal prefigures the trembling of the two figures at the moment of meeting. The sestet runs as one unit and is not divided into two triplets. Yet the unity that is promised in the moment when the two separate figures come together is threatened: both figures are drawn out of their security of intact being. What was light becomes heavy, the pulse of the poem quickens from its measured opening, and the internal rhyme highlights the difficulty of meeting — 'Daß keine Hand die andre fand'.

Weltgeheimnis speaks of a primal unity of which man was once part. In that unity men and women did not need speech — 'Einst waren alle tief und stumm'. Yet that unity has now (the 'jetzt' of stanza two) been forfeited. Men and women now have language which is a ghostly echo of that pre-verbal condition ('Zauberworte', 'nicht begriffen'): but words are pebbles with the jewels locked inside. The 'einst' of primal unity is but a dream to the discourse of the modern world.

Ballade des äußeren Lebens is dominated by the conjunction 'und' with which it opens. It lists the profusion of experience as something disparate and inauthentic. The children already have the 'deep eyes' of death, and the deep eyes know nothing. Natural organisms fulfil their cycle, the wind blows, men and women talk and feel. Stanzas five and six ask after the meaning of this process of separate, dissociated being – 'und gleichen / Einander nie? und sind unzählig viele?' The question is asked by the 'wir' of stanza six, figures who are isolated and aimless. In stanza seven an answer is forthcoming:

> Und dennoch sagt der viel, der 'Abend' sagt.

We note the contrast between the devalued speech of stanza three ('und reden viele Worte') and this act of 'saying' which amounts to much; and which, in the final line of the poem, is associated with distilled richness and sweetness. The word 'Abend' refers to time, it acknowledges, therefore, the transience that has been lamented in stanzas one to four. Yet the 'Trauer' is linked by alliteration to 'Tiefsinn'. There is sorrow but also insight. Evening, we may suggest, is a time when, with the waning of daylight, objects lose their separateness, their hard edges. A kind of unity is possible. And, paradoxically, unity is achieved by this poem which is about disunity. For it employs the complex rhyme scheme of *terza rima*, which links one stanza to the next. The utterance that is 'saying much' is the utterance of the poet (the 'wir' of stanza six).

Terzinen über Vergänglichkeit I. The poem, again in *terza rima*, opens with two stanzas of horror-struck lament at the ineluctability of transience. The incredulity ('Wie kann das sein') produces the disbelieving repetition of the final line of the first stanza. The third stanza speaks of personal change as the 'ich' moves from child to man. Yet, paradoxically, if the poet's childhood self is 'mir . . . unheimlich stumm und fremd', earlier ancestors are part of him, physically present with him. The pain of transience comes from man's knowing that nothing lasts. But the knowing is inseparable from memory, which means that man lives with a sense both of change and continuity, of a past that is 'fremd' and of other pasts that are 'verwandt'.

Manche frelich . . . begins with a distinction between two kinds of people in the ship of life: those 'down below', the oarsmen, and those who navigate and steer. Metaphorically, the contrast is made in terms of heavy and light: the first category are those who are close to the heavy matter of life, while those above know of realms beyond the earthly ('Vogelflug und die Länder der Sterne'). Lightness also implies light, insight ('Sibyllen'); its opposite is the tangle of life at its roots ('Bei den Wurzeln des verworrenen Lebens'). But the last three stanzas of the poem countermand the distinction just established. The 'heavy' and the 'light' are bound together: and the 'ich' speaks of knowing of past peoples, sharing their weariness, and of sensing the fall of distant stars. And the poem ends with the image of the 'ich' as embedded in a multiplicity of lives and destinies. And his lot is linked with the flame, agent of transformation, and lyre, symbol of the poet's song. The 'ich', as poet, affirms his task to be the utterance of the totality of experience, from 'light' to 'heavy', from distant past to distant future.

Rainer Maria Rilke (1875–1926) grounds his whole poetic career in a quest for that unity which he felt modern man had lost, a unity that could embrace life and death, the visible and the invisible. Time and time again the lament is heard for the banality and hollowness of man. In this respect Rilke is very close to T. S. Eliot, although he lacks the latter's ability to incorporate into his poetry the clichés and tired cadences of everyday speech. What Rilke and Eliot have in common is an aversion to the subjectivism of modern poetry: for both of them the poet is a craftsman, a maker who is heir to a long tradition of literary utterance. Moreover, Rilke's distrust of the 'ich' (particularly in the poems of the *Neue Gedichte*) has to do with his sense that man is a fragmented creature, shamed by the greater integrity of plants, animals, *objets d'art*. Yet, for all the attempt to keep human subjectivity out of his picture, Rilke also knows – and this will be the centre of the *Duineser Elegien* – that the material world can only be redeemed by the uniquely human act of transforming the world into pure 'saying'. Behind this quest there vibrates, as with Yeats and Eliot, a need to find again a faith that can answer the spiritual negativity of the modern world. Where Eliot's quest takes him to the institutional forms of Christianity, Rilke's metaphysic lacks institutional identity: it is, rather, an artistic redemption in and through the poetic labour of love.

Ich fürchte mich so vor der Menschen Wort. An early poem (November 1897) which sees language as bound up with clarity, knowingness, with qualities that, by naming, isolate things and rob them of their magic. In the third stanza the poet praises the music of things, and denounces language as the murderer of things. (Compare Hofmannsthal's *Weltgeheimnis*). Note the heavy irony of the alliteration in the line –

ihr Garten und Gut grenzt grade an Gott

and the grandiloquent self-assertion of the poet in 'ich will immer warnen und wehren'.

Herbsttag explores the relationship between men and nature. Autumn is seen both as a time of destruction (the shadow falling on the sundial, the winds released like hunting dogs) and as one of fulfilment (stanza two with its resonant depictions of fruition and rich sweetness). Stanza three turns to man. He is subject to the winds of autumn, to solitude, homelessness, to the brittleness of the leaves. Yet he seems to be denied the fruition of autumn: he partakes of natural rhythms, but without the richness that is vouchsafed to the fruits and grapes. Man knows 'es ist Zeit': but his knowing impoverishes him. Time and time again Rilke will return to the curse of consciousness as a disjunctive agent.

Fortschritt, as the title indicates, registers a growth in man, a deepening of his being. The poem (from *Das Buch der Bilder*) looks forward to some of the key preoccupations of the *Neue Gedichte*. The first four lines are dominated by adjectives or adverbs in the comparative mode ('lauter', 'breitern' 'verwandter', 'angeschauter'). This sense of growing and becoming is linked with a complicity in the nameless truth of natural phenomena — 'wie mit Vögeln', 'wie auf Fischen stehend'. The 'ich' is increasingly related to things, objects, scenes.

The *Neue Gedichte* celebrate the intensity of being of which modern man has only rare intimations. A number of the poems are directed towards the simple integrity of things and objects, others concern animals. Where human experience is invoked, it tends to be of a particular kind — one that demands from (or enforces on) the people concerned an inner-directed, or self-absorbed life. The encapsulation of the experience is the measure of its intactness. And that intactness is mirrored in the frequently employed sonnet form.

Der Panther depicts the situation of the caged animal. Stanzas one and three are concerned with the gaze of the animal: the bars form a barrier between the animal's consciousness and everything that is outside its circular movement. In the final stanza, the curtain over the eyes is briefly lifted. The rhythm changes, the repeated 'geht' stresses the moment of receptivity, the circular padding in the cage stops. But the tension relaxes in the final line: the image from the outside world is swallowed up by the heart. The middle stanza concerns the movement of the caged animal − the fusion of power, suppleness, and containment, the grace that is 'wie ein Tanz von Kraft um eine Mitte'. The poem captures with amazing vividness the behaviour of the caged panther. There is no human self in the poem: the consciousness that concerns the poet is that of the animal − 'Ihm ist'. No judgment is made (on, for example, whether it is right or wrong to keep animals in cages). The poem seeks, rather, to capture a pattern of circular movement which contains the body and mind of the animal.

Die Gazelle. The poem consists of one extended sentence. The octet celebrates the gazelle as a metaphor for enchanted perfection − 'alles Deine geht schon im Vergleich' − an incarnated poem ('Reim', 'Laub und Leier', 'Liebeslieder'). If the gazelle is (metaphorically) like the love song, the love song (metaphorically) invites the reader, in his mind's eye, to see the gazelle. The sestet begins weightily − 'um dich zu sehen'. And what follows is an extraordinary fusion of physical description and metaphor: each running movement of the animal is loaded with the contained nervousness of leaps and bounds. ('Lauf' has the double meaning of run and barrel of a gun − a gun which would not fire − 'schösse nur nicht ab'). What contains this febrile energy is the neck holding the head as the animal listens. Rilke captures the dynamic at the heart of this motionless pose by the accusative of 'das Haupt *ins* Horchen hält'. And the final lines, in an amazing vision of physical poise, capture the gazelle interrupted (literally − interrupting herself) at bathing. The face is turned, and the limpidity of the gaze contains the lake within it. Few poets have equalled Rilke in his ability to employ metaphors which both go beyond and yet also celebrate the physical.

Römische Fontäne expresses the circular pattern of movement enacted by the water in a fountain. In that perfect cycle, the water is constantly at home with and at one with itself (hence the 'heimlich', 'ohne Heimweh', hence the concluding line which speaks of a smile made possible by 'Übergängen' − transitions). Implicitly, the contrast is made with man who feels 'Heimweh', who is uncomfortable at the transitions of his life. The poem is one long sentence: most of the verbs are present participles, expressing not one discrete event, but an uninterrupted process. The language enshrines the perfect reciprocity of the various stages of the water's cycle – 'übersteigend' answers 'neigend', 'redend' answers 'schweigend', 'sich niederlassend' answers 'von unten lächeln macht'. The poem moves to a magical closing cadence with the enjambement that crosses the stanza division at

> träumerisch und tropfenweis
> sich niederlassend . . .

As with *Der Panther*, the final cadence is signalled by 'nur manchmal': a process reaches its end, but it is not, strictly speaking, the end of the process itself. The poem as linguistic artefact comes to an end, not the circular movement it expresses.

Das Karussell evokes, again, circular movement – the roundabout. It is peopled by animals from fairy tales – horses, lions, elephants. The poem captures the consciousness of the children – 'ein böser roter Löwe', 'ein Hirsch, ganz wie im Wald'. And, as the movement quickens, as the specific details – the white elephant – dissolve into a blissful pattern of shapes and colours, the children too become abstracted. Their eyes look fixedly, vacantly 'irgendwohin, herüber', and that vacant gaze becomes the blissful smile, occasioned by, yet going beyond, the 'atemloses blindes Spiel'. The use of the accusative with 'verschwenden' is a characteristically Rilkean coinage, expressing, as it does, an abundance of bliss that far exceeds the simple cause (the roundabout). Perhaps it is not necessary to add that this poem captures an extraordinary – but totally familiar – experience which every parent has had when watching his child on a roundabout.

Archaïscher Torso Apollos spells out what is often implicit in so many of the *Neue Gedichte*: that integrity of being, once glimpsed, is a reproach to man in his imperfection and fragmentation. The poem celebrates a torso from the oldest period of Greek statuary. It is a fragment: there is no head on the torso. Yet the whole glows as though the absent gaze has gone inward to that 'Mitte' which makes life. Without the radiance, the torso would be but an incomplete thing. But with that radiance, the torso sees man, and passes implicit judgment on his life. The authority of the statue is given voice at the end of the poem.

The *Duineser Elegien* are a cycle of ten poems which constitute Rilke's most impassioned reckoning with the deprivation of modern man. The legacy of Hölderlin can be felt — not least in the alternation of lament and affirmation. I offer here two extracts that will serve to suggest the spiritual landscape of the *Elegies*.

Wer, wenn ich schriee . . . is the opening of the cycle. The angel is, as the poems make clear, not to be understood in a Christian sense. Rather, the angel is the direction of the poetry; the angel represents that oneness of being which obliges man to know his own deprivation. The elegy opens with the key notion of utterance — in this case, the scream of pain. But the angels would hardly hear, and if they did, man could not bear their fullness of being. And man can find so little help in his attempt to communicate with the angels: animals immediately sense that man is not at home in the world of common interpretations and assumptions. This strand of lament continues to dominate elegies one to six. Yet, miraculously, the seventh elegy brings a note of affirmation. A new kind of utterance is envisaged — no longer the 'Schrei' of the opening elegy, but also no longer 'Werbung', the cry that woos, that asks for something. Rather, there is now a showing, a disinterested saying of what man has been able to achieve. And the notion of past achievement ripens, in the ninth elegy, into a sense of a present task that man, uniquely man, can accomplish.

Elegy 9, which is printed in its entirety, begins with a question, and the sequence of question and answer recurs throughout the elegy. The question concerns the difference between the simple integrity of the laurel and man who is doomed to be disunited. But an answer is forthcoming, the purpose of human destiny is both form-ulated and validated. The seven lines beginning 'Aber weil Hiersein viel ist' suggest that man, precisely because he is transient and knows that he is transient (and that knowledge makes him the more transient — 'uns, die Schwindendsten'), can redeem the fleetingness of the world. The passage is wonderfully poised: we hear the lament for the 'once and once only' of passing time, yet tentatively (the 'scheint' is as much affirmation as is offered) the worth of the fleeting is attested. Yet immediately a warning note is struck. We — humankind, that is — try to achieve this, and our willing comes up against the unsayable, 'lauter Unsägliches'. But then, with the characteristic qualifier 'vielleicht', an aim for man is announced ('Sind wir vielleicht hier, um zu sagen'). And our saying will be of modest and simple things – 'Brücke, Brunnen, Tor'. The notions of the 'here' and the 'sayable' define man's task on earth. The world is losing experiencable things, just as human activity becomes abstract and shapeless ('Tun ohne Bild'). In saying the sayable, in saying the modest things of the earth, man can celebrate 'ein Unsriges', and even the angel will stand amazed. The paradox that has been announced before is repeated: man, by virtue of his known, and therefore compounded, transience can give utterance to 'diese von Hingang lebenden Dinge'. This is entrusted to 'uns, den Vergänglichsten', which echoes the phrase 'uns, die Schwindendsten' of line eleven. The earth, consistently personified, endorses this role for man ('Erde, ist es nicht dies, was du willst . . .', 'Ist es dein Traum nicht . . .', 'dein drängender Auftrag', 'Immer warst du im Recht'). In that consonance between man and the existing world the poet has the sense of fuller existence, as in the formulation, which could hardly be simpler, 'Siehe, ich lebe'. And the elegy closes with the celebration of the 'überzähliges Dasein' – the being beyond number – which fills the heart. The elegy finely captures a sense of urgency and elation as each stage of the argument is registered in phrases of quickened emotion and perception: 'Warum dann / Menschliches müssen?', 'Oh, nicht, weil Glück ist . . .', 'Nicht aus Neugier . . .', 'Aber weil Hiersein viel ist . . .', 'Und so drängen wir uns . . .', 'Wem es geben?', 'Also die Schmerzen', 'Sind wir vielleicht hier . . .', 'was ists für zwei / Liebende . . .', 'Drum zeig / ihm das Einfache . . .', 'Erde, du liebe, ich will'. There is no shortage of commentaries which chart the thematic and philosophical territory of the *Duineser Elegien*. What often goes unremarked is the little particles of almost colloquial speech in which the urgency of the poetic argument finds its immediate, and immediately human, expression.

Die Sonette an Orpheus continue the current of affirmation that the elegies achieve. The fearsome otherness of the angel as direction for the poetic utterance is now replaced by the much closer figure of Orpheus: man and supreme singer, at home in the realm of both the living and the dead. And in the song offered to Orpheus Rilke finds the symbol and justification of his poetic quest, which is both explored and embodied in the rich variations on the sonnet form.

Ein Gott vermags argues the contrast between the song of man and the song of the god. What the god can do ('Ein Gott vermags', 'Für den Gott ein Leichtes') is asking a great deal of fragmented man. How should he be able to sing the song of existence, given that his own existence is so precarious? The italicization of the verb 'to be' insists on the being that is so rarely vouchsafed to man. Yet the sonnet ends with a promise of truthful singing. The three nouns of the final line of the poem show a gradual increase in intensity — from 'Hauch', to 'Wehn', to 'Wind'. True singing would, then, have the strength and the simplicity of a natural phenomenon. It is important to note the various definitions of humankind in this sonnet — 'Mann', 'wir', 'Jüngling', 'du'. The disinterested quality of the true song will allow the poet to sing for man and the generality of his world.

O Brunnen-Mund, du gebender speaks of that natural utterance that is not so much a song of being as being transforming itself into utterance. The water in the fountain speaks 'unerschöpflich Eines, Reines'. The assonance links the purity with the oneness. The water flows through the mouth of a marble mask into a basin which is likened to an ear. The spring is talking to itself. The heavy rhyme patterns of 'davor', 'Ohr', 'Marmorohr', 'Ohr der Erde' suggest the totality of this communion. The man-made artefact, the marble mask and basin, are one with nature in the sense that they make possible the dialogue of nature with herself, in which the history of man, too, has a part (the aqueducts, the legends). But the pronoun that dominates at the end is 'sie': nature's communion with herself.

Georg Trakl (1887–1914). In his well nigh obsessive concern with the themes of sickness and decay, Trakl may be associated with the European generation of decadent poets (Swinburne, Dowson). Yet in Trakl's hands, the modish themes become rich and disturbing. The decline of both body and soul and nature and God gives the sense of hurtful extremity to Trakl's oeuvre. Yet the decay coexists with a strangely affirmatory quality. All of which imparts a sense of weighty spiritual drama to his art. The decay may signal not only collapse but also the possibility of a new beginning. The language is often strangely dislocated, images coexist in associative, rather than argued juxtapositions, exclamations and parataxis abound. The fragmentariness is, however, frequently housed within a strict form with end rhymes and metrical regularity (iambic pentameter). The tension between chaos and order accounts for the power of the poetry.

Die Bauern. A poem that achieves an extraordinary blend of realistic detail and metaphysical urgency as the natural landscape is contrasted with the human scene. The first line registers not a particular landscape but a broad sweep of interrelated sound and sight ('tönendes Grün und Rot'). In the second stanza we read 'Die Äcker flimmern in einem fort'. By contrast, the dwelling and life of the peasants is seen realistically in its oppression and meanness. In the final stanza, the two worlds are brought together — 'Und wieder ins Feld'. Nature is overwhelming in its power — the 'Ähren-gebraus' — and the work process (the scythes) becomes a 'geisterhaft' intimation of mortality.

Verklärter Herbst depicts the power and abundance of autumn. The affirmation of the beauty and goodness coexists with the insistent rhetoric of loss and ending — 'endet', 'zum Ende', 'hinunter', 'unter'.

De profundis. As the title implies, the poem is a cry from the depths. We are offered a series of images with no reassuring continuity to them. Figures appear — 'die sanfte Waise', 'Hirten', 'den süßen Lieb', the 'ich' as a shadowy wanderer. But the poem is held together by metaphors that juxtapose aridity, blight, death on the one hand and the intimation of salvation on the other. The poem opens with the laconic, inert depiction of the dead landscape. But the second stanza brings pictures of life: at a physical level, the harvest is tentative ('noch spärliche Ähren'): but metaphorically (spiritually) there is a richer harvest — 'ihre Augen weiden rund und goldig'. The assonance of 'Waise' and 'weiden' suggests perhaps that this harvest is only there for those who are homeless and vulnerable, who look for a heavenly family. But the waiting of the girl is also symptomatic of deprivation. The promise coexists with its negation. The sweet body (stanza three) is now rotten: the 'ich' drinks from the well — but it is God's silence that he tastes. His head, heart, and mouth are constricted, attacked, closed. In the final stanza the symbols of Heaven become so much 'Unrat und Staub'. Yet the sound of angels is heard. The adjective 'kristallne' vibrates unsettlingly: does the sound have the purity of crystal, or is it merely a tinkling? Blight and promise, past (stanzas three and six) and present (stanzas one, two, four, and five) mingle to form a set of images that both trouble and console.

Der Herbst des Einsamen works with similar juxtapositions.

Autumn is depicted as a season of 'Frucht und Fülle'. The decay that is part of the season promises release ('Ein reines Blau tritt aus verfallener Hülle'). The 'blue', associated here with purity, is invoked in the second stanza (the blue wing of night), and in the third (the blue eyes of the lovers). Moreover, there is a gentleness and peace that bespeaks fulfilment, and not inertia − 'milde Stille', 'leiser Antwort', 'es ruht . . . ruhige Geberde', 'sehr leise', 'still Bescheiden', 'leise', 'sanfter'. The intimations of beauty and value are unmistakable. Yet the poem ends with two shattering lines in which the physical presence of death and terror is described with extraordinary power − one notes the fierce dynamic of the 'anfällt'. The horror ends the poem: yet the word 'Grauen' rhymes with 'Brauen' and 'blauen' − with the very intimations of promise.

Ein Winterabend speaks of the security of the laid table, the solid house in wintertime. To that home come wanderers, and the poem closes with the picture of bread and wine on the table 'in reiner Helle'. The picture is both of a simple meal, and of the sacrament (prefigured in stanza two with the reference to the 'Baum der Gnaden'). And the final stanza associates the pain and exclusion of the wanderer with the splendour of the bread and wine. 'Versteinerte' is the only verb in the past tense, and it expresses the result of lengthy processes. The threshold is the point at which the exposed realm and the protected realm meet. The threshold can be a place of entry or one of exclusion. It is those who are excluded who notice the threshold as a barrier and who constitute it by their pain. Yet their pain is also a tribute to the beauty from which they are excluded, a beauty which transforms the homely comfort ('wohlbestellt') of the laid table into the sacramental radiance of the bread and wine. The double meaning of the threshold as place both of admission and exclusion is captured in the syntactical ambiguity of the opening line of the final stanza. If we take 'tritt' as the third person singular of the present tense, the wanderer does cross the threshold and enter the house. But we can also read 'tritt' as the imperative form: the wanderer is urged to enter, but whether he does or can is left open. If he does not, then his pain will add another layer to the stone of the threshold.

Grodek invokes Trakl's experience of the First World War as a medical orderly at the hospital in Grodek, a Galician town near Lemberg and the scene of savage battles in the autumn of 1914. The

poem expresses death and destruction ('die wilde Klage / Ihrer zerbrochenen Münder'). The plural 'Münder' as opposed to the more
usual singular powerfully suggests the sheer number of broken
mouths. Yet nature brings a measure of consolation ('Doch stille
sammelt . . . '), a consolation that is immediately relativized by the
apocalyptic line 'Alle Straßen münden in schwarze Verwesung'. But
immediately afterwards, the note of promise is heard again, both in
nature ('unter goldnem Gezweig'), and also in the human sphere. Yet
even that promise is ambivalent. The shadowy figure of the
mythological sister greets the dead as the flutes of autumn sound. Is
she a caring, protective figure? Or is she a warrior woman, a
Valkyrie, whose promise to future generations ('die ungeborenen
Enkel') is not of a new and regenerate mankind but of further
sacrifices on the 'ehernen Altäre' of the War God? What is the force
of the comparative in 'O stolzere Trauer'? What kind of greater pride
is this? We are left with uncertainty. Will there be future generations
or will they, of necessity, remain unborn? And if they are born, will
they bring a new hope for mankind, or will they, in their turn, be can-
non fodder?

Gottfried Benn (1886–1956) shares with Trakl a sense of the decay inherent in all matter. And like Brecht, he is sceptical of the hallowed
place of feeling in lyric poetry. Benn can write with a dispassion that
contrasts devastatingly with his at times overwhelmingly immediate
vision of human catastrophe. The one value he affirms is the self —
but this is not so much a proud assertion of individualism as a poet's
affirmation of the creative self that makes the poem. And the poem
inhabits a realm divorced from the familiar one of everyday experience. The poem, by its mode and theme, becomes almost a
disparagement of the human condition; poetry is the one value in a
futile world. The link between aestheticism and inhumanity is one of
the most disturbing features of Benn's poetry, and of the age through
which he lived. (He was briefly a member of the Nazi party.) But
there is, at the same time, a remarkable drama to Benn's lyric oeuvre:
on many occasions the poetry expresses not so much the triumph of
the hermetic imagination as its struggle with the forces ranged
against it. (Benn is poles apart from Mallarmé — not least in the extent to which he draws on modern slang, the jargon of sport or
technology, for his poetry.)

Mann und Frau gehn durch die Krebsbaracke The man speaks and shows the woman round the cancer ward, urging her calmly (the 'ruhig' of stanzas two and three) to inspect the varieties of physical decay. One notes the insistent address to the woman (and, by implication, also to the reader) — 'hier', 'komm', 'steh', 'fühl', 'du siehst'. The poem is laconic — particularly in the last two stanzas short sentences predominate. The final stanza is a vision of the decay of the body as the ineluctable law of matter — 'Acker', 'Land', and 'Erde'.

Wer allein ist praises the loneliness of the man of form and image (that is, the poet). His solitariness is symptomatic of his dwelling with the creative (procreative) flood of images. The metaphor of sexuality is sustained into the second stanza: he is big with the intellectual dissection and destruction of life, of 'Menschliches, das nährt und paart'. The organic self-renewal of the earth is a matter of indifference to him: perfection is static, abstracted form, not the flux of living processes. The penultimate line of the poem is, of course, a taking back of the secret announced in Goethe's *Selige Sehnsucht*, 'stirb und werde'. Goethe's and Benn's poem repay careful comparison: Benn challenges the Goethean view of the mind as implied (and implicated) in the energy of natural processes.

Einsamer nie contrasts the 'Erfüllungsstunde' of nature in August with the state of man excluded from the natural splendour. 'Wo' points up the crucial distinction — in the first two stanzas it has the force of 'where', in the final stanza it implies 'whereas'. The human sphere — 'Glück', love, wine, the abundance of things — is repudiated in favour of the 'Gegenglück' of 'Geist'. The poem asserts this service as the true condition of the 'du': but the poem acknowledges the beauty of the things repudiated and the price paid — 'einsamer nie'.

Gedichte. The first and last stanzas open with a parodistic reference to Goethe's poem *Prooemion* which begins 'Im Namen dessen, der Sich selbst erschuf!' Goethe's poem views God as an ever-present force at work in nature and man. Benn's poem celebrates an experience that questions the value of the created world, that takes things from their place in the world and remakes them in the mystical realm of the poetic word. The poem bypasses human history, the Mount of Olives, the Anjouin conquest of Naples (the Posilipo being a nearby chain of hills), the heroic past ('Stauferblut'), in favour of a new crucifixion, a new redemption of the material world — in poetic song. The final stanza celebrates the privileged hour which yields the song, as something set against the gravel and scree ('Geröll') of history.

Verlorenes Ich expresses the onslaught on the 'ich' by the world of modern physics: gamma rays and atomic particles are the new version of infinity (the old one was the stone of Notre Dame). The world and time spirals 'ohne Schnee und Frucht': distance and time become relative. The primitive world, what has been claimed as the inalienable ground of being, all this is swallowed up. Our age has 'die Welt zerdacht', our myths are false, all our 'Unendlichkeiten' and 'Ewigkeiten' are simply functions of the new mechanics. And the poet looks for a mode that still remains to him to express man's condition: no Dionysian hymn ('Evoë'), no requiem will work any more. The final two stanzas lament the passing of a centred world which made possible an integrity of being, feeling, and thinking. But in place of the Lamb of God (stanza seven) we know only the 'Gamma-Strahlen-Lamm' (stanza one). The anguish and deprivation issue in the predominantly exclamatory mode of the poem. This is poetry made out of cultural history, and its potent ancestor is Hölderlin.

Was schlimm ist is a catalogue of experiences, all of which are variations on the theme expressed in the title — a lament for what really is bad about life. The list moves imperturbably from what might seem minor frustrations (the English detective story) to profounder discontents (the repeatability of what we take for unique experiences, stanza four). The category is then intensified to 'sehr schlimm' (to have to go out when one would rather stay at home) and finally we reach the superlative 'Am schlimmsten'. The worst thing is to fail to get one's dying right. And that rightness has to do with the clarity and efficiency of the dying process. The poem stays close to colloquial speech; employing mundane language for mundane discontents. Yet the final stanza gives a dark relief to the whole poem, implying, as it does, that the ultimate frustration in a life full of frustrations is not to be able to get out of it when (literally) the going is good. The catalogue of irritants acquires, in hindsight, a strange weightiness. The poem works as an updated version of a Baroque lament for the vanity (in modern terms: triviality) of the world.

Leben — niederer Wahn. The poem opens with a Baroque slogan on the folly of the world. And subsequent metaphors sustain that argument: life is but a dream, an excitation of the senses (stanza two), an impermanent thing (stanza three). The rhetorical questions directed at the self imply incredulity that any knowing self could be taken in by the false promises of life. And the poem closes with a definition of both 'Glaube und Tat' which do keep their experiential promise. Form is the only value: form made by men, but ultimately standing separate from the human sphere. ('Doch dann den Händen entführt. . . .') The weighty assonance in the final line underpins the point (and the paradox): only statues bear the living seed.

Bertolt Brecht (1898–1956) was a superb lyric poet who distrusted lyric modes and themes. Nature and love recur throughout his poetry, yet he makes his verse out of the sense that it is largely illegitimate, in his time and place, to derive poetry from such experiences. In the process he produces low-key, understated poetry, informed by a simplicity of diction that is neither arch nor sentimental. One might summarize the linguistic and moral situation of Brecht's lyric output with a quotation from the *Svendborger Gedichte*:

> In den finsteren Zeiten
> Wird da auch gesungen werden?
> Da wird auch gesungen werden,
> Von den finsteren Zeiten.

Vom ertrunkenen Mädchen. There has been no shortage, in this anthology, of poems in which nature is celebrated as an order of being that underscores and corroborates man's moods. In one sense Brecht shares this sense of the kinship between man and nature. But he is also critical of what he sees as the sentimentality of much previous nature poetry, a sentimentality which regards the natural world as existing for man's benefit. Brecht is untiring in his assertions of the otherness of nature – and at the same time insists on the physical kinship between man and the natural world: both are organic matter. *Vom ertrunkenen Mädchen* describes a oneness between the human organism and nature after death. And Brecht insists that this oneness is, precisely, not metaphysical but physical. The first stanza describes the corpse being carried downstream, and then refers to the colour of the sky. The notion of a metaphorical link between the two (the sky *pacifying* the corpse) is invoked, thereby implying a natural universe that is caring, protective of man. Stanza two concentrates on the body, and on the physical closeness between weeds, plants, fish and the corpse. Stanza three invokes the second of the two elements with which the poem opens – the sky which grows light towards morning 'daß es auch / Noch für sie Morgen und Abend gebe'. Again we have the notion of the sky as related (and relating) to man. The final stanza expresses the total union of human body and nature: a unity that is physical dissolution. The ultimate architect of the pathetic fallacy – God as the maker of the natural world for man's benefit – loses track of the girl's body. The sky, then, is the sky, part of the natural order of things; the sky is not the Christian – or any other kind of – heaven. The poem is dominated by weighty 'a' sounds – 'opal', 'wundersam', 'ward', 'Fahrt', 'vergaß', 'Haar', 'Aas'. The poem is not ghoulish: rather, there is a resonant yet dispassionate observation of the authority of natural phenomena.

Erinnerung an die Marie A. is a poem which wonderfully challenges a whole number of conventions and expectations. The opening stanza recalls a moment of young love – and associates it with the brief appearance of a cloud. Perhaps the cloud symbolizes the impermanence of the love which one knows 'wie einen holden Traum'? Perhaps the memory remains of first love, undiminished by the years? Stanza two converts the poem into a hard-bitten statement – the colloquial 'fragst du mich, was mit der Liebe sei' gives the tone of worldly wise, perhaps even cynical, repudiation of the (by implication, sentimental) mood of the first stanza. Yet the third stanza modifies the poem again by the assertion of what the poet still knows – and by virtue of what. The word 'weiß' in its double meaning ('know' and 'white') dominates the second and third stanzas. The knowing is linked with the white cloud. Strangely, all the things that would appear to be humanly essential – the girl, the scene of that kiss, the trees, the kiss itself – have faded. Yet paradoxically, an insubstantial, and seemingly insignificant, detail remains enshrined in the memory (and in the poem). This is, perhaps, a kind of last-ditch love poem: if the traditional centres of love poetry, the girl, the man, anthropomorphic nature, will not hold, the periphery does. The contingent physical detail is raised into the lasting consciousness of art – the cloud becomes (in spite of the odds) a symbol. The poem registers the shift of priorities – both linguistic and experiential – in the genre of love poetry.

Liturgie vom Hauch has for its refrain four lines borrowed from

Goethe's *Über allen Gipfeln*, lines which celebrate the peace of nature. In Brecht's poem that peace coexists with the brutally enforced peace of a repressive society (captured in the ominous refrain of 'da kam . . . einher' / 'da sagte . . . nichts mehr'). The red bear declares war on the natural world (and also, by implication, on the human world): he promises a revolution that will break the existing mould of both man-made and natural realms. Similarly, Brecht's poem, in its borrowings from Goethe, breaks the crucial order of Goethe's line sequence, an order which incarnates the hierarchical progression from 'Gipfel' to 'Wipfel' to 'Vögelein' to man. In the process Brecht challenges the implications of necessity and rightness in Goethe's poem, and thereby he invites us to reflect critically on the kind of thinking that legitimates a social order by investing it with the aura of natural inevitability.

Fragen eines lesenden Arbeiters. A poem that, through the mind and consciousness of the working man, asks questions about the traditional kinds of historiography, replete with the doings of great men. The poem ends with the quizzical juxtaposition of 'Berichte' and 'Fragen'; Brecht makes the point that 'reports' or 'accounts' are not simply the unmediated recapitulation of facts. Rather, they are facts rendered pertinent by certain assumptions as to the workings of history. The poem juxtaposes historical facts − and the questions to which those facts, as formulated, can offer no answer.

An die Nachgeborenen. A poem in which Brecht imagines himself explaining his life and times to a group of readers who live well after him. The point of the poem is not to seek immortality, but to hope for an age to which the experiences reported in the poem will be both foreign and reprehensible. The opening stanza chronicles a world that is out of joint in the sense that innocence, an untroubled brow, laughter indicate stupidity, insensitivity, or ignorance. And the first section of the poem chronicles the outrageousness of a world in which to speak of nature, to be well fed, to repudiate violence, and to answer evil with good is unwise, unacceptable, naive. The second section has a refrain which registers time as something allotted to man − the constant invocation of 'finstere Zeiten', 'was sind das für Zeiten', 'zur Zeit der Unordnung' insists that 'meine Zeit' was not the time chosen by or wished by the poet, but the time given to him. The final section expresses anguish at the distortions of humanity which these times have exacted − features twisted, the voice hoarse with rage. The poem is moving in its bad conscience, in the undertow of pain which is hardly assuaged by the argument that the times are to blame. The painful tautology of 'meine Zeit / Die . . . mir gegeben war' insists on the 'mine' and the 'me' of a selfhood that suffers for what it does ('Und doch esse und trinke ich').

Schlechte Zeit für Lyrik. A poem about the possible themes for poetry, which acknowledges the continued existence of the experiences and the sensibility that, traditionally, engender lyric poetry — happiness, boats on water, girls' breasts, the apple tree. Yet the poem ends with the insistence that the horror at Hitler's speeches (the 'Anstreicher' of the final stanza) fuels the writing process. We hear in this poem Brecht's need to turn his back on lyric utterance as traditionally defined (a rhyme, stanza four tells us, would be arrogant), yet we also hear the voice of perceptual and experiential loss in the 'sehe ich nicht' of stanza three, and the regret that, even where there still is 'Begeisterung', it counts less than the horror at public events. The tension is characteristic of so much of Brecht: between a full-blooded, impassioned sensibility, and the determination to give public, socio-political concerns pride of place in his feeling, thinking, and writing.

Der Radwechsel expresses a single, contained situation as an aphoristic illumination of experience. And, as so often in Brecht's poetry, questioning is the dominant mode of utterance. The poet asks himself why he is impatient at the interruption of a journey whose starting point and destination bring him no contentment. The poem poses a riddle and offers no answer. The moment when the particular past and future concerns of the life are in abeyance is, we might say, a privileged one: yet it is a privilege that cannot be grasped. The poem summarizes, in the briefest compass, the self-understanding that informs so much of Brecht's lyric output.

Der Rauch. Again a situation is treated as an aphorism. In five lines of extraordinary simplicity (which was only achieved before him by Goethe) Brecht sketches a scene, and makes a brief comment. The scene finds its justification not as a picture of nature but as the housing of man (the smoke from the chimney). Without that sign of human habitation, the scene would be desolate. The whole poem pivots about the central line — 'fehlte er' — which is the precondition of all the other details in the poem having value and meaning. The poem asserts the primacy of man housed, man dwelling in the practical everyday world (the smoke suggests the fire needed for warmth and cooking). No one celebrated more movingly than Brecht the poetry of those modest needs and experiences.

Paul Celan (1920–1970) or Antschel ('Celan' was an anagram under which he published his first poems in 1947) was born at Czernowitz, Rumania in 1920. In 1941 his parents were deported to a concentration camp. Celan managed to escape but was drafted to a labour camp. After the war he settled in Paris where he committed suicide in 1970. By any standards. Celan's poetry is difficult, and that difficulty has to do with his desperate attempt to wrest language both from the debased currency of the common world and from the silence which crowds in upon any and every attempt at poetic utterance. Celan once wrote: 'das Gedicht zeigt, das ist unverkennbar, eine starke Neigung zum Verstummen.' Yet against this we should set his remarks about the poem needing to establish communication – 'das Gedicht will zu einem Anderen, es braucht dieses Andere, es braucht ein Gegenüber.' One feels that the dialogue partner is a public that does not – or not yet – exist. Celan at one point uses the metaphor of the poem being a message in a bottle. Celan's use of language is uncompromising precisely because he seeks an uncompromised hearer and an uncompromised language (and German was compromised like no other language because of its complicity in the holocaust).

Espenbaum operates with motifs from folk poetry. The poem consists of five couplets: in each, the second line is devoted to the mother, to her pain and violent death. Three times we hear of the negation that has consumed the mother's life – 'nimmer', 'kam nicht heim', 'kann nicht kommen'. The first lines speak of experiences that in themselves are not menacing. Yet the negation of the second lines flows back into the first, in spite of the implied contrast. Even the motifs of the aspen leaves, the dandelion, the cloud, the star, the door lifted from its hinges cannot assuage the grief that is heard in the urgently flowing second lines.

Todesfuge opens with the shattering paradox of milk that is black. All the associations of milk – purity, nourishment, naturalness –

are negated in this world of imprisoning evil. Details recur and constitute the fugal structure of the poem. And that omnipresent recurrence expresses the theme: the repetitive, brutalizing routine of the death camp. In this world gone crazy, where milk is black, where graves are located in the air (the smoke from the ovens), normality (the man who lives in a house and writes home to Germany) becomes monstrous. The golden hair of the German girl contrasts with the ashen hair of her Jewish counterpart. In the one rhyme of the poem ('sein Auge ist blau' / 'er trifft dich genau') the blue eyes of the Aryan master of death become the one eye looking along the sights of the gun. For that man the prisoners have no humanity, as is suggested in the assonance of 'Rüden' and 'Juden'. The details of the poem vibrate from the precise and concrete to the metaphorical and abstract (the man who 'plays with snakes' both flicks his whip and plays with evil; the music of death is both the camp orchestra and the Dance of Death; Margarete with her golden hair is both the man's girlfriend and the symbol of Aryan Germany). The poem evokes a world that is unhinged, yet completely, brutally organized; and the theme is mirrored in the poem's formal argument.

Sprich auch du. A poem concerned with language, which suggests that language, like human experience generally, needs negation alongside affirmation, darkness alongside light, silence alongside utterance. Hence 'Beim Tode!' occurs in immediate proximity to 'Lebendig!' Hence 'Mitternacht' is robbed of its middle syllable in order that its sound value moves close to that of its opposite 'Mittag'. The final stanza envisages a kind of transcendence: language pared down, spun out to a fine thread which can allow the star to descend into the shifting matter ('Dünung') of words.

Tenebrae. The word that forms the title means darkness, and it is also the name for a Roman Catholic service. The poem is a prayer which insistently invokes the name of the Lord ('Herr') and asserts a closeness between man and God. The closeness is made of pain — the 'greifbar' of the second line is immediately taken up in the 'gegriffen' of line three. The human bodies are clawed together as though part of the Lord's body (the rhyme links 'Herr' and 'wär'). The closeness is made of clenched hands and limbs. The third stanza inverts the normal associations of closeness through prayer, for it is the Lord who is invited to pray to men. The next five stanzas are in the past tense. They speak of those who bent over hollows and lakes ('Maar' is the geological term for a volcanic lake), who went to be watered ('zur Tränke') and who saw blood in the trough, and in the blood, the image of the Lord. The final stanza returns to the present command of 'Bete Herr'. The past tenses that invoke blood and horror are linked with the nearness to God, as is suggested by the weighty assonance of 'war' and 'nah'.

Weggebeizt addresses an unidentified 'du'. That 'du' commands a language that, like acid, burns away the 'bunte Gerede des An- / erlebten'. The implications are of inauthentic experience, inauthentic language — and these implications are reinforced by the appositional noun 'das hundert- / züngige Mein- / gedicht, das Genicht'. The 'Mein' has presumably the force of 'my own' — but also of falsity, as in the compound noun 'Meineid' which means a false oath, i.e. perjury. The falsity of *that* poem means that it is a negation of poetry, a 'Genicht'. The second stanza opens, as does the first, with a past participle. The wind of the language that emanates from the 'du' whirls a way through a snow landscape to glacial places. Yet, surprisingly, in the glacier are 'Stuben' (the word implies intimacy and comfort) with tables. The ice proves 'gastlich'. And in that ice the crystal made by human breath issuing into the fierce cold is a true, unchallengeable witness to the 'du'. Once again, at the very extremity of the humanly habitable world, there are intimations of comfort and fruitfulness — in the references to 'Wabeneis', honeycombed ice. The crystalline is, it would seem, the last repository of authentic experience and language. The poem invokes processes that are over and done with ('weggebeizt', 'ausgewirbelt'), and leaves, in the one main verb 'wartet', a fixed witness caught in the cleft of time.

Ich kann dich noch sehn. A poem concerned with parting. The first stanza speaks of the 'du' as hardly a presence, as an echo that can yet be reached and charted by words. The notion of an 'Abschieds- / grat' presumably implies a ridge beyond which the 'du' has passed, leaving only the echo behind, yet the opening line speaks of the 'ich' still being able to see the 'du'. The notion of visibility is maintained into the second stanza. The 'du' recoils from the brightness of that place in the 'ich' where to say 'never' is most painful. We cannot be sure of the intimations here. Does the 'du' recoil from the clarity and force with which the 'ich', in spite of the pain, says 'never'? This would imply that the negation which would sunder the relationship for ever is resisted by the 'du' — resisted, paradoxically, in an act of recoiling from the 'ich'. Or does the bright light imply a taking back of the 'never': does the 'du' recoil from the refusal to call an end to the relationship? We cannot be sure. But what we can say is that the poem is both about, and in its ambivalence is situated on, the 'ridge of leavetaking'. On that ridge, and to either side of that ridge, are gestures of separation and of coming together.

Ein Blatt. The poem is a reply to the second stanza of Bertolt Brecht's *An die Nachgeborenen*. It opens with a punning reference to Brecht's 'Gespräch über Bäume': for Celan's poem is a 'Blatt' (a leaf of paper) which belongs to no tree. Celan, to pursue the pun, takes a leaf out of Brecht's book and indicts the conversation for saying too much. Brecht's point is that to talk of trees is a crime when there are so many more urgent things to talk about. Whereas Celan argues that talking about any kind of sayable matters may be a crime — a crime against the unsayable things that need to be said. What looks at first sight like a simple polemical inversion of Brecht's sentiment proves more complex than that: common to both poets is the need to make poetry say the things that it all too easily leaves unsaid.

Hans Magnus Enzensberger (born 1929) once wrote: 'Poesie heute setzt nicht nur Kenntnis, sondern auch Kritik der modernen Poesie voraus', and he went on to add: 'ja Produktion und Kritik sind nicht mehr voneinander zu trennen'. The critical stance of which he speaks is directed both at prevailing modes and conventions of lyric poetry and at the encroaching bureaucratization and inhumanity of the modern world.

Geburtsanzeige. A bitter denunciation of the world which is waiting to 'process' the newly born baby. The poem plays with double meanings throughout. 'Wurf' means a litter of animals. In the first stanza, the baby is not born, it is 'geworfen', which both implies that it has little better than animal status and that it is randomly flung into the world. The priest is perfunctory in his welcome, as is the doctor who performs the forceps delivery. The dealer cashes the draft ('zieht die Tratte'), and ink and blood flow at the child's birth. (A 'Zettel' is a small piece of paper: but 'verzetteln' means to waste.) And even as the baby howls ('plärrt') in the clinic, the strategists from the military are arranging its call-up. The child is already insured and lost, wasted ('vertan'). In stanza four we learn that its future is unavailable, 'vergriffen' (as of a book that has gone out of print), that the child is already repudiated ('verworfen') and trapped in a net and lost ('verwirkt'). Even the baby who dies cannot, as the next stanza tells us, escape being registered ('verbucht'), declared ('verhängt', as of a decree, but 'Verhängnis' means destiny), trapped ('verstrickt'). The final stanza brings a sombre warning: if the child cannot fill up the hole ('die Grube überhäuft') which we have made for it, cannot resist the aggression and everything else that we have in readiness for it, then it is betrayed. The penultimate line does envisage a kind of counter-offensive that would be possible – to describe the meagreness of the times with unheard-of writing. And that possibility is, we might say, embodied in this poem. The subversive play with double meanings in the refrain-like verbs beginning in 'ver—' suggest the resistances of unheard-of writing (that is, writing that deviates from all the other kinds of writing – bureaucratic paper work – that the poem chronicles). The poem generates an unsentimental affection for the child ('Bündel', 'häßlich rot und zart', 'mit krummer Hand'), and in the use of 'wir', three lines from the end of the poem, implies that the poet too is part of the processing of the child. The title, 'Geburtsanzeige', means the announcement of a birth: in the context of the poem, however, the other, more sinister, meaning of 'Anzeige' – an accusation passed to the authorities – also makes itself heard.

Ins Lesebuch für die Oberstufe. A poem that subverts all notions of what might constitute a 'suitable' poem for sixth-form use. The poet warns his son to prepare early for the business of survival in modern society. Odes are less use than timetables. One should not draw attention to oneself, because those who stand out will appear on lists, will have signs ('Zinken') fixed to their chests. Mobility is all-important, and the poet commends frequent changes of address (Viertel' is a district), of face, of passport. Only those who have the will and the wit to fight can produce the fine dust that will eventually block the lungs of the powerful. Both in theme and mode the poem is indebted to Brecht, who also advocated tactical resistance in preference to martyrdom. And, like much of Brecht, this poem also expresses, together with its hard-bitten attitude, a sense of pain at the betrayals involved – 'lern mehr als ich', 'Versteh dich auf den kleinen Verrat, / die tägliche schmutzige Rettung', 'Wut und Geduld sind nötig'.

Küchenzettel. The first three stanzas give three images of a kitchen seen through an open door. The first stanza, in the present tense, depicts the kitchen in the poet's house; the second, presumably a Dutch interior, portrays a similar view into a kitchen; the third stanza, again in the past tense, describes a similar glimpse into a similar kitchen in a summerhouse in the Soviet Union. All three images have in common a feeling of simple, solid domesticity. Yet all three images contain a detail that has entered the domestic realm from the world outside – a telegram, a letter, a newspaper. The domestic idyll remains intact as long as the message is not received. Yet the final stanza suddenly bring destruction. There is, presumably, no need to read the telegram, the letter, the newspaper. For the events outside have now invaded the domestic frame. If the homely world unites humanity across different historical periods and different cultures – Germany, the Dutch painting, the Soviet Union – so too do the disturbances of the domestic: wars, rockets, class struggles. The penultimate stanza places the 'Brotkörbe' between rockets and class struggles, and the poem closes on the one detail that was common to all three domestic interiors: the cat's dish.

Weiterung. Enzensberger offers here a commentary on and continuation of Brecht's *An die Nachgeborenen*. Where Brecht could envisage generations who would come after his, Enzensberger examines the unimaginable possibility with which we live: that there will be nothing to come after our Armageddon. The poem opens with a sequence of question and answer. The first voice asks who will be left. The second voice replies soothingly that a little more time, a little more progress will tell: that when 'it' happens ('wenn es erst soweit ist') 'it' will become clear. Yet the soothing voice envisages a future which will deny man any future. And gradually the standard terms for future events ('bis auf weiteres', 'so weiter') become unreal, aimless palliatives. There will be no 'Nachgeborenen' who can look back to our times (in context, 'Nachsicht' vibrates with implications of 'hindsight'), with forgiveness ('Nachsicht'), or with any other emotion. This seemingly simple poem, with its manifold variations on 'weit', 'weiter', 'weiteres' is a wonderfully economical exploration of our vague acquiescence in a future which houses the possibility of complete extinction. The colloquial phrases reveal their ludicrous inadequacy.

Zwei Fehler. A poem which again makes reference to Brecht's *An die Nachgeborenen*. The poem invokes the proverbial expression in German for 'to take a sledgehammer to crack a nut' — 'mit Kanonen auf Spatzen schießen'. The proverb appears in inverted form in the first stanza, and it expresses the ineffectuality of poetry — like sending sparrows to attack cannons. But stanzas three, four, and five repudiate the conclusion that might be drawn from the helplessness of poetry: that one should be silent altogether. And the final stanza repudiates the other kind of radical conclusion that might be drawn: to align poetry with the language of the powerful. In its understated way, the poem offers an impassioned defence of poetry: it is as little a crime (and, we might add, as much a necessity) as 'Schlafen, Luftholen'.

Nicht Zutreffendes streichen has as its title the familiar instruction on forms to 'delete that which is inapplicable'. The poem offers the portrait of somebody who is so concerned not to say anything inapplicable (or, we might add, inappropriate) that what is said is 'flach', 'dünn', 'blechern'. The poem implies a denunciation of the intellectual who dares not risk saying anything unimportant, stupid, derivative, anything that could be misunderstood, or welcomed by the 'wrong' people. Beyond that, the poem, in its concern with language, by implication countermands the notion that poetry must be of sublime austerity and difficulty, unique in its sentiments and diction. The poem warns against thinness and dryness, and urges the taking of (human and linguistic) risks.

It is not an unworthy note on which to end this selection from 170 years of German poetry.

SELECT BIBLIOGRAPHY

Adorno, T. W. 'Rede über Lyrik und Gesellschaft', in *Noten zur Literatur*, Frankfurt am Main, 1981, pp. 48–68

Allemann, Beda. *Über das Dichterische*. Pfullingen, 1957

Anderle, Martin. *Deutsche Lyrik des neunzehnten Jahrhunderts*, Bonn, 1979

Austermühl, Elke. *Poetische Sprache und lyrisches Verstehen*, Heidelberg, 1981

Benjamin, Walter. *Ursprung des deutschen Trauerspiels*, Frankfurt am Main, 1963

Blackall, E. A. *The Emergence of German as a Literary Language*, Cambridge, 1959

Boulton, Marjorie. *The Anatomy of Poetry*, 2nd edition, London, 1982

Brooks, Cleanth. *The Well-Wrought Urn*, New York, 1947

Closs, A. *The Genius of the German Lyric*, 2nd edition, London, 1962

Easthope, Antony. *Poetry as Discourse*, London, 1983

Eliot, T. S. 'Tradition and the individual talent', in Eliot, *Selected Essays*, New York, 1950

Empson, William. *Seven Types of Ambiguity*, London, 1930

Fraser, G. S. *Metre, Rhyme, and Free Verse*, London, 1970

Friedrich, Hugo. *Die Struktur der modernen Lyrik*, Reinbek bei Hamburg, 1956

Gnüg, Hiltrud. *Entstehung und Krise lyrischer Subjektivität*, Stuttgart, 1983

Grundlehner, P. *The Lyrical Bridge: Essays from Hölderlin to Benn*, Rutherford, New Jersey, 1979

Hamburger, Michael. *The Truth of Poetry*, London, 1969

Häublein, Ernst. *The Stanza*, London 1978

Haupt, Jürgen. *Natur und Lyrik: Naturbeziehungen im zwanzigsten Jahrhundert*, Stuttgart, 1983

206

Heller, Erich. 'The hazard of modern poetry', in *The Disinherited Mind*, Harmondsworth, 1961, pp. 227–57
The Poet's Self and the Poem, London, 1976.

Heukenkamp, Ursula. *Die Sprache der schönen Natur: Studien zur Naturlyrik*, Berlin and Weimar, 1982

Hinck, Walter. *Von Heine zu Brecht: Lyrik im Geschichtsprozeß*, Frankfurt am Main, 1978

Hinderer, Walter (ed.). *Geschichte der Deutschen Lyrik*, Stuttgart, 1983

Horn, András. *Das Literarische*, Berlin 1978

Kayser, Wolfgang. *Geschichte des deutschen Verses*, Berne and Munich, 1960

Klein, Johannes. *Geschichte der deutschen Lyrik*, Wiesbaden 1957

Ledanff, Susanne. *Die Augenblicksmetapher: über Bildlichkeit und Spontaneität in der Lyrik*, Munich, 1981

Lewis, C. Day. *The Poetic Image*, London, 1947

Link, Jürgen. *Die Struktur des literarischen Symbols*, Munich, 1975

Lotman, Yury. *Analysis of the Poetic Text*, ed. and transl. by D. Barton Johnson, Ann Arbor, 1976

Ludwig, Hans-Werner. *Arbeitsbuch Lyrikanalyse*, Tübingen, 1981

Marsch, Edgar. 'Die lyrische Chiffre: ein Beitrag zur Poetik des modernen Gedichts', *Sprachkunst* 1 (1970), 207–40

Mecklenburg, Norbert (ed.). *Naturlyrik und Gesellschaft*, Stuttgart, 1977

Nowottny, Winifred. *The Language Poets Use*, London, 1962

Pestalozzi, Karl. *Die Entstehung des lyrischen Ich*, Berlin, 1970

Prawer, S. S. *German Lyric Poetry*, London, 1952

Rey, William H. *Poesie der Antipoesie*, Heidelberg, 1978

Richards, I. A. *Practical Criticism*, London, 1929

Rogers, William Elford. *The Three Genres and the Interpretation of Lyric*, Princeton, 1983

Sorg, Bernhard. *Das lyrische Ich*, Tübingen, 1984

Spinner, Kaspar. *Zur Struktur des lyrischen Ich*, Frankfurt am Main, 1975

Staiger, Emil. *Grundbegriffe der Poetik*, Zürich, 1946
Die Kunst der Interpretation, Zürich, 1955

Todorov, Almut. *Gedankenlyrik*, Stuttgart, 1980

Welsh, Andrew. *Roots of Lyric: Primitive Poetry and modern Poetics*, Princeton, 1978

Wiese, Benno von. *Die deutsche Lyrik*, 2 vols., Düsseldorf, 1957

Wimsatt, W. K. *The Verbal Icon*, Lexington, 1954
Yates, W. E. *Tradition in the German Sonnet*, Berne, 1981
Ziolkowski, Theodore. *The Classical German Elegy*, Princeton, 1980